New Approaches
in
Psychological Measurement

New Approaches in Psychological Measurement

Edited by
P. Kline

Reader in Psychometrics,
University of Exeter

JOHN WILEY & SONS

London · New York · Sydney · Toronto

Library of Congress catalog card number
73-2787

ISBN 0 471 49120 9

Printed in Great Britain at
The Aberdeen University Press, Aberdeen

CONTRIBUTORS

DON BANNISTER

Clinical research psychologist in charge of the MRC Unit at Bexley Hospital and Visiting Professor of Psychology in the University of Surrey.

MICHAEL BOTT

Consultant psychiatrist, Hellingly Hospital, Hailsham

JOHN BUTCHER

Professor of Developmental Psychology in the University of Sussex.

ANTHONY GALE

Senior Lecturer in Psychology, University of Wales Institute of Science and Technology.

JASPER HOLLEY

Professor of Psychology, University of Lund, Sweden.

JOHN HUNDLEBY

Professor of Psychology, Department of Psychology, University of Guelph, Canada.

PAUL KLINE

Lecturer in Psychology, Department of Psychology, University of Exeter.

PHILIP LEVY

Professor of Psychology, University of Lancaster.

BORIS SEMEONOFF

Reader in Psychology, Department of Psychology, University of Edinburgh.

ACKNOWLEDGEMENTS

THE editor gratefully acknowledges the assistance of the following publishers who have granted permission for the reproduction of extracted material quoted in the text, sources being given in the References at the end of each chapter:

Academic Press Inc., London.
Addison-Wesley Publishing Co., Reading, Mass.
American Psychological Association Inc., Washington, D.C.
Annual Reviews Inc., Palo Alto, California.
Cambridge University Press, London.
Haughton Mifflin, Boston, Mass.
Institute for Personality and Ability Testing, Champaign, Illinois.
Prentice-Hall Inc., Englewood Cliffs, New Jersey.
Princeton University Press, Princeton, New Jersey.

INTRODUCTION

OVER the last decade there has been a massive increase in the number of psychological tests of every kind. The huge twin volumes of the latest *Mental Measurement Year Book* (Buros 1972) are eloquent witness of this proliferation. This means that many psychologists, both researchers and practitioners, not to say students, have to take many aspects of psychological testing on trust.

Thus what has been attempted in this book is to scrutinize new developments in key areas of psychological measurement. The definition of new has been left deliberately loose so that it embraces in part recent (meaning the last five years) and in part novel. Perhaps little known might best describe it. We have also placed great emphasis on the notion of scrutiny, so that these chapters are not mere lists or reviews of literature, the bane of theses, but are critical examinations of new methods and techniques such as can be carried out only by specialists in the relevant area. This is the reason for the symposium form of the book. Few psychologists are equally at home in all aspects of psychological measurement, none is equally involved in on-going research. This careful scrutiny enables us, we hope, to choose what is valuable from the new developments rationally rather than intuitively.

It is against this background that the rationale and purpose of each chapter can be understood. For these chapters were written to a specific plan. We begin first with Levy's study of the relation between test theory and psychology. This chapter is quite fundamental to any discussion of psychological measurement, which is why it appears first. In it the concepts of reliability and validity are examined in the light of the theoretical models these concepts imply and the theoretical models of the objects of measurement. The implications of the apparent disparity for psychological measurement are fully driven home.

Next come two chapters concerned with two most important applications of psychological testing—intelligence and personality. Butcher gives us a clear summary of the most recent developments in the field of intelligence. Here we can find a critical appraisal of the most recent and important work by Cattell and Guilford on the structuring of abilities, and a discussion of the controversy over racial differences in intelligence. Chapter 3 by Hundleby deals with objective measures of personality and motivation. Despite the gargantuan compendium of such tests by Cattell and Warburton (1967) these instruments have been neglected, although they overcome so many of the disadvantages of personality questionnaires which seem to have reached their limit of development.

From these two areas of test application we turn to a type of psychological test which has received considerable opprobrium from experimental psychology—projective tests, celebrated by Eysenck (1959) as the vehicles for the riotous imagination of clinicians. In Chapter 4 Semeonoff surveys the most recent developments in projective tests and fits them into a useful frame of reference, which provides a healthy counterargument to the overhasty condemnation of such instruments. Chapter 5 attempts a task of perhaps even greater difficulty. Holley presents some results of his investigations into the validity of the Rorschach test and justifies the use of his G index for such studies. Those who would condemn the Rorschach must be able otherwise to account for the findings presented in this chapter.

Our first five chapters have covered some important aspects of psychological testing, perhaps the most important. Now, as a jolt to psychometric pride, Bannister and Bott challenge all the logical assumptions of such psychological testing, presenting the Kellian, phenomenological view backed up with some impressive case studies.

Our last two chapters are concerned again with psychological measurement but in fields, unlike those of intelligence and personality, where measurement is often thought to be difficult or of little value. In Chapter 7, Kline discusses the application of various test procedures in the elucidation of psychodynamic theory—especially that of Freud and Jung. The interest of this chapter lies in the fact that these theories are far from untestable (hence unscientific) and that the means of putting parts, at least, of psychodynamic psychology to the test are already at hand. Our final chapter is concerned with psychophysiological measurement. Here Gale demonstrates how such measurement can be highly useful in helping to answer both physiological and psychological questions. Ultimately, perhaps, this specialized branch of psychology may provide superior measures of personality and even other mental states than the more conventional methods discussed earlier in the book. The whole book is rounded off by a brief conclusion.

Such then, in outline, is *New Approaches in Psychological Measurement*. For whom is it intended? We hope that all those who are in any way concerned with psychological testing will find this book valuable. This means, therefore, that both academic and professional psychologists, research students and perhaps final-year undergraduates can be expected to use it.

Finally, in this introduction thanks must be paid to the contributors of this symposium who, despite their other burdens, did produce their manuscripts, and without whose efforts there would have been no book.

PAUL KLINE
University of Exeter

CONTENTS

1

ON THE RELATION BETWEEN TEST THEORY AND PSYCHOLOGY

Philip Levy

University of Lancaster

Introduction

THIS CHAPTER offers an idiosyncratic—and perhaps unfair—review of psychological test theory. The general question is: what is uniquely 'psychological' about psychological measurement by tests? It is concluded that we might be more thoughtful about test construction in aid of our theories, and especially about the use of tests in making statements about individuals.

The domain of discussion is well defined by a limited set of references. The texts by Cronbach (1970) and Lord and Novick (1968) effectively summarize the background thinking on most of the issues to be raised. Although cognitive testing is our principal concern, some reference will be made to other types of test.

First, a brief flirtation with the beginnings of psychological measurement to remind us where we have come from. In 1885 Galton hung up a poster announcing the establishment of his Anthropometric Laboratory at the South Kensington Museum (Anastasi 1965, p. 21, Pearson 1924, p. 358). The poster read, in part, as follows:

> 'This laboratory is established for . . . the use of those who desire to be accurately measured in many ways, either to obtain timely warning of remediable faults in development, or to learn their powers . . . and for obtaining data for statistical discussion'.

Cattell (J. McK.) defined the purpose of psychological measurement as follows:

> 'Psychology cannot attain the certainty and exactness of the physical sciences, unless it rests on a foundation of experiment and measurement. A step in this direction could be made by applying a series of mental tests and measurements to a large number of individuals. The results could be of considerable scientific

1

value in discovering the constancy of mental processes, their interdependence, and their variation under different circumstances. Individuals, besides, would find their tests interesting, and perhaps, useful in regard to training, mode of life or indication of disease. The scientific and practical value of such tests would be much increased should a uniform system be adopted, so that determinations made at different times and places would be compared and combined' (Cattell 1890, quoted in Anastasi 1965, p. 24).

Galton commented as follows:

'One of the most important objects of measurement is hardly if at all alluded to here and must be emphasised. It is to obtain a general knowledge of the capacities of a man by sinking shafts, as it were, at a few critical points. In order to ascertain the best points for the purpose, the sets of measures should be compared with an independent estimate of the man's powers. We may thus learn which of the measures are the most instructive . . .' (Anastasi 1965).

Thus, between them, Galton and Cattell eloquently anticipated the many directions in which the testing movement has gone. With little need to allow for stylistic changes, they mention all the issues that have occupied us over the years. How far then have we advanced the goals of mental measurement? Or more pointedly, since Galton charged three or four pence for performing and recording the measurements, if we were to display his poster today, might not some cynic bring charges under a Trade Descriptions Act or the like for false representation of our skills and powers?

The problems of psychological measurement by tests may be viewed at three levels, namely, the characteristics of items, the properties of scores from a single test, and the questions we attempt to answer when two or more scores are available. The relationships between psychological theory and test theory are questioned at each level.

Characteristics of Items

Typically, an investigator envisages some trait, assembles a pool of items likely to represent that trait, and applies the trial test to some group of persons. The items of an ability test are said to have two characteristics, namely, difficulty and discriminating power. The method by which characteristics of pass–fail or dichotomous items are examined has not changed in principle since the early days of test construction. We may imagine Binet and Simon plotting graphs like those in Figure 1 to show how success rate on each item varied with age, just as a modern test constructor following Birnbaum (1968) or Lord (1968) might estimate the parameters of item-characteristic curves. Item difficulty may be indicated by the pass rate for persons of average ability; and item's discriminating power may be assessed by the rate at which difficulty changes with ability. The labelling of the horizontal axis might vary: for Binet and Simon it would have been chronological age; for others it might be a total score on the test; and for others a measure of some latent trait. While there are important distinctions to be made among total score, true score and latent trait (Lord and Novick 1968, pp. 386–7 and Chap. 24), models by Guttman, Rasch, Lazarsfeld and Birnbaum may all be regarded as defining a relationship between success rate and a score and may be compared in this form.

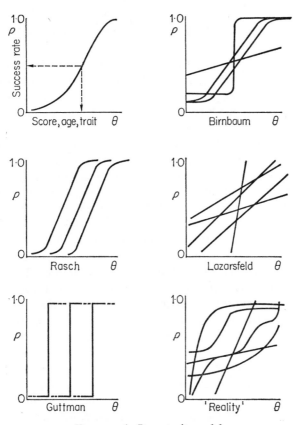

FIGURE 1. Item–trait models.

Birnbaum's (1968) latent trait model is the more general. The three-parameter version assumes that the probability of success is a (logistic) function of item difficulty, the testee's ability and a guess-rate parameter. It is also the least presumptive model in terms of psychological theory, a feature which may be seen as good or bad depending upon one's point of view. Rasch's (1966) theory for dichotomous items leads to a special case of Birnbaum's model in which items have equal discriminating power but varying difficulty (Lord and Novick 1968, p. 402). Guttman's (1950) model, by contrast, refers to a structure in the manifest data in which for the 'perfect scale' a dual conditional relationship holds: that persons who pass a particular item will pass all easier items, and that persons who fail an item will fail all harder items. If Rasch's items were sufficiently distinct in their difficulty the perfect scale would be the result; if they were not distinct we would have a probabilistic version of Guttman. The particular case of Lazarsfeld's (1950, 1960, Lazarsfeld and Henry 1968) latent trait model shown is also a special case of Birnbaum's model (Lord and Novick 1968, p. 404). In contrast to the Guttman and Rasch models, Lazarsfeld items may change in difficulty at different rates, and hence the difficulty order of the items may change with the level of the latent trait under examination. Thus only those subsets of the items having non-intersecting traces will show the restricted range of response patterns permitted by the perfect scale. This much is well documented; not so explicitly discussed in the literature are the differences among the models as representatives of psychological theory.

Item-discriminating power has been assessed by a variety of methods in the past. Many indices of item–total score association exist, and factor analysis of more than one kind of inter-item correlation coefficient has been used. By and large, pragmatic accounts abound in our textbooks, and only now are some of the relations among the indices and among the methods becoming recognized. We note in passing just a few technical curiosities. Lord and Novick (1968, p. 378) have shown that a simple function of the biserial correlation between item and total test score provides a good first estimate of the slope parameter in Birnbaum's model. Lord (1963) has explored the properties of the Brogden–Clemans estimator, a generalized biserial coefficient which assumes nothing about the underlying bivariate distribution of item response and test score. He has shown that this coefficient more efficiently estimates the underlying product-moment correlation than does the usual biserial correlation coefficient, even when the bivariate normal distribution assumed by the latter coefficient is present in the population. Lord (1970) has also demonstrated that there is little to choose between parameter estimates which assume item-characteristic curves of Birnbaum's logistic form and those found assuming nothing about the form of the curves. Centroid factor analysis of inter-item phi coefficients gives first centroid loadings which are approximately the same as the point-biserial correlations between items and total score, whereas the first centroid loadings for inter-item tetrachoric correlation coefficients are similar to item–test biserial correlation (Henrysson 1962). Some order is emerging from the mess of the semi-intuitive practices of the past.

At a more fundamental level, however, a number of problems remain. The nature of item difficulty and the dimensionality of psychological traits are discussed in turn.

Item Difficulty

Figure 1 shows a reflexive relationship between success rate and ability: the difficulty of an item may be described in terms of the ability required to give a specified success rate, and ability may be defined in terms of items passed or failed. In this sense we might ask what it is that makes for differences in difficulty among items; and, equivalently, what it is that the test measures. Curiously, we are able to construct tests with little or no formal reference to this point. We must deal with this issue at some length.

Item difficulty may be regarded, perhaps unfairly, as a mere curve-fitting parameter in Birnbaum's model. It has a clearer substantive role in the development of Rasch's model in which, if its rather restrictive conditions hold, item difficulties may be estimated independently of the characteristics of a particular sample of persons used, and a person's ability may be estimated independently of the sample of items used. (For a practical example see Anderson *et al.* 1968.) Rasch's theory specifies a particular way in which the parameters for items and persons interact to produce the item–person response matrix which has an identifiable, although probabilistic, structure. Lazarsfeld's latent class model for dichotomous data (e.g. Stouffer 1950, pp. 19–33) has many 'difficulty' or endorsement rate parameters which are its only parameters, and an ordering of the latent classes to form a latent trait may emerge as a secondary feature of the analysis in appropriate cases. Guttman's scale analysis specifies no parameters as such, but the response matrix for the perfect scale clearly gives reflexive roles to item-difficulty order and the rank order of the respondents. Guttman's specification of the response matrix in terms of the principal component weights for items and persons is also reminiscent of Rasch's model. Further, that the two least squares problems of assigning weights to items and scores to persons in order to maximize appropriate variances have identical solutions (Guttman 1950, pp. 334–40, Torgerson 1958, pp. 338–43) reinforces the view that persons and items have a reflexive role in the Guttman model. These relationships refer, however, to the manifest data, whereas Birnbaum deals with an asymmetrical or regression relationship between item responses and a latent trait. Lord (1965a, 1965b) has been careful to point out the distinction between item–total score regression and item–latent trait regression. Potentially, therefore, item difficulty plays a different role in each model.

But frankly, we are still left with the question: what is difficulty? Consider the following analogy item as an example:

sheep is to lamb as cow is to ——.

How would we make such an item either easier or more difficult?

First, we could vary the form of the item, giving it a conventional or symbolic form as in, *sheep : lamb :: cow :* —— (1). We could vary the position of the missing element as in, *sheep :* —— *:: cow : calf* (2). Or omit two elements as in, *sheep* : —— :: —— : *calf* (3). Or offer a multiple-choice format as in, *sheep* : *lamb* :: *cow* : —— (*foal, chicken, calf*) (4). We could probably modify difficulty by offering different types of multiple-choice options such as, (*ewe, bull, ram, calf*) (5); or (*car, cough, calf*) (6); or (*cat, pig, calf*) (7); or (*farm, milk, calf*) (8); or by offering a double multiple choice as in:

sheep : *lamb*

   horse   cow   farm   ::   *tractor   donkey   calf* (9).

We could perhaps make the item easier by, *dog* : *puppy* :: *cow* : —— (10); or, *owl* : *owlet* :: *pig* : —— (11); but what about the item, *pig* : *piglet* :: *cut* : ——? Or we could make the items more difficult as in, *swan* : *cygnet* :: *eel* : —— (12); and, *tadpole* : *frog* :: *caterpillar* : —— (13). But, more generally, we could consider the whole range of relationships normally represented in such analogy items. The elements might be common words but the required relationship obscure; or the elements could be obscure but the relationship obvious if only the elements were understood.

The point is that items may vary in difficulty for a multiplicity of reasons and we have often been rather thoughtless about identifying those reasons; yet the 'dimensions' of difficulty tell us what we are measuring. Variations in content, form, and relationship are surely not trivial options? Recall formats (e.g. 1) and recognition formats (e.g. 4) imply psychologically distinguishable processes; the merely pragmatic issue that multiple-choice tests are easier to score must not be allowed to obscure this difference. The given set of multiple-choice options also helps define the dimensions of measurement; selection of a wrong answer in examples (4) to (8) implies different kinds of errors. Vocabulary difficulty, an expression which disguises several dimensions of difficulty, is varied in other examples. It is often said that items 'sample behaviour'; or, more elegantly, that items are selected to represent some behavioural domain or universe of behaviour; or, as Galton put it, 'sinking shafts'. This point has received much lip-service but little formal attention.

It is left for the reader to 'vary the difficulty' of the following item from the Verbal Reception subtest of the Illinois Test of Psycholinguistic Abilities (Kirk, McCarthy and Kirk 1968):

Do dogs bark?

If the attempt makes you question what 'Verbal Reception' means, how we have come to distinguish so readily between ability and achievement, and what the item domain is, the point is made (cf. Cronbach 1970, pp. 145–8).

Now undoubtedly our item-analysis procedures can create a test having a solid core of common trait variance (cf. Guttman 1950, p. 183, 1971, p. 343). The dimensions of difficulty to be found among items having similar manifest content and format are likely to be correlated; but should we not ask why this is so? The simplest answer is rarely mentioned: children developing in a particular culture are likely to accrue knowledge, processes or whatever at different rates but in a similar order. No apology is offered for introducing a psychological assumption.

The most commonly implied advice for test construction is that items should have a spread of difficulty and high discriminating power (but see Birnbaum 1968, Chaps. 19 and 20, Cronbach 1970, pp. 145–8). In the limit this prescription leads to the Guttman perfect scale shown in Table 1. It has

TABLE 1. Data Illustrating the Perfect Scale for an Ability Test of Four Dichotomous Items

Persons	Items			
	1	2	3	4
1	1	1	1	1
2	1	1	1	0
3	1	1	0	0
4	1	0	0	0
5	0	0	0	0

1, pass; 0, fail.

not always been recognized that every perfect scale response pattern strongly implies a developmental trend. One of the original demonstrations of the scalogram technique referred to data which showed how soldiers under fire report different physical reactions to the dangers of battle (e.g. Coombs, Dawes and Tversky 1970, pp. 39–41, Stouffer 1950, pp. 13–14). The reactions to stress occurred with different frequencies (cf. difficulty) and soldiers responded with different numbers of reactions. Although the data are cross-sectional, the quasi-perfect scale form of the soldier–reaction response pattern strongly implies a temporal order in which reactions might appear in a single soldier as stress is increased. The items ordered according to their endorsement frequencies might well correspond to a 'depth of autonomic arousal' scale. Similarly, in the cross-sectional study of specialist departments in business and civic organizations by Pugh *et al.* (see Levy and Pugh 1969), there was a tendency towards a simplex pattern in the specialism–organization response matrix. The implication is that as organizations develop and grow larger, not only do they add more specialist departments, but they add them in a particular order. More directly, much of Piagetian theory would predict the response pattern of a perfect scale, even in cross-sectional data, as an important sign of development. If vocabulary items, arithmetic items, perceptual items, and so on, differ in their difficulty and show good scalability with respect to a collection of similar items, how can we have avoided taking note of the developmental implications? Actually, the failure in this direction cannot be held to be serious: test constructors usually report age trends in test scores when they occur. Rather, the failure is in the other direction: few tests have been constructed in which items and hence their associated difficulties have been developed under the control of an explicit developmental theory. It is certainly interesting to learn that scores increase with age, but when 'item difficulty' is undefined we must explain the results *post hoc*. On the other hand, when item difficulty is created *a priori* under the control of some developmental theory and employing content analysis, the demonstration of an age trend in the data strengthens belief in that developmental theory. The Guttman perfect scale represents, therefore, a fundamental kind of unidimensional measurement structure for psychological data.

Most real tests, however, are composed of items having only moderate discriminating power. What substantive theory might exist for these? Three types of factor might cause departures from the perfect scale, namely, 'error', effects specific to particular items, and multidimensional behaviour on items. We shall deal with these in turn.

Items: the Errorful Simplex

Consider a set of items which, in principle, form a perfect scale, or, let us say, a simplex. The observed data may depart from the simplex pattern because of guessing. There are now good arguments and some evidence for believing that guessing is a function of the ability of the testee and the difficulty of the item. In particular, the effects of guessing upon errors of measurement may be worse at higher levels of difficulty for testees of lower ability (Lord and Novick 1968, p. 233, Traub, 1967, 1968).

Leaving aside this systematic source of error, item-discriminating power will be lowered by what we might conceive of as momentary fluctuations in ability occurring independently on each item. Guttman (1950, Chap. 6) rather scorns the use of item analysis, in its conventional sense, for examining internal relations in a test; yet in errorful data item-analysis indices have a clear relation to, and are sensitive to, Guttman's notion of a 'gradient' of errors (Suchman 1950, pp. 159–63). Many of us have tended to neglect the simplex, perhaps regarding it as impractical; yet if we seek items having high discriminating power through conventional item analysis, then item-culling causes the response matrix to move closer to the simplex pattern. Moreover, the simplex is the simplest and most plausible model we have for psychological unidimensionality. A prerequisite for psychological measurement is the existence of some qualitative structure in the data; the Guttman simplex is one such structure. By contrast the indices of conventional item analysis have only latterly found formal justification in terms of their relationship with a factor model (Henrysson 1962) and with the item-characteristic curve type of model (Lord and Novick 1968, Chap. 16).

A certain neglect, perhaps even psychometric prejudice, is evident for the

Guttman model. Cronbach (1970), for example, indexes just one brief reference to its use in a developmental context (p. 261); and Lord and Novick (1968), who otherwise give it several fair mentions, offer a symmetrical contingency table for two items of *equal difficulty*, saying: 'This table shows how far such typical items are from forming a Guttman perfect scale (p. 337)'. Undoubtedly the strength of Guttman's attack on conventional analyses and the high standards he demanded from real data have hindered his cause in some quarters (cf. Solomon 1960, p. 294). Actually, as Guttman (1971) has reminded us, the core of his attack is upon item analysis as a *post hoc* procedure. We shall have more to say on this point later.

Items: Specific Factors

Consider the possibility that items detect specific factors in addition to some common trait. We may think of the specific factors as due to specific representations of the common trait in the real world for which not all testees have had, let us say, relevant experiences. The total score on a test may then be taken to represent an average across the several representations. Such a view is plausible but hardly novel. We can, however, gain a closer sighting of a behaviour theory implied by item analysis if we reconsider some data used by Stouffer (1950, Chap. 1) to illustrate Lazarsfeld's latent dichotomy model. Table 2 reproduces data for four items concerning attitude to the army. Against each of the 16 possible response patterns is shown the proportion of respondents estimated to possess the latent character (favourable attitude to the army). The response patterns are ranked in the final column according to this proportion. Five of the 16 response patterns (1, 4, 9, 12, 16) form a simplex and simultaneously maximize the number of observed response patterns which fit (67 per cent). How then might we account for the discrepant patterns which certainly appear in the analysis of typical items analysed in any number?

The final column in the table gives the total score for each response pattern on the test of just four items. The scores are clearly related to the rank ordering of the proportions estimated to possess the latent character. Thus a score of four ($+ + + +$) corresponds to the highest value (0.996) and a score of zero ($- - - -$) to the lowest value (0.011). Between these extremes response patterns showing scores of 1, 2 and 3 items marked favourably correspond to successively higher proportions. It would seem, therefore, that a given level of latent trait in a person may be developed (or exhibited) by various routes (or signs). The Lazarsfeld items behave as though they are approximately equivalent signs of the latent character, any three of which indicate roughly the same high probability of possessing the latent character. There may be, for example, many different alternative expressions for essentially the same attitude, just as there may be many different experiences which aid development of some numerical concept or the development of conservation of volume. Several distinct subsets of experiences or exemplars may be *sufficient* for learning, no single experience or exemplar being in itself a *necessary* precondition.

TABLE 2. Illustrative Data for Lazarsfeld's Latent Dichotomy Analysis (Adapted from Stouffer 1950, p. 22)

Response pattern Items 1 2 3 4	Observed number of cases	Proportion possessing latent character	Rank	'Total score'
+ + + +	75	0.996	1	4
+ + − +	42	0.971	2	3
+ − + +	55	0.953	3	3
− + + +	69	0.940	4	3
+ + + −	3	0.938	5	3
+ − − +	45	0.736	6	2
− + − +	60	0.680	7	2
+ + − −	10	0.674	8	2
− − + +	96	0.568	9	2
+ − + −	8	0.561	10	2
− + + −	16	0.494	11	2
− − − +	199	0.152	12	1
+ − − −	16	0.148	13	1
− + − −	25	0.117	14	1
− − + −	52	0.076	15	1
− − − −	229	0.011	16	0

When we examine the discrepancies between the scores and the proportions more closely, we could account for these in terms of the departures from equivalence of the four items. The values for patterns having three favourable responses range only from 0.938 to 0.971, but the values for two favourable responses show wide variation. Within a score category the proportion is lower if item 3 is one of the scored responses. The rather sharp break in continuity between ranks 8 and 9 corresponds to the division between the three response patterns having two favourable responses which include item 3 and the three which do not. More generally, the ordering of the response patterns within a score category may be accounted for by supposing that item 4 is the dominant item, followed by items 1 and 2 in that order, and lastly item 3. Scoring weights for the items are readily found so that when response patterns are scored their rank order is reproduced exactly. For example, using the weights 1.0, 0.9, 0.75 and 1.1, pattern + + + + scores 3.85, pattern + + − + scores 3.0, and so on. Actually, there is nothing remarkable about this finding, because Lazarsfeld determines the proportions which are ranked as the product of four proportions, and taking logarithms gives an additive representation. Our purpose in this discussion has been to show what meaning we might develop for scoring tests the way we do.

Thus, although it is tempting to regard the specific behaviour of items in the rather non-theoretical way that specific factors are treated in factor analysis, we may in some cases be able to employ the much stronger notion of behavioural equivalence; that is to say, there are alternative routes through (the simplex of) development, or that certain experiences or behaviours are for some purposes the equivalents of others. At least, this is one possible interpretation of our many tests whose items have only moderate discriminating power, and offers some justification for giving the same or similar scores to different response patterns.

Items: Dimensionality of the Latent Space

We have sometimes failed to recognize that a unidimensional latent space for items is not necessarily to be identified with a one-dimensional solution in factor analysis (Lord and Novick 1969, pp. 381–2). The matrix of product-moment (phi) coefficients for items of a perfect scale, shown in Table 3, has as many principal components as there are items, and these are simple polynomial functions of difficulty order.

TABLE 3. Product-Moment Correlations (Phi) for Nine Items of a Simplex and their Principal Components (Incomplete)*

Items	Items						Principal components				
	1	2	3	4	5	...	I	II	III	IV	...
1	1.00	0.67	0.51	0.41	0.33		0.52	0.55	0.48	−0.35	
2	0.67	1.00	0.76	0.61	0.50		0.70	0.55	0.24	0.06	
3	0.51	0.76	1.00	0.80	0.65		0.80	0.42	−0.05	0.27	
4	0.41	0.61	0.80	1.00	0.82		0.85	0.22	−0.26	0.22	
5	0.33	0.50	0.65	0.82	1.00		0.87	0.00	−0.34	0.00	
6	0.27	0.41	0.53	0.67	0.82		0.85	−0.22	−0.26	−0.22	
7	0.22	0.33	0.43	0.53	0.65		0.80	−0.42	−0.05	−0.27	
8	0.17	0.25	0.33	0.41	0.50		0.70	−0.55	0.24	−0.06	
9	0.11	0.17	0.22	0.27	0.33		0.52	−0.55	0.48	0.35	
p	0.9	0.8	0.7	0.6	0.5	Root	5.0	1.7	0.83	0.50	

* Since the item difficulties are $p = 0.1\ (0.1)\ 0.9$, the complete matrix of correlations is doubly symmetrical.

Following a certain amount of controversy (Ferguson 1941, Guilford 1941, Wherry and Gaylord 1944, Carroll 1945, Gourlay 1951, see also Carroll 1961), it is clear that the matrix of tetrachoric correlations among items will have the required unit rank when the items form a perfect scale, but this is the outcome of a search for a coefficient which gives such a numerical solution and not the result of some psychological argument. With real data the tetrachoric correlations may form an improper (non-Gramian) set; they suffer when responses are errorful; they can be misleading when their sometimes gratuitous distributional assumptions are not met; and, as we shall see, they offer only a limited generalization to the multidimensional case. What meaning there might be in a factor analysis of tetrachorics is discussed by Lord and Novick (1968, Chap. 16), who conclude:

> 'The dimensionality of the complete latent space does not depend upon distributional assumptions, nor on a choice of a measure of interitem correlation, nor on any choice of transformation of the latent variables. Thus the dimensionality of the complete latent space is a more basic concept than is the number of common factors' (p. 382).

Curiously, much argument has centred on the problem of 'removing' the effects of difficulty order from the coefficients, yet difficulty order is the *sine qua non* of the simplex.

The neatest algebraic demonstration of the existence of a perfect scale is to be seen in the inverse of the matrix of product-moment correlations. When the items are arranged in order of difficulty, the inverse has the form shown in Table 4. The structure of the inverse matrix and its relation to the problem of

TABLE 4. Inverse of the Phi Matrix of Table 3*

Item	1	2	3	4	Item 5	6	7	8	9
1	1.80	−1.20							
2	−1.20	3.20	−1.83						
3		−1.83	4.20	−2.25					
4			−2.25	4.80	−2.45				
5				−2.45	5.00	−2.45			
6					−2.45	4.80	−2.25		
7						−2.25	4.20	−1.83	
8							−1.83	3.20	−1.20
9								−1.20	1.80

* Zeros where blank.

predicting one variable (item) from other variables in the matrix confirms that all that item 3 has in common with the remaining items may be accounted for by items 2 and 4, the adjacent items in the difficulty order. Hence an argument may be developed for estimating parameters which would minimize the complexity of the inverse matrix rather than minimizing the number of factors in the original matrix (e.g. Guttman 1953, 1958a). If simple error were to be added to the data, some moderate predictive value would be obtained from items more distant in difficulty but the diagonal structure of the inverse matrix should be discernible.

Recent developments in matrix analysis have featured methods for studying special kinds of covariance structures (e.g. Jöreskog 1969, McDonald 1969, Jöreskog 1970a, Mukherjee 1970), including that of the simplex (e.g. Kaiser 1962, Mukherjee 1966, Gibson 1967, Jöreskog 1970b, Proctor 1970, Schöne-mann 1970, Groen 1971). The simplex may find greater favour now that its algebra and associated computational algorithms have been more fully explored.

If we have sometimes confused factorial unidimensionality with latent space unidimensionality, we have more often failed to recognize that a multi-dimensional factor analysis implies just one of the several possible multi-dimensional theories of behaviour, namely, the compensatory theory (Torgerson 1958, pp. 349–55, Coombs 1964, pp. 259–64). Consider the data given in Table 5. Several items and persons are specified in terms of two

TABLE 5. Item and Person Specification in a Two-dimensional Latent Space

Item No.	Latent values w_1	w_2	Person No.	Latent scores s_1	s_2
1	0	1	1	0	0
2	0	2	2	0	1
3	0	3	3	0	2
4	0	4	4	0	3
5	1	0	5	0	4
6	1	1	6	1	0
.	.	.	.	.	.
.	.	.	.	.	.
.	.	.	.	.	.
23	4	3	23	4	2
24	4	4	24	4	3
			25	4	4

numbers. The two numbers for a person represent scores on two latent traits. Let the two numbers for an item represent weights to be applied to a person's latent scores; and consider the item weights to be so scaled that the criterion to be met by a person to achieve a pass is that the weighted sum of his scores, $w_1 s_1 + w_2 s_2$, must be at least as high as some fixed value, say, 8 points. Thus the item makes demands upon the person as specified by the weights, but the person may compensate for a shortage in one latent score by having enough of the other to satisfy the criterion. The operation of the model is displayed in Figure 2(a). Persons are points in a two-dimensional latent space, and items

are conveniently represented as lines which divide the person space into areas
to the top and right, where persons pass the item, and bottom left, where they
fail. The four areas produced by the crossing of the item lines contain the four
frequencies a, b, c, d of a typical 2 × 2 contingency table for these items.

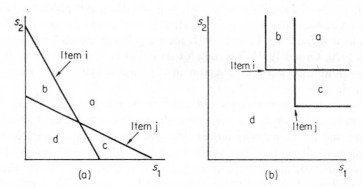

FIGURE 2. (a) The compensatory model. (b) The conjunctive model.

If certain distributional assumptions hold, factor analysis of the matrix of
tetrachoric correlation coefficients has a sensible outcome for perfect data
produced under this model: a two-dimensional factor solution is obtained
which has a reasonable relation to the parameters of the input data. This
result should not surprise us; after all, factor analysis, as a system of linear
equations, necessarily implies a compensatory theory of behaviour. On the
other hand, factor analysis generally makes a nonsense of data generated
under other multidimensional models. Coombs (1964, pp. 251–9) has discussed two other models. The conjunctive model for our data requires that a
person satisfy the item's demands on both latent trait 1 and latent trait 2
independently. A pass on the item is thus achieved only by a logical conjunc-
tion of two latent passes. Person 5 fails item 5 on one count even though he
has more than enough of latent trait 2. A verbally stated arithmetic problem
(Four men took three days to plough twenty acres; how long would it take
two men to plough six acres?) requires that the candidate be able *both* to
decode the verbal presentation *and* to perform the necessary arithmetic.
Presumably it would be possible to vary components of the verbal and arithmetic difficulty independently.

The action of the conjunctive model is displayed in Figure 2(b). Again, we
may imagine the latent space filled with person points. An item is represented
by two lines at right angles, held parallel to the latent axes, and meeting at the
crucial point where candidates just have sufficient of each ability to pass the
item. Again, the letters a, b, c and d indicate areas corresponding to cells of a
2 × 2 contingency table relating two items. Whatever the distribution, tetra-

choric correlation coefficients are inappropriate for this model. It is entirely possible for the following correlations to occur between three items 1, 2 and 3:

$$r_{12} = 1 \qquad r_{13} = 1 \qquad r_{23} = 0.4.$$

The tetrachorics would have it that two variables (items) which are perfectly correlated can have different correlations with a third variable. Such data place a strain upon commonsense, let alone the usual distance axioms, and even the normally very tolerant factor analytic methods begin to groan (cf. Guttman 1950, pp. 195–9, Coombs 1964, p. 247).

A third multidimensional model is the disjunctive case. Here persons may satisfy the demands of an item by having sufficient ability *either* on one latent trait *or* on the other. A person in Table 5 who has latent scores of 2 and 3 passes item 6 on both counts, passes item 4 for one reason, and fails item 24 for two reasons. The model supposes, therefore, that there are optional reasons for the same behaviour: a boy may collect stamps as an investment, for aesthetic pleasure, because it is a popular activity in his peer group, or for any combination of reasons. The disjunctive model is clearly the inverse of the conjunctive model: what is necessary for the one is more than sufficient for the other.

Solutions for these models are not easy, but there have been suggestions in the deterministic case (Coombs 1964, Coombs, Dawes and Tversky 1970). The Guttman–Lingoes series of non-metric programs (see Guttman 1968) are said to 'solve' them in the probabilistic case; but work by Tversky and Krantz (1970) leads us, like Fleiss and Zubin (1969), to question how clearly these programs are linked to explicit representations of psychological theory. Rozeboom (1966) has speculated about the existence of multidimensional theory for item responses, and Lord and Novick (1968, Chaps. 16 and 24) introduce some general considerations, but concentrate on the unidimensional case. Another approach to a solution is suggested by image theory (Guttman 1953). Just as the inverse of the matrix of phi coefficients has interest in the case of the perfect scale, so it does for the conjunctive and disjunctive cases. With perfect data, values appear in the inverse matrix only for those items most adjacent to each other in the latent space.

The general point is that three models exist where many have used a single analysis that will only (sometimes) disentangle one of them. The choice of analysis must surely be made on psychological grounds. Factor analysis of phi coefficients does have some empirical meaning, since such factors can be estimated by item-scoring; the problem of their psychological meaning may remain, however, since factor analysis of phi coefficients corresponds in no simple way to the latent space of any of the above models. The nearest approach has been that of McDonald (1962, 1965, 1967a, 1967b, 1967c), whose non-linear (i.e. polynomial) factor analysis may expose their non-linearity. But since two of the models are not in the mould of this kind of algebra, should we not start

elsewhere? On the other hand, Einhorn (1970) has found hyperbolic trans-
forms which approximate the action of the conjunctive and disjunctive
models.

The conjunctive and disjunctive models may be construed to be the result
of the joint operation of several simplexes. Table 6 gives an illustration for

TABLE 6. Two Latent Simplexes, A and B, Acting Conjunctively to
Produce Response Matrix C

	A (a_{ij}) Items						B (b_{ij}) Items						C $(a_{ij} \times b_{ij})$ Items					
	1	2	3	4	5	6	1	2	3	4	5	6	1	2	3	4	5	6
Persons 1	1	1	1	1	1	1	1	1	1	1	1	1	1	1	1	1	1	1
2	1	1	1	1	1	1	1	1	1	0	1	0	1	1	1	0	1	0
3	1	1	1	1	0	0	1	1	1	1	1	1	1	1	1	1	0	0
4	1	1	1	1	0	0	1	1	1	0	1	1	1	1	1	0	0	0
5	1	1	1	1	0	0	0	1	0	0	0	0	0	1	0	0	0	0
6	1	0	0	0	0	0	1	1	1	0	0	0	1	0	0	0	0	0
7	1	0	0	0	0	0	0	1	0	0	0	0	0	0	0	0	0	0

the two-dimensional case. Both of the hypothetical response matrices A and
B exhibit simplex form, although the rows and columns of B require reorder-
ing to show this. Matrix C is formed as the element-by-element product of A
and B and represents the conjunctive case. To obtain a response matrix for
the disjunctive case, the 1's and 0's in A and B are interchanged before the
elements are multiplied, and then the 1's and 0's are reversed again.

The simplex is a special case of all three models. In the compensatory case,
any set of items represented by lines in Figure 2(a) which do not cross within
the space of the person points form a perfect scale. In the conjunctive and disjunctive cases, items lying on any track progressing outwards from the origin
in a positive direction in Figure 2(b) also form a perfect scale. Thus in all three
models there may be many subsets of items which form simplexes, but the
'discovery' of a simplex pattern does not in itself imply latent trait unidimensionality. For example, the two-dimensional series of items specified by
(0,0), (0,4), (1,4), (2,4), (6,4), (6,8) would give a simplex within the conjunctive model. Hence our concern earlier with the nature of item difficulty.

Items: General Considerations

It should be clear that neither scale analysis nor item analysis defines content (cf. Guttman 1950, Chap. 3, Guttman 1971). The various technologies of
item analysis, scalogram techniques, latent structure analysis, and the more
recent latent trait models, only have meaning through prior study of content

and through clarity of psychological purpose. Constructors of educational tests have increasingly accepted that analysis of content to study the likely dimensions of difficulty and hence of learning is a necessary prior condition for the meaning of measurement (e.g. Bloom 1956, Bormuth 1970). It is not clear how psychological tests are so distinctively different as to be excused from such a prior analysis. As Bock and Wood (1971) said: 'Considering the faith we place in test item responses as valid tokens of behaviour, it is surprising how little we know about the psychological properties of items. If we knew what made items work, then we might be able to design them rationally or at least produce similar kinds of items at will. Unfortunately, neither capability is securely within our grasp. Test theory has glossed over this disconcerting state of affairs by invoking words such as "equivalence", "homogeneity", "parallel", and "unifactor" to describe item populations which do not actually exist' (p. 212).

Nevertheless, and in spite of Loevinger's (1965) doubts, things are happening on this front. Guttman and Schlesinger (1967a, 1967b) have demonstrated the power of rational item design by facet analysis (Guttman 1955, 1971, Foa 1965, 1968); Bormuth (1970) has shown us how we might systematically vary the content of verbal items; Foa (1965, 1968), Butt and Fiske (1968) and Neill and Jackson (1970) have described such efforts with personality items; and Harreldon, Jordan and Horn (1972) applied facet analysis to a study of attitudes. Undoubtedly there are many more references in this 'growth area', and facet analysis is clearly the key to development. A facet is to test design what a factor is to an experiment: a facet has elements where a factor has levels, and a multifaceted design implies combinations of facet elements, interactions, and all the other ramifications of explicit, operationally meaningful and manipulative experimental design. Perhaps facet analysis will lead to a conjoint measurement approach (Krantz *et al.* 1972) to the scaling of the components of difficulty.

Much of what we have said above refers to cognitive tests of the 'power' variety, but many cognitive tests are designed to be speed tests in which items have little or no difficulty, and thus discriminating power in the sense of Figure 1 is a meaningless concept. Test theory for speeded tests is not well developed (Bock and Wood 1971, p. 216, but see Rasch 1960, Meredith 1971). Worse, most real tests behave like speeded tests for some groups or some persons. The speed *versus* power dichotomy is an unhappy technical distinction whose psychological basis is hardly touched upon in our textbooks (but see Lord and Novick 1968, pp. 131–3, Cronbach 1970, pp. 147, 286). Further, we have sometimes been advised to construct tests having items of a given level of difficulty. Such 'peaked' tests may be justified from a practical point of view when a selection quota for a job is known and fixed. From a theoretical point of view, a test made up of items of similar content and difficulty may be viewed as a special case of behavioural equivalence discussed above.

Paradoxically, latent trait technology, developed primarily for cognitive tests, might more readily apply to the so-called non-cognitive areas of personality, attitudes and interests. For one thing, endorsement rate (cf. difficulty) and discriminating power have an existence free from the dangers of a factor like 'speededness'. For another, the notion of behavioural equivalence discussed in connection with items of moderate discriminating power is possibly more easily justified in these areas. More generally, though, it is surprising that special technologies have not been developed for the construction of personality questionnaires. One would suspect that we should have different views of the operation of items in relation to personality traits from those we adopt for cognitive traits in the light of the separateness of the associated theories; yet, apart from some rather empirically oriented work on such topics as forced-choice formats, social desirability, and *post hoc* research on response biases, no special construction theory has emerged. Indeed, from an inspection of Buros (1965), the most used tests in this area are empirically produced tests like the MMPI and some projective tests. Similarly, the most used interest questionnaire is the empirically derived Strong. Some contrast is to be seen in attitude measurement, where scalogram technique, latent structure analysis, Thurstone–Chave and Likert techniques, and Coombs' unfolding (e.g. Hall 1970) have been applied. Better still, specific theories of attitude have given rise to special kinds of algebra for examining their behaviour samples (e.g. Heider 1946, McGuire 1960, Fishbein 1967), which might lead us to believe that some attitude measurement is where it ought to be, that is, embedded in substantive theory.

Finally under this head, and in summary, should we not expect that the different purposes for which we use tests would influence more explicitly the technology of test construction at the item level?

Characteristics of Tests

Classically, the principal characteristics of whole tests are said to be their reliability and validity. Each has its paradoxes. The best-known for reliability is the attenuation paradox; that is, as a test is made more 'consistent' by discarding the items of lower discriminating power and substituting those of higher discriminating power, there may come a point where the test's correlation with some external criterion decreases (Lord and Novick 1968, p. 344). Birnbaum (1968, Chap. 19) has offered a technical specification of the problem; but content analysis may inhibit the effect if we refuse to discard items thoughtlessly (cf. Cronbach 1970, p. 147).

A second reliability paradox concerns the choice among our psychological purposes for measurement: why do we build tests having high stability when many of us wish to detect change? The current answer seems to be that unless we can measure a trait reliably we cannot reliably measure change in the trait.

The two uses of the term 'reliably' in such a statement might well have different meanings. Perhaps, though, the internal consistency and stability of a test are linked characteristics, and our item-analysis procedures, designed to improve the item–trait correlations, also lead to higher stability or 'stodgi_ness' in our tests. Support for this view may be found in the work of Jinks and Fulker (1970), who found high heritabilities and a lack of evidence for cor_related environments and genotype–environment interactions in a range of psychological tests (p. 347). Eaves (1972), also working in the framework of biometrical genetics, found that some individual items of Eysenck's PEN test have remarkably high heritability coefficients. Goldberg (1963) and Jones and Goldberg (1967) have pointed to a relation between stability and endorse_ment rate characteristics of personality test items. Although we probably seek temporal stability in some of our tests as a *post hoc* matter, internal consistency may not be an independent characteristic.

Imagine, if you will, that we are developing a scale of 'persecution mania'. The following range of items, with alternative contents to make additional items indicated in brackets, might be considered: (a) My *wife* poisoned the *soup* last evening (husband, son, landlady/gravy, cocoa); (b) The *KGB* is *watching* me (CIA, Secret Police/following, trying to kill); (c) My *neighbour* is out to get me (boss, brother, income tax inspector); (d) *People* look at me strangely in the *street* (neighbours, some people/works, club); (e) Someone is trying to do me some kind of harm; (f) I am not very happy; (g) I am suspic_ious of strangers; (h) A *colleague* stole my *best research idea* (the Russians/ watch, girl-friend); (i) I am dying and doctors refuse to help me; (j) I have never been given credit for my genius; (k) I am being persecuted.

We might guess that item analysis would first eliminate the more specific items, say, item types (a), (b), (c), (h), (i) and (j); although descriptive of somebody's problem, they may be too rarely endorsed, even among the 'persecuted', to be useful items. According to Goldberg (1963), these might be among the most stable responses. Next, the more specifically stated, although more commonly occurring, types of persecution might be eliminated on grounds of their low discriminating power: behavioural equivalence lowers the usual indices. The items left might be the rather general ones, say, items (e), (f), (k) and perhaps (g). Thus the more we improve internal consistency by item elimination the less informative might be the score, the more we might build in a lack of sensitivity to the treatments or environmental changes we might hope to evaluate, or the more we might risk measuring something other than that which we intended to measure. To prevent this, a stronger notion of the structure of the universe of items and stronger statements of the purposes of measurement are required.

A third paradox of reliability is that the Kuder–Richardson Formula 20 for reliability is maximized, other things being equal, when all items have a 50 per cent difficulty; yet there is a (Guttman) sense in which internal consistency is maximized when there is a spread of difficulties. Like most paradoxes, this one disintegrates when the alternative assumptions are exposed. Taken to the limit, a high KR-20 would indicate a 'peaked test' in which the structure of relations among items and the nature of the trait measured might well be different from those intended by the test constructor. Our earlier discussion would suggest that the choice is between an 'equivalence behaviours' test and a test having a strong dimension of difficulty; or, some planned compromise of these styles of test. Meanwhile, test constructors may well quote their KR-20 with pride when they had intended to adopt different assumptions and a different measurement model.

A paradox of validity concerns the general striving towards high predictive validity. If, in some industrial study, hand-span were found to have a correlation of 0.6 with worker output, then would we not best serve the company by attempting to redesign the job so that hand-span had reduced validity rather than by using it as a selection measure? Similarly, those who chastise educational selectors because their procedures have less than perfect validity should pause to consider what perfect validity would imply: that several years of the educational process do nothing to alter the rank order at entry! (Of course, some might regard this as desirable.) We might also question the expectations of those who correlate, say, attitude measures with behaviour, or infant performance with adult performance. If they were to achieve high validities, should we not ask, in the first case, about the distinctiveness of the concepts of 'attitude' and 'behaviour', and, in the second case, about the nature of the environment that provides and maintains such immutable individual differences? In other words, the higher the predictive validity the more we might suggest the need for engineering, educational or social manipulations to undo that predictability (cf. Cronbach 1957), or the more we might question the definitions of our variables and our purposes.

Further, the operational distinction between reliability and validity is not as clear as our elementary texts would have it. Suppose that an investigator assesses the ability of the same group of children at age 7 and again at age 11 using the same test. Is this a study of reliability (stability) or of validity (prediction)? Actually, this is a silly question in the absence of a statement of intent by the investigator and some declaration of belief concerning the meaning of 'same test', but many psychologists can be tempted to give definite answers without such information. By and large, test theory contains some good pragmatics but has a questionable relation to any psychological theory.

Let us, for the moment, abandon the terms 'reliability' and 'validity' and consider the internal structure of the two tests shown in Table 7. Test 1 has three items and all the eight possible answer patterns occur with equal frequency. The items have equal difficulty and pairs of items have zero association whichever coefficient is used to show this. Kuder–Richardson Formula 20 or Coefficient Alpha (Cronbach 1970, p. 161) would indicate zero internal consistency. Item–score correlations are zero when a correction is applied for the inclusion of items in the total score. Thus some of the usual indicators suggest no hope for this test; yet there are circumstances in which such a test might have positive correlation with another test.

TABLE 7. Two Item–Person Response Matrices

		Test 1 Items					Test 2 Items			
		1	2	3	Score		1	2	3	Score
Persons	1	0	0	0	0	Persons 1	1	1	1	3
	2	1	0	0	1	2	1	1	0	2
	3	0	1	0	1	3	1	0	0	1
	4	0	0	1	1	4	0	0	0	0
	5	1	1	0	2	p	0.75	0.50	0.25	
	6	1	0	1	2					
	7	0	1	1	2					
	8	1	1	1	3					
	p	0.5	0.5	0.5						

Suppose first that the items of Test 1 refer to the presence or absence of certain 'experiences', that persons differ in the number of experiences, and that items are strictly sampled from a much larger pool of such items. A person with a low number of experiences is likely to have a low score on two such tests, and a person with a high number of experiences is likely to have a high score on both tests. The larger the sample of items in each test, the higher the correlation. Clearly, such an example is close to the classical notion of parallel tests, but it is better handled within the style of generalizability theory of Cronbach *et al.* (1972), who rephrased the issue as follows: '*An investigator asks about the precision or reliability of a measure because he wishes to generalise from the observation in hand to some class of observations to which it belongs* (Cronbach, Rajaratnam and Gleser 1963, p. 144)'. When the universe of content is well defined by substantive considerations, sampling of behaviour —items, conditions of measurement—becomes a reality. There is a growing literature on generalizability and the associated techniques of item-sampling (e.g. Osburn 1967, 1968, 1969, Lord and Novick 1968, Chap. 11, Shoemaker and Osburn 1968, 1969, Cahen, Romberg and Zwirner 1970, Sirotnik 1970, 1972).

Suppose next that all experiences are equivalent with respect to attaining some concept, and that the more experiences the higher the score on some test of the concept. A positive correlation would exist between the total score on a sample of items and the test of concept attainment. As the sample of items is increased this correlation would increase. In conventional terms, then, Test 1 has some poor internal characteristics, yet it can correlate positively both with a sample of items from the same universe of items and with a test based upon another universe of items. Apparently Test 1 has, in one sense, zero reliability, yet it can have a positive validity. Further, the external validity of a long version of Test 1 could be very high even though some indicators of internal validity would remain at zero. There is no problem here so long as we free ourselves from parts of the older technology.

Test 2 exhibits the familiar simplex form. Item–score correlations by Brogden–Clemans estimator are perfect, although KR-20 is not. The information given by each item at its point of difficulty is clearly very good. Consider two such tests, Tests 2(a) and 2(b), where the ability measured by the one is the developmental prerequisite for that measured by the other. When a score on Test 2(a) is necessary for, but not sufficient for, the same score on Test 2(b), a scattergram like that shown in Figure 3 will result. Only some of

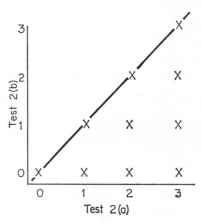

FIGURE 3. A conditional relationship between two tests.

those who score, say, 3 points on Test 2(a) score 3 points on Test 2(b), and no-one scores higher on Test 2(b) than they scored on Test 2(a). Although the developmental 'validity' of the tests is obviously high, the correlation between the tests is far from perfect. Indeed, the stronger the developmental or conditional nature of the relationship, the more curvilinear the regression of Test 2(b) on Test 2(a), and the lower the conventional linear correlation coefficient of validity.

Guttman and Schlesinger (1967a, pp. 26–35) and Guttman (1970) have demonstrated the existence of such pairs of tests. Fisher (1959), Storms (1960) and Jensen (1970, pp. 132–4) have discussed such a scattergram under the name of the 'twisted pear'. This simplex type of principle is increasingly employed in a variety of developmental studies (e.g. Wohlwill 1960, Kohen-Raz 1967, Peel 1967, Ridberg, Parke and Hetherington 1971).

Thus conventional test theory has had a hard time dealing with at least two testing situations which have a plausible basis in psychological theory. Future definitions of reliability and validity will rest upon the distinction between one and two universes of behaviour. Whether we have one or more universes of behaviour is a substantive issue concerning content analysis, and requires a clear statement about the investigator's intentions and the kinds of interpretations he would wish to make.

Relations among Two or More Tests

Given two or more test scores, several things can be done with them. If criterion scores are available we may study how well various combinations of test scores predict the criterion scores, and well-known computational procedures are available for this task. More generally, a taxonomy of the practical uses to which tests are put is given by Cronbach and Gleser (1965), who give prominence to the institutionally, rather than individually, valued decisions. With regard to the theoretical uses of test scores, psychologists typically intercorrelate the tests in the expectation of concluding something about the meaning of one or more of the tests in terms of the remainder, perhaps using factor analysis. In other uses of test scores we may draw up profiles of scores for individuals, and note 'discrepancies' among scores; or we may study differences among scores achieved over time, perhaps assessing 'change'. The first use concerns construct validity and the second concerns tests in the service of individuals. We shall deal with these in turn.

Construct Validity

Construct validity concerns the psychological meaning of test scores. The process of construct validation is concerned with the role of tests in the development of psychological theories. Following Cronbach (1970, pp. 143–4), the methods and procedures by which the construct validity of a test may be studied are as follows: (a) inspection of items; (b) administration of the test to individuals who 'think aloud'; (c) correlation with practical criteria; (d) correlation with other tests (and factor analysis); (e) internal correlations among items and subtests; (f) studies of group differences; (g) studies of the effect of treatment on scores; and (h) stability of scores on retest.

Each method has its problems. The manifest content of an item may not always give the right clues as to process. For example, the materials of the WAIS Block Design subtest are three-dimensional, but three-dimensional thinking may not be involved; and items of a Guilford divergent ability test include girls' names, but knowledge of girls' names may be irrelevant to the required process. The processes of individuals who are asked to 'think aloud' while performing the items may be different from those of the silent testee. Although there is some degree of plausibility in the argument that the traits we measure should have stability over time, perhaps this is not true of all traits, for example 'fickleness', 'responsiveness to treatment'. These are, however, obvious and relatively trivial points.

A test's correlation with other tests is usually given most attention in construct validation. Typically, we seem to want to understand the meaning of one test in terms of several other tests whose own 'construct validities' may not be well understood. Almost as a consequence of our frustration with the multiple meanings of the mass of data collected, we follow up with a factor analysis which may well confuse the issues more than it illuminates them. Studies of group differences may also founder on the lack of a unique interpretation of why the groups differed in the first place; and experimental treatments may have complex multiple effects on the scores.

The more basic problem is that construct validation requires prior statement of a theory about what is being measured; yet most of the methods appear to be applied *post hoc*. Apparently tests are to be constructed and their properties are to be examined. Should not the theory as part of its specifications indicate how the test items might be constructed? If the theory refers to a structure of relations among variables, should not the theory also specify how those variables might be operationalized, and should not construct validity refer to that structure of relations?

Several lines of theoretical and empirical work on construct validity have been converging over the past 15 years or so. The source paper by Cronbach and Meehl (1955) featured the notion of a nomological network. Influenced by Meehl (1945), Coombs (1953), Peak (1953), Guttman (1954) and a preprint of Guttman (1958b), Loevinger (1957) found the Cronbach–Meehl network too loose and proposed a more direct structural component of validity in which the 'structural relations between test items parallel the structural relations of other manifestations of the trait being measured'. The Campbell and Fiske (1959) procedure for convergent and discriminant validation by the multitrait–multimethod matrix continues to generate new illustrations and developments (e.g. Boruch *et al.* 1970). Path analysis (e.g. Werts and Linn 1970) is a form of structural analysis relating both to true score theory and construct validity. Guttman has long sought to discover qualitative structures in data: facet theory (e.g. Guttman 1955, 1971, Foa 1965, 1968) promises to do for test design and analysis what Fisherian logic did for experimental design and analysis. Humphreys (1962) has acted as a helpful publicist for facet analysis in the area of cognition; and Foa has given examples in personality and social behaviour. The generalizability theory of Cronbach *et al.* (1972) adopted the term 'facet', and employs a rational, structured approach to the old problem of reliability. Indeed, reliability becomes just one aspect of construct validity, and Boruch and Wolins' (1970) paper on multitrait–multimethod is simultaneously an exercise in generalizability theory and facet analysis.

Meanwhile, classical forms of factor analysis continue to be the principal type of structural analysis for many others, and *post hoc* at that. We should also add a reminder that a qualitative structure among variables is not always to be found by a structure of linear equations. Although some would seem to require methods of analysis which produce results untouched by human thought, many structures of relationships are readily visible to the naked eye if an appropriate experiment has been conducted. Some examples follow.

Construct Validation by Psychological Decomposition

Hopkins (1971) wanted to understand what might be measured by the Digit–Symbol subtest of the WAIS. It might be hypothesized that performance on this test is influenced by such factors as writing speed, motivation, speed of eye-movements and perhaps ability to learn the relations between the digit and symbols. It is very tempting, in the mould of conventional construct validation, to construct tests of these attributes, or to seek out available tests which might be related to these attributes, or to correlate the test of interest with every other test in sight. Thus, what starts as a problem of understanding something about one test becomes a multiple act of construct validation. Indeed, there is the danger that we might know less about the tests we drag in to help us understand the test of interest than we already know about that test.

Hopkins' solution was to construct tests in the style of the Digit–Symbol subtest. Holding constant the format, instructions, practice test format, timing and scoring of the test, he varied the relations between digits and symbols to capture different processes. 'Writing speed' was assessed not by just any measure of writing speed, but the speed of writing the same symbol repeatedly for 90 seconds within the usual digit–symbol response frame and under the usual instructions. 'Eye-movement' was assessed by a test in which only two symbols were assigned randomly to digits. Twenty-five 'digits' were used to reduce the chances of the testee learning which of the two symbols was associated with each 'digit' within the 90-second test. As soon as a testee saw the task and attempted the practice items, he appreciated that only two symbols are involved. His task is therefore one of scanning the panel to discover which of the two symbols he is to write in the current response box. Hopkins constructed further tests to study the effect of 'learning', employing repeated trials with the same digit–symbol relations, and other tests where there was some discoverable semi-logical relation between digits and symbols. He also repeated the original WAIS subtest. The principal results, being the correlations between the WAIS subtest and Hopkins' decompositions of the test, are shown in Table 8.

Strictly speaking, we should more accurately describe the writing speed test as 'writing speed and motivation', for within the style of this operational decomposition of the test how can we assess a relevant version of 'motivation' separate from writing speed? Similarly, the eye-movements test includes writing speed, and the 'learning' tasks include both. Given these limitations, it is notable how well the eye-movements form of the digit–symbol task accounts for the original WAIS subtest, particularly in the light of the retest correlation for the group of testees used. It is also interesting to see that the correlations with repeated trials of a digit–symbol task diminish the more opportunity and encouragement there is to learn the digit–symbol relations. The point is that the task of understanding an available test has been handled by relatively controlled and manipulative experimentation with features of the test, rather than by the looser classical psychometric approach.

TABLE 8. Correlations with WAIS Digit–Symbol Subtest
(Hopkins 1971)

Test	Correlation
Writing speed	0.47
Eye-movements	0.68
WAIS Digit–Symbol (repeat)	0.81
Learning 1	0.30
Learning 2	0.13
Learning 3	0.07

For a second example we shall refer briefly to an unpublished study of two creativity tasks, carried out in an undergraduate practical class. It was thought that the two Guilford-style tests (cf. Getzels and Jackson 1962), 'Uses for Things' (e.g. uses of a brick) and 'Word Associations' (e.g. bolt), both verbal tests, might relate differentially to the speed–power dimension of conventional verbal ability tests. The creativity tasks were administered alongside three verbal ability tasks, which may be regarded for the group tested as speeded (V_1), speed–power (V_2) and power (V_3) tasks. The results recorded in Table 9

TABLE 9. Selected Correlations between Two Creativity Tests (C)
and Three Verbal Ability Tests (V)

Tests	V_1	V_2	V_3
C_1	0.53	0.27	0.08
C_2	0.04	0.08	0.20

show that while the correlations are generally low for this highly selected group those for 'Uses for Things' (C_1) increase with power, and those for 'Word Associations' (C_2) increase with speededness. We suggest that this style of experimentation and 'eyeball' analysis may give more immediate meaning to the differences among tests than factor analysis of whole tables of correlations among miscellaneous and unmatched tests.

For a third example of how we might understand available tests by devising operational decompositions of their processes, we refer to a study of the WAIS Block Design subtest by Chatterton and Perkins (1971). They constructed three multiple-choice paper-and-pencil tests in which they attempted to simulate some aspects of the WAIS task. The items of each test called upon the testee to identify which of six alternative block designs matched an example. Test 1 was a simple recognition task. Test 2 required the testee to identify what design would be produced by moving blocks together. Test 3 called for the matching of a rotated block design. The correlations between these three tests and WAIS Block Design proper are displayed in Table 10.

TABLE 10. Correlations between Three Paper-and-Pencil Tests and WAIS Block Design Subtest (Chatterton and Perkins 1971)

Test	Correlation
1. Simple recognition	0.43
2. Exploded recognition	0.48
3. Rotated recognition	0.70

Clearly, the simple processes represented in the paper-and-pencil tests, which require no manual manipulations of blocks, go some way towards accounting for performance on the Block Design subtest. In addition, we ought to have spotted at the design stage the possibility of a fourth test—'exploded and rotated recognition'—which would complete the 2×2 structure of the study shown in Table 11. There is a structural implication in Table 11 that the fourth

TABLE 11. Data of Table 10 Rearranged to Expose the Incomplete Design

		'Explosion'	
		0	+
'Rotation'	0	0.43	0.48
	+	0.70	?

test would have an even higher correlation with Block Design than the other tests. We now turn to other studies in which similar structural implications are examined.

Construct Validation by Structural Analysis

One of the most quoted structural views of intelligence is Guilford's structure-of-intellect model. Fisher and Guthrie (1971) devised or adapted tests to represent four cells of Guilford's 120-cell structure. All four were divergent tests but varied in their Content (semantic, symbolic) and their Products (units, classes). The expectation was that if Guilford's view of intellect held and the tests were properly constructed then a certain structure of relationship would be found among the four tests. Pairs of tests with one feature in common (e.g. semantic Content) should have higher intercorrelation than tests with no feature in common. The data of Table 12 show that the

TABLE 12. Fisher–Guthrie (1971) Data on Four Divergent Ability Tests

Tests	SU	MC	MU	SC	Structured data
SU	—	0.29	0.54	0.44	Products M S (Contents)
MC		—	0.34	0.53	U ×—0.54—×
MU			—	0.26	0.34 0.29 0.44
SC				—	C ×—0.53—× 0.26

Structural diagram:

Contents: M (semantic), S (symbolic)
Products: U (units), C (classes)

U: ×—0.54—×
        0.29
0.34 ×   × 0.44
        0.26
C: ×—0.53—×

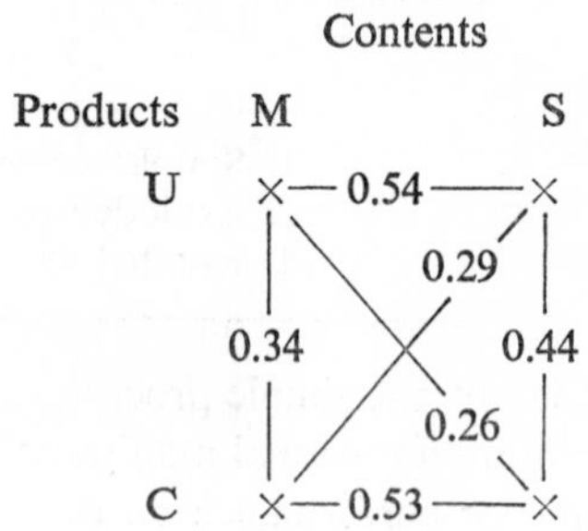

M, semantic; S, symbolic; U, units; C, classes.

basic expectations were fulfilled and a degree of simple structural validity was demonstrated. The test pairs with either units or classes as Products in common had the highest correlations, the test pairs with either symbolic or semantic Contents in common had the next highest correlations, and the two pairs of tests with nothing in common had the lowest correlations. For the group tested and the tests used, the Contents formed a weaker bond across tests that the Products.

To obtain even this primitive degree of confirmation, Fisher and Guthrie had to spend a great deal of time considering how compatible were their tests in format and administration and how well the items represented the hypothesized processes. Few such simple structural expectations are fulfilled by those parts of Guilford's data which we have examined. The results of some of Guilford's factor analyses are surely less satisfactory when a simple eyeball search for a structure supposedly represented by the tests in a logical manner does not discover it.

Similar remarks might be made about the structural theory behind the Illinois Test of Psycholinguistic Abilities (Kirk, McCarthy and Kirk 1968). Several factor analyses largely confirm the existence of a strong common factor in the ITPA. Given its theory and the labels applied to the subtests, we should be able to expect certain relationships to hold. For example, pairs of tests calling upon auditory input ought to correlate more highly than pairs not having such a feature in common (cf. Jones and Wepman 1961). If simple validation of this kind does not work, then either the theory is wrong, or the tests are unrepresentative of the theory, or the theory applies to some group of persons other than those tested, perhaps some lower age-group. The point is that the structural theory suggests an experimental–manipulative approach to test construction and validation. If four sequential tests, compounded of auditory and visual inputs and vocal and motor outputs, were constructed then we might expect that the correlations among pairs of tests would have the structure shown in Figure 4. Double bonds are used to suggest the higher

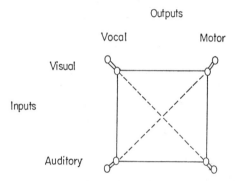

FIGURE 4. Expected structure of relationships among four tests.
O = test, e.g. visual–motor sequencing test.

correlations to be expected among pairs of tests representing the same process ('reliability'), single bonds represent the lower correlations which ought to be found among pairs of tests having an input or an output mode in common, and the broken-line bonds link pairs of tests having nothing but a sequential process in common.

One attempt to verify this structure of relationships failed in part, and that failure was instructive. Either we failed to inject real motor difficulty into the tests carrying that label, or we failed to represent the sequential process equally throughout the various input–output modes. The attempt also brought to our attention the fact that while the original ITPA auditory–vocal test calls upon temporal sequencing (digit-span type), the visual–motor test probably calls for spatial sequencing. Such an 'incompatibility' may or may not be intended.

Surtees and Tennant (1972) explored properties of the Memory-for-Designs (MFD) type of task in a structured way. Using a series of designs, shown for two different exposure times and to be copied from memory after two different delay times, they intercorrelated performances on the four tests implied. Table 13 shows that higher correlations were found for pairs of tests

TABLE 13. Intercorrelations among Four 'Memory-for-Designs' Tests Presented under Two Exposure Times (*E*) and Two Delay Times (*D*) (Surtees and Tennant 1972)

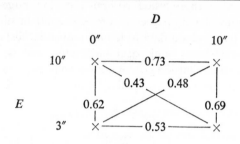

having the same level of a factor in common (cf. Figure 4). Surtees and Tennant had intended to examine a standard MFD test in relation to their own manipulations of the task, but unfortunately the test failed to discriminate among the subjects used. Had they been able to do so they would have been able to examine a 'validity surface' across the exposure times, delay times, scoring methods and item types that they used.

The Chatterton–Perkins data of Table 11 suggest an incomplete validity surface. Cope (1972) was able to complete one for features of spontaneous speech in four-year-olds. She devised four matched tests—Vocabulary Production, Grammar Production, Vocabulary Comprehension and Grammar Comprehension—and correlated each with children's total speech production in a 15-minute observation period. The results are shown in Table 14. Cope

TABLE 14. Correlations between Four Tests, Based on the Facets Vocabulary (V) *versus* Grammar (G) and Production (P) *versus* Comprehension (C), and Total Speech Production (Cope 1972)

	V	G
P	0.79	0.55
C	0.66	0.21

also found interesting validity surfaces for other observed measures of speech such as interrogative and imitative speech. Had the tests not been constructed with the appropriate degree of compatibility, we could not be confident that the differences found among the correlations were directly meaningful.

The above are rather simple examples drawn from short-term student projects and may be somewhat lacking in psychological importance. Nevertheless, they illustrate the ways in which either well-known tests might be better understood or representations of multivariate theories might be examined. In neither case is elaborate statistical engineering required. The more rational the development of tests purporting to represent a theory, the less arduous are the statistical gymnastics required to test the truth or falsity of the theory and its representation. In particular, variables which form the networks of strongly structural theories are best represented by tests developed in concert. The tests should have suitable compatibilities and only relevant incompatibilities. If tests being compared differ unsystematically among themselves in too many features, who knows what they measure?

Comparing Scores: Discrepancies and Profiles

Given two or more scores for an individual, what meaning can we attach to the differences among the scores? We might calculate that an observed difference between scores is 'reliable', or that it is rare in some defined population, or that one score departs reliably from an 'expected' score based upon another (Payne and Jones 1957). About a score profile we might be able to say that the individual is more like some defined group of persons than he is like some other group. Generally, the statements we attempt to make about an individual on the basis of two or more scores are norm-referenced statements, correct in their empirico-statistical way, but ill defined in their reference to any psychological theory and uncertain in their relevance to any clinical problem.

The notion of a 'discrepancy' between two scores is a persistent one: a child's reading ability is said to be below his intelligence; or his verbal scale score is said to be above or below his performance score; or his listening comprehension is better or worse than his vocabulary level. Superficially, all that such statements require is that two scores have been standardized within some group. Why then do we not say that a child's height is below his vocabulary level? Presumably it is because the correlation between height and vocabulary level is almost zero within an age group; and, further, that within age groups height differences have no obvious relevance to the acquisition of vocabulary. Now intelligence tests tend to have strong correlations with reading tests; but this pragmatic justification is insufficient. The development of intelligence is presumably considered to contain the necessary preconditions for learning to read. Should we, then, use a verbal intelligence test or a non-verbal intelligence test as a basis for judging the standard of reading performance? Should we say that the two scores differ by so many standard points, or should we use the intelligence test score to estimate an expected reading score? Essentially atheoretical answers have been given to such questions. For example, it has been argued that the regression method should be used for calculating the discrepancy between ability and performance because such discrepancies will, by construction, be uncorrelated with ability level; but an overachiever in one classroom may be an underachiever in the normative context of another (e.g. Levy and Tucker 1972). It has also been argued that a non-verbal predictor should be used, because otherwise the predictor might be confounded with the criterion. (If the predictor were made sufficiently non-verbal and unconfounded with reading performance, perhaps the correlation would be zero. *Reductio ad absurdum*.) We would seem to lack a sufficiently clear statement of theory about discrepancies such that the fundamental measurement problem may be solved; mere pragmatics abound in an area of considerable psychological importance.

It is a curious fact that the expression 'individual tests' denotes a test which is merely procedurally more appropriate to administer to an individual than it is to a group of individuals. How much of the technology of its design is specifically geared to aiding the decisions to be made about individuals in a clinical setting is open to question. So long as we borrow tests, developed independently and for other purposes, the meaning of differences, regressed or otherwise, will remain obscure. Discrepancy scores present a new and higher-level problem of construct validity. As Gunzberg (1970) concluded: 'there is little doubt that, neither individual tests . . . nor large assortments of tests . . . provide ready made answers to questions which the psychologist is likely to be asked in individual cases' (p. 309). A new start is required in this area.

One approach is to build up tests in tandem from the item level. Suppose, to take a simple example, that the discrepancy between a person's recall and recognition abilities in some area of memory is thought to be of interest, one set of items could be given first in a recall mode and then in a recognition mode. The meaning of the discrepancy assessed in this way is determined by inspection of the items and consideration of the operational procedures used. Experimentalists have often used such a procedure; perhaps psychometricians have been too bound by the dogmas of test construction.

A second approach appropriate to the clinical–individual setting is to prepare pairs of items, rather than tests, to examine particular hypotheses. Consider the following rather simplistic example. A child is given a card with the oral instruction: 'Do what it says on this card'. Let us suppose that the child does nothing. Now the child is told to stand up and he does so. Since the card contains the message 'Stand up' we have a discrepancy in behaviour: the child responded to the oral message but not to the written message. Perhaps the child cannot read, he may be blind, he may not have understood the instructions for the first item, or, to the second item he may have stood up in response to the tester's manner rather than the message. Whatever is true, we have further hypotheses to test about the meaning of the original discrepancy in behaviour; we need no reference to standardized and normed tests; and we are limited, not by the limited library of available tests, but only by our inventiveness as psychologists. This clinical style of psychometrics, in which discrepancies within the individual are sought and hypothesis tested, is well illustrated in the work of Luria (e.g. 1966, Part III).

A third approach might be to bring notions from generalizability theory, Guttman, and item-sampling to the problem. Consider the hypothetical situation shown in Table 15. A class of behaviours A is suspected to provide

TABLE 15. Dependencies between Matched Items of Two Behaviour Classes

(a) Data			(b) Complete dependence				(c) Partial dependence			

	A	B
Item 1	1	1
Pairs 2	1	0
3	0	0
.	.	.
.	.	.
.	.	.
100	1	0

(b) Complete dependence

		A		
		1	0	
B	1	50	0	50
	0	10	40	50
		60	40	100

(c) Partial dependence

		A		
		1	0	
B	1	40	10	50
	0	20	30	50
		60	40	100

the developmental prerequisite for class of behaviours B in one individual. Classes A and B may be represented by a universe of pairs of items such that a discrepancy is directly meaningful for any pair of items and for the individual. Suppose, now, that behaviour over 100 pairs of items is tabulated in a 2×2 table. The appearance of the 'one-person simplex pattern' of Table 15(b) would indicate a strong type of developmental dependance, whereas the data in Table 15(c) would indicate another sort, perhaps that development may have occurred through optional routes and that there are equivalence classes in behaviour.

Much the same style of comment applies to profiles of test scores insofar as they purport to represent multiple discrepancies within a person. Just as there has been argument about whether or not to regress discrepancies, so there has been controversy about whether or not the scales making up a profile should be orthogonalized (e.g. Overall 1964, Heerman 1965). Again, profile interpretation is normative at root rather than truly intra-individual: we are tempted to say that a person is better at A than he is at B; what we really mean is that the person is higher on scale A relative to the population than he is on scale B relative to the population. No doubt the latter statement has some value, but its meaning is more limited than we would like for some purposes. Looking at bumps and hollows in profiles has become a new phrenology. Again, it is suggested that the task of developing *post hoc* meaning and comparability for a collection of scales is too difficult; witness the struggle over the years to determine the meaning of profiles for the MMPI, a test which had the benefit of empirical construction. Better that our psychological intentions are embedded in scales at the item-construction level.

Comparing Scores: Change

The measurement of change requires a theory about change, about what is changing, and about what causes change. Clearly, the measurement of change is important in psychology and education; yet, like the study of discrepancies, the measurement of change has usually taken as its starting point some available test scores. Similar problems, and perhaps pseudo-problems, therefore arise. Should a gain score be orthogonal to the initial measurement? Are gains made by different individuals comparable? In what sense can scales have high reliability yet be responsive to change-inducing environments or treatments? If we are uncertain about the meaning of the original test scores, what meaning do the gain scores have?

Recent discussion of change (Harris 1963) shows little inclination to ask why we should want to measure change and whether we might have more than one purpose. Statistical solutions abound to problems of uncertain psychological origin. Cronbach and Furby (1970) doubted whether we should measure change; at least, they suggest that we examine our intentions.

One substantive area of interest in change is the well-worn problem of the differentiation of intelligence with age. Reviewers (e.g. Anastasi 1958, pp. 357–61, Vernon 1961, p. 140) have continued to find the evidence contradictory and the studies beset with methodological difficulties. One approach might be to ask of each test participating in such a study: What do the improvements in score with age mean? Or, equivalently, how is the implied difficulty scale induced? Several answers seem possible. For example, items may increase in difficulty because they call upon differentiating skills (e.g. increasingly calling upon knowledge or vocabulary in specific areas); or, the items may call for increasing coordination or integration of old skills (e.g. simultaneous application of previously learned principles); or, older persons may simply be faster as though through practice. As Anastasi (1967) said: '. . . attempts to subsume all such age changes under the single principle of either differentiation or generalization of ability represents an over-simplification. It would seem more realistic to expect some functions to become more differentiated, others less so, with time, depending upon the nature of intervening experiences in a particular cultural context' (p. 303). Such explanations may appear obvious but we have seemed reluctant to try them, preferring rather to examine the external evidence of relations among whole tests by factor analysis in search of a simple overall answer. Foa (1968), arguing in the style of facet analysis, has also discussed ways of detecting change in qualitative structures and has given examples outside the field of ability-testing.

Another substantive area of interest concerns the detection of change in individuals *qua* individuals. Some of the approaches suggested in the previous section may apply here.

The scale of measurement for change is said to be an issue. Almost every textbook on psychological measurement by tests (including Lord and Novick 1968, p. 21) gives a discussion of scales of measurement—nominal, ordinal, interval and ratio scales—and the 'permissible' numerical operations, but no convincing explanation of how to achieve such scales (cf. Guttman 1971, p. 339). Several texts have rather limply claimed that test scores give interval scale measurement when a normal distribution obtains. By contrast, Cronbach (1970) said that '. . . the shape of the distribution depends upon the scale of measurement . . .' (p. 99), although here he was questioning the assumption that all scales automatically give rise to normal distributions. Bock and Wood (1971, pp. 194–5) drew attention to the scale properties flowing from the Lord–Novick–Birnbaum latent trait models, saying that they '. . . offer the advantage of measurement on a scale with a well-defined metric. This means that the ability estimates, or any one-to-one transformation of them which theory may dictate, may be used to measure growth and change. Traditional methods of scoring tests are markedly deficient in this respect and have hindered the study of growth in ability and in other latent traits' (p. 195). It is not clear, though, how we can have a 'well-defined metric' without the intrusion of any substantive issues such as the purpose of measuring change and some discussion of approaches to item-content analysis. As Coombs, Dawes and Tversky (1970) said: 'A closer examination of the problem (of metric) reveals that no measurement theory for intelligence is available. Consequently no representation theorem can be established and no meaning can be given to the uniqueness problem' (p. 17).

Much remains to be done in this area. One promising line is the elaboration of models and methods for the multivariate Guttman scale by Coombs and Smith (1972). Their model would allow us to view development as the acquisition and deletion of behaviours or processes, and also permits alternative routes to the same end-point in development. Thus change (acquisition/ deletion) is a feature of a structure rather than of a single scale.

Another line of development is the application of generalizability theory (Cronbach *et al.* 1972) to the study of change in an individual. For example, Butterfield (1970) studied the use of behaviour-rating scales to detect change in a child under treatment. Before treatment began she determined the relative sizes of baseline errors, using seven nurses to rate the child on a five-point scale on each of 21 items on two occasions. The component variances, shown in Table 16 alongside the usual mean squares of analysis of variance, are

TABLE 16. Mean Squares and Estimated Component Variances
for Ratings of a Single Child (Butterfield 1970)

Sources	MS	Component variances
Nurses (N)	8.38	0.12
Items (I)	3.57	0.11
Occasions (O)	10.00	0.05
$N \times I$	1.13	0.36
$N \times O$	3.36	0.14
$I \times O$	1.15	0.11
$N \times I \times O, E$	0.41	0.41

estimated assuming that 'items' is a fixed factor but that 'nurses' is a random factor. It may be calculated from these data that the error variance—relative to whatever changes one would hope to induce in a five-point scale—for generalizing from one nurse using 20 items is 0.35; using two nurses and 20 items the error variance is 0.20, but using 20 nurses who are randomly assigned one item each the value is 0.11. Thus the error variance for generalizing across nurses is lower in the last case when just 20 units of information are gathered than in the second case where there are 40 units, a result difficult to spot within the classical mould of reliability theory.

Concluding Remarks

Psychological measurement should derive from psychological theory; but in some areas the development of technique has outstripped psychological analysis and in other areas the development of psychological theory is far ahead of any proper representation of its variables by tests and similar instruments. There are many signs of this. Classical procedures for construct validation, though plausible, are flabby and *post hoc*. It is as though tests crystallize out of the stream of research and are then analysed to see what structures they contain. We are good at developing some single tests, but we are bad at representing multivariate theories. The holy cows of item analysis, standardization and indices of reliability appear to receive more attention from test constructors than elucidation of meaning. We have become so concerned with creating the 'uniform system . . . so that determinations made at different times and places would be compared and combined' (Cattell 1890) that we have lost distinctiveness of purpose. Statistical manipulation of test results is sometimes used as a poor substitute for operational control of item content and format at the test development stage. Much needed are tests constructed to test hypotheses, and fewer hypotheses about tests. In particular, the goal of making sensible statements about an individual *qua* individual needs a stronger representation of theories about individuals to guide test construction. One might also expect very distinctive modes of test construction to develop in different areas of psychology.

This review has indeed been idiosyncratic. It has also been unfair in not emphasizing the achievements of Lord and Novick in bringing good statistical order to the looser formulations of former decades (but see Guttman 1969); and it has not given credit to Cronbach for the coherence which his account of tests and testing has brought to many students. Perhaps other contributors will redress the balance?

References

Anastasi, A. (1958), *Differential Psychology: Individual and Group Differences in Behavior*, New York, Macmillan.

Anastasi, A. (1965), *Individual Differences*, New York, Wiley.

Anastasi, A. (1967), 'Psychology, psychologists, and psychological testing', *American Psychologist*, **22**, 297–306.

Anderson, J., Kearney, G. E., and Everett, A. V. (1968), 'An evaluation of Rasch's structural model for test items', *British Journal of Mathematical and Statistical Psychology*, **21**, 231–8.

Birnbaum, A. (1968), 'Some latent trait models and their use in inferring an examinee's ability', in F. M. Lord and M. R. Novick, *Statistical Theories of Mental Test Scores*, New York, Addison-Wesley.

Bloom, B. S. (1956), *Taxonomy of Educational Objectives*, New York, Longmans, Green.

Bock, R. D., and Wood, R. (1971), 'Test theory', *Annual Review of Psychology*, **22**, 193–224.

Bormuth, J. R. (1970), *On the Theory of Achievement Test Items*, Chicago, University of Chicago Press.

Boruch, R. F., Larkin, J. D., Wolins, L., and MacKinney, A. C. (1970), 'Alternative methods of analysis: Multitrait–multimethod data', *Educational and Psychological Measurement*, **30**, 833–53.

Boruch, R. F., and Wolins, L. (1970), 'A procedure for estimation of trait, method, and error variance attributable to a measure', *Educational and Psychological Measurement*, **30**, 547–74.

Buros, O. K. (1965) (Ed.), *The Sixth Mental Measurements Yearbook*, New Jersey, Gryphon.

Butt, D. S., and Fiske, D. W. (1968), 'Comparison of strategies in developing scales for dominance', *Psychological Bulletin*, **70**, 505–19.

Butterfield, T. (1970), Unpublished Report, University of Birmingham.

Cahen, L. S., Romberg, T. A., and Zwirner, W. (1970), 'The estimation of mean achievement scores for schools by the item-sampling technique', *Educational and Psychological Measurement*, **30**, 41–60.

Campbell, D. T., and Fiske, D. W. (1959), 'Convergent and discriminant validation by the multitrait–multimethods matrix', *Psychological Bulletin*, **56**, 81–105.

Carroll, J. B. (1945), 'The effect of difficulty and chance success on correlations between items or between tests', *Psychometrika*, **10**, 1–19.

Carroll, J. B. (1961), 'The nature of the data, or how to choose a correlation coefficient', *Psychometrika*, **26**, 347–72.

Cattell, J. McK. (1890), 'Mental tests and measurements', *Mind*, **15**, 373–408.

Chatterton, C., and Perkins, E. (1971), Unpublished Report, Department of Psychology, University of Birmingham.

Coombs, C. H. (1953), 'Theory and methods of social measurement', in L. Festinger and D. Katz (Eds.), *Research Methods in the Behavioral Sciences*, New York, Dryden.

Coombs, C. H. (1964), *A Theory of Data*, New York, Wiley.

Coombs, C. H., Dawes, R. M., and Tversky, A. (1970), *Mathematical Psychology: An Elementary Introduction*, New Jersey, Prentice-Hall.

Coombs, C. H., and Smith, J. E. K. (1972), 'On the detection of structure in attitudes and development processes', Michigan Mathematical Psychology Program Reports No. 72–8.

Cope, H. (1972), Unpublished Report, Department of Psychology, University of Birmingham.

Cronbach, L. J. (1957), 'The two disciplines of scientific psychology', *American Psychologist*, **12**, 671–83.

Cronbach, L. J. (1970), *Essentials of Psychological Testing* (3rd ed.), New York, Harper and Row.

Cronbach, L. J., and Furby, L. (1970), 'How should we measure "change"—or should we?', *Psychological Bulletin*, **74**, 68–80.

Cronbach, L. J., and Gleser, G. C. (1965), *Psychological Tests and Personnel Decisions* (2nd ed.), Urbana, University of Illinois Press.

Cronbach, L. J., Gleser, G. C., Nanda, H., and Rajaratnam, N. (1972), *The Dependability of Behavioral Measurements: Theory of Generalizability for Scores and Profiles*, New York, Wiley.

Cronbach, L. J., and Meehl, P. E. (1955), 'Construct validity in psychological tests', *Psychological Bulletin*, **52**, 281–302.

Cronbach, L. J., Rajaratnam, N., and Gleser, G. C. (1963), 'Theory of generalizability: A liberation of reliability theory', *British Journal of Statistical Psychology*, **16**, 137–63.

Eaves, L. (1972), Personal Communication.

Einhorn, H. J. (1970), 'The use of nonlinear, noncompensatory models in decision making', *Psychological Bulletin*, **73**, 221–30.

Ferguson, G. A. (1941), 'The factorial interpretation of test difficulty', *Psychometrika*, **6**, 323–9.

Fishbein, M. (1967), 'A behaviour theory approach to the relations between beliefs about an object and the attitude toward the object', in M. Fishbein (Ed.), *Readings in Attitude Theory and Measurement*, New York, Wiley.

Fisher, J. (1959), 'The twisted pear and the prediction of behaviour', *Journal of Consulting Psychology*, **23**, 400–5.

Fisher, J., and Guthrie, J. S. (1971), Unpublished Report, Department of Psychology, University of Birmingham.

Fleiss, J. L., and Zubin, J. (1969), 'On the theory and methods of clustering', *Multivariate Behavioral Research*, **4**, 235–50.

Foa, U. G. (1965), 'New developments in facet design and analysis', *Psychological Review*, **72**, 262–74.

Foa, U. G. (1968), 'Three kinds of behavioural change', *Psychological Bulletin*, **70**, 460–73.

Getzels, J. W., and Jackson, P. W. (1962), *Creativity and Intelligence*, New York, Wiley.

Gibson, W. A. (1967), 'A latent structure for the simplex', *Psychometrika*, **32**, 35–46.

Goldberg, L. R. (1963), 'A model of item ambiguity in personality assessment', *Educational and Psychological Measurement*, **23**, 467–92.

Gourlay, N. (1951), 'Difficulty factors arising from the use of tetrachoric correlations in factor analysis', *British Journal of Psychology* (Statistical Section), **4**, 65–76.

Groen, G. J. (1971), 'Stochastic processes and the Guttman Simplex', *Psychometrika*, **36**, 289–302.

Guilford, J. P. (1941), 'The difficulty of a test and its factor composition', *Psychometrika*, **6**, 67–77.

Gunzberg, H. C. (1970), 'Subnormal adults', in P. Mittler (Ed.), *The Psychological Assessment of Mental and Physical Handicaps*, London, Methuen.

Guttman, L. (1950), in S. A. Stouffer *et al.*, *Measurement and Prediction*, Princeton, Princeton University Press.

Guttman, L. (1953), 'Image theory for the structure of quantitative variates', *Psychometrika*, **18**, 277–96.

Guttman, L. (1954), 'A new approach to factor analysis: The radex', in P. F. Lazarsfeld (Ed.), *Mathematical Thinking in the Social Sciences*, Glencoe, Illinois, Free Press.

Guttman, L. (1955), 'An outline of some new methodology for social research', *Public Opinion Quarterly*, **18**, 395–404.

Guttman, L. (1958a), 'To what extent can communalities reduce rank?', *Psychometrika*, **23**, 297–308.

Guttman, L. (1958b), 'What lies ahead for factor analysis?', *Educational and Psychological Measurement*, **18**, 497–515.

Guttman, L. (1968), 'A general nonmetric technique for finding the smallest coordinate space for a configuration of points', *Psychometrika*, **33**, 469–506.

Guttman, L. (1969), 'Review of F. N. Lord and M. P. Novick, Statistical theories of mental test scores', *Psychometrika*, **34**, 398–404.

Guttman, L. (1970), 'Integration of test design and analysis', in *Proceedings of the 1969 Invitational Conference on Testing Problems*, Princeton, N.J., Educational Testing Service.

Guttman, L. (1971), 'Measurement as structural theory', *Psychometrika*, **36**, 329–48.

Guttman, L., and Schlesinger, I. M. (1967a), *The Analysis of Diagnostic Effectiveness of a Facet Design Battery of Achievement and Analytical Ability Test* (Project Report), Jerusalem, Israel, The Israel Institute of Applied Social Research.

Guttman, L., and Schlesinger, I. M. (1967b), 'Systematic construction of distractors for ability and achievement test items', *Educational and Psychological Measurement*, **27**, 569–80.

Hall, R. F. (1970), 'An application of unfolding theory to the measurement of attitudes', *Educational and Psychological Measurement*, **30**, 621–37.

Harreldon, L. E., Jordan, J. E., and Horn, H. (1972), 'An application of Guttman facet theory to the study of attitudes toward the mentally retarded in Germany', *Journal of Psychology*, **80**, 323–36.

Harris, C. (1963) (Ed.), *Problems in Measuring Change*, Madison, University of Wisconsin Press.

Heerman, E. F. (1965), 'Comments on Overall's "Multivariate methods for profile analysis"', *Psychological Bulletin*, **63**, 128.

Heider, F. (1946), 'Attitudes and cognitive organisation', *Journal of Personality*, **21**, 107–12.

Henrysson, S. (1962), 'The relation between factor loadings and biserial correlations in item analysis', *Psychometrika*, **27**, 419–24.

Hopkins, N. (1971), Unpublished Report, Department of Psychology, University of Birmingham.

Humphreys, L. G. (1962), 'The organisation of human abilities', *American Psychologist*, **17**, 475–83.

Jensen, A. R. (1970), 'Hierarchical theories of mental ability', in W. B. Dockrell (Ed.), *On Intelligence*, Toronto, Ontario Institute for Studies in Education.

Jinks, J. L., and Fulker, D. W. (1970), 'Comparison of the biometrical genetical, MAVA, and classical approaches to the analysis of human behaviour', *Psychological Bulletin*, **73**, 311–49.

Jones, L. V., and Wepman, J. M. (1961), 'Dimensions of language performance in aphasia', *Journal of Speech and Hearing Research*, **4**, 220–32.

Jones, R. R., and Goldberg, L. R. (1967), 'Interrelationships among personality scale parameters: Item response stability and scale reliability', *Educational and Psychological Measurement*, **27**, 323–33.

Jöreskog, K. G. (1969), 'A general approach to confirmatory maximum likelihood factor analysis', *Psychometrika*, **34**, 183–202.

Jöreskog, K. G. (1970a), 'A general method for analysis of covariance structures', *Biometrika*, **57**, 239–57.

Jöreskog, K. G. (1970b), 'Estimation and testing of simplex models', *British Journal of Mathematical and Statistical Psychology*, **23**, 121–45.

Kaiser, H. F. (1962), 'Scaling a simplex', *Psychometrika*, **27**, 155–62.

Kirk, S. A., McCarthy, J. J., and Kirk, W. (1968), *Illinois Test of Psycholinguistic Abilities: Examiner's Manual* (Revised Edition), Illinois, University of Illinois Press.

Kohen-Raz, R. (1967), 'Scalogram analysis of some developmental sequences of infant behavior by the Bayley Infant Scale of Mental Development', *Genetic Psychological Monographs*, **76**, 3–21.

Krantz, D., Luce, R. D., Suppes, P., and Tversky, A. (1972), *Foundations of Measurement*, Volume 1, New York, Academic Press.

Lazarsfeld, P. F. (1950), in S. A. Stouffer *et al.*, *Measurement and Prediction*, Princeton, Princeton University Press.

Lazarsfeld, P. F. (1960), 'Latent structure analysis and test theory', in H. Gulliksen and S. Messick (Eds.), *Psychological Scaling: Theory and Applications*, New York, Wiley.

Lazarsfeld, P. F., and Henry, N. W. (1968), *Latent Structure Analysis*, Boston, Houghton Mifflin.

Levy, P., and Pugh, D. S. (1969), 'Scaling and multivariate analyses in the study of organisational variables', *Sociology*, **3**, 193–213.

Levy, P., and Tucker, J. (1972), 'Differential effects of streaming on primary school attainment', *British Journal of Educational Psychology*, **42**, 75–9.

Loevinger, J. (1957), 'Objective tests as instruments of psychological theory', *Psychological Reports*, Monograph Supplement Number 9.

Loevinger, J. (1965), 'Person and population as psychometric concepts', *Psychological Review*, **72**, 143–55.

Lord, F. M. (1963), 'Biserial estimates of correlation', *Psychometrika*, **28**, 81–5.

Lord, F. M. (1965a), 'A note on the normal ogive or logistic curve in item analysis' *Psychometrika*, **30**, 371–2.

Lord, F. M. (1965b), 'An empirical study of item–test regression', *Psychometrika*, **30**, 373–6.

Lord, F. M. (1968), 'An analysis of the verbal scholastic aptitude test using Birnbaum's three-parameter logistic model', *Educational and Psychological Measurement*, **28**, 989–1020.

Lord, F. M. (1970), 'Item characteristic curves as estimated without knowledge of their mathematical form—A confrontation of Birnbaum's logistical model', *Psychometrika*, **35**, 43–50.

Lord, F. M., and Novick, M. R. (1968), *Statistical Theories of Mental Test Scores*, New York, Addison-Wesley.

Luria, A. R. (1966), *Higher Cortical Functions in Man*, London, Tavistock.

McDonald, R. P. (1962), 'A general approach to non-linear factor analysis', *Psychometrika*, **27**, 397–415.

McDonald, R. P. (1965), 'Difficulty factors and non-linear factor analysis', *British Journal of Mathematical and Statistical Psychology*, **18**, 11–23.

McDonald, R. P. (1967a), 'Numerical methods for polynomial models in nonlinear factor analysis', *Psychometrika*, **32**, 77–112.

McDonald, R. P. (1967b), 'Factor interaction in nonlinear factor analysis', *British Journal of Mathematical and Statistical Psychology*, **20**, 205–15.

McDonald, R. P. (1967c), 'Nonlinear factor analysis', *Psychometric Monographs*, Number 15.

McDonald, R. P. (1969), 'A generalized common factor analysis based on residual covariance matrices of prescribed structure', *British Journal of Mathematical and Statistical Psychology*, **22**, 149–63.

McGuire, W. J. (1960), 'Cognitive consistency and attitude change', *Journal of Abnormal and Social Psychology*, **60**, 345–53.

Meehl, P. E. (1945), 'The dynamics of "structured" personality tests', *Journal of Clinical Psychology*, **1**, 296–303.

Meredith, W. (1971), 'Poisson distributions of error in mental test theory', *British Journal of Mathematical and Statistical Psychology*, **24**, 49–82.

Mukherjee, B. N. (1966), 'Derivation of likelihood-ratio tests for Guttman quasi-simplex covariance structures', *Psychometrika*, **31**, 97–123.

Mukherjee, B. N. (1970), 'Likelihood ratio tests of statistical hypotheses associated with patterned covariance matrices in psychology', *British Journal of Mathematical and Statistical Psychology*, **23**, 89–120.

Neill, J. A., and Jackson, D. N. (1970), 'An evaluation of item selection strategies in personality scale construction', *Educational and Psychological Measurement*, **30**, 647–61.

Osburn, H. G. (1967), 'A note on design of test experiments', *Educational and Psychological Measurement*, **27**, 797–802.

Osburn, H. G. (1968), 'Item sampling for achievement testing', *Educational and Psychological Measurement*, **28**, 95–104.

Osburn, H. G. (1969), 'The effect of item stratification on errors of measurement', *Educational and Psychological Measurement*, **29**, 295–302.

Overall, J. E. (1964), 'Note on multivariate methods for profile analysis', *Psychological Bulletin*, **61**, 195–8.

Payne, R. W., and Jones, H. G. (1957), 'Statistics for the investigation of individual cases', *Journal of Clinical Psychology*, **13**, 107–14.

Peak, H. (1953), 'Problems of objective observation', in L. Festinger and D. Katz (Eds.), *Research Methods in the Behavioral Sciences*, New York, Dryden.

Pearson, K. (1924), *The Life, Letters and Labours of Francis Galton* (Volume II), Cambridge, Cambridge University Press.

Peel, E. A. (1967), 'A method for investigating children's understanding of certain logical connectives used in binary propositional thinking', *British Journal of Mathematical and Statistical Psychology*, **20**, 81–92.

Proctor, C. H. (1970), 'A probabilistic formulation and statistical analysis of Guttman scaling', *Psychometrika*, **35**, 73–8.

Rasch, G. (1960), *Probabilistic Models for some Intelligence and Attainment Tests*, Copenhagen, Danmarks Paedogogiske Institut.

Rasch, G. (1966), 'An item analysis which takes individual differences into account', *British Journal of Mathematical and Statistical Psychology*, **19**, 49–57.

Ridberg, E. H., Parke, R. D., and Hetherington, E. M. (1971), 'Modification of impulsive and reflective cognitive styles through observation of film-mediated models', *Developmental Psychology*, **5**, 369–77.

Rozeboom, W. W. (1966), *Foundations of the Theory of Prediction*, Homewood, Illinois, Dorsey.

Schönemann, P. H. (1970), 'Fitting a simplex symmetrically', *Psychometrika*, **35**, 1–22.

Shoemaker, D. M., and Osburn, H. G. (1968), 'An empirical study of generalizability coefficients for unmatched data', *British Journal of Mathematical and Statistical Psychology*, **21**, 239–49.

Shoemaker, D. M., and Osburn, H. G. (1969), 'Computer-aided item sampling for achievement testing: A description of a computer program implementing the universe defined test concept', *Educational and Psychological Measurement*, **29**, 165–72.

Sirotnik, K. (1970), 'An analysis of variance framework for matrix sampling', *Educational and Psychological Measurement*, **30**, 891–908.

Sirotnik, K. (1972), 'Estimates of coefficient alpha for finite populations of items', *Educational and Psychological Measurement*, **32**, 129–36.

Solomon, H. (1960), 'A survey of models in factor analysis', in H. Solomon (Ed.), *Mathematical Thinking in the Measurement of Behaviour*, Glencoe, Illinois, Free Press.

Storms, L. H. (1960), 'Rationales for the "twisted pear"', *Journal of Consulting Psychology*, **24**, 552–3.

Stouffer, S. A. (1950), in S. A. Stouffer *et al.*, *Measurement and Prediction*, Princeton, Princeton University Press.

Suchman, E. A. (1950), 'The utility of scalogram analysis', in S. A. Stouffer *et al.*, *Measurement and Prediction*, Princeton, Princeton University Press.

Surtees, P., and Tennant, L. (1972), Unpublished Report, Department of Psychology, University of Birmingham.

Torgerson, W. S. (1958), *Theory and Methods of Scaling*, New York, Wiley.

Traub, R. E. (1967), 'A note on the reliability of residual change scores', *Journal of Educational Measurement*, **4**, 253–6.

Traub, R. E. (1968), 'Comment on Glass' response', *Journal of Educational Measurement*, **5**, 343–5.

Tversky, A., and Krantz, D. H. (1970), 'The dimensional representation and the metric structure of similarity data', *Journal of Mathematical Psychology*, **7**, 572–96.

Vernon, P. E. (1961), *The Structure of Human Abilities* (2nd ed.), London, Methuen.

Werts, C. E., and Linn, R. L. (1970), 'Path analysis: psychological examples', *Psychological Bulletin*, **74**, 193–212.

Wherry, R. J., and Gaylord, R. H. (1944), 'Factor pattern of test items and tests as a function of the correlation coefficient: content difficulty and constant error factors', *Psychometrika*, **9**, 237–44.

Wohlwill, J. F. (1960), 'A study of the development of the number concept by the scalogram analysis', *Journal of Genetic Psychology*, **97**, 345–77.

2

INTELLIGENCE AND CREATIVITY

H. J. Butcher

University of Sussex

Introduction

IT IS OBVIOUSLY very difficult to give an adequate account of such a large topic within a single chapter. Rather than attempt the almost impossible, I have thought it more useful to confine myself to a few aspects. Thus there will be little account in this summary of the nature of ability tests, of how they are constructed and administered, or of their specific merits and defects. Nor will it be possible to say much about the arguments concerning how such terms as 'intelligence' should be defined; nor about the recent spate of sociological and cross-cultural studies. Given the general context of this book, I have concentrated mainly on two areas of study that have recently attracted the interest of psychologists and, to a large degree, of the general public. These are (a) the renewed dispute, stimulated by the writings of Arthur Jensen, about the extent to which differences in ability are inherited, and particularly about the extent to which subgroups may differ in genetic potential; (b) the recently very flourishing field of divergent thinking and creativity. This latter area is a huge one in itself, so that even within it one faces the same dilemma—whether to attempt a broad but necessarily somewhat superficial survey or to select one or two aspects and provide slightly more detail. Here again it has seemed preferable to impose a degree of selection rather than aim at comprehensive coverage, but even so, the volume of recent work has made it necessary to allocate far more space to it than to the other section.

These two currents of research—into genetic aspects of ability and into divergent thinking and creativity—have not, since the work of Francis Galton in the late nineteenth century, closely mingled. Psychologists such as Holzinger, and more recently Jensen in the US and Sir Cyril Burt in Britain, who have aimed to tease out the respective contributions of hereditary and environmental factors to observed differences in human ability, have based their studies primarily on the results of conventional intelligence tests. The much newer and still highly experimental techniques that are designed to assess originality and similar qualities have not yet been employed in the kinds of experiment (e.g. twin studies or large-scale longitudinal surveys) that would throw light on genetic and environmental components.

If this chapter had been confined to these two themes they would necessarily have appeared arbitrarily separate, and the reader unfamiliar with the trend of research in the preceding 50 years might well wonder why they had become so prominent. There is indeed a kind of arbitrariness in the course of research, especially perhaps in infant sciences or near-sciences such as cognitive psychology (the theories of Kuhn 1962 about the stretching and eventual breaking of overfamiliar paradigms are very suggestive), but this degree of apparent arbitrariness can only be evaluated in the light of earlier history. I have therefore thought it most useful to precede sections on the two themes already briefly described with a more general and historical section.

Empirical Studies of Intelligence and Ability Since 1900

The idea of a general mental trait describable as intelligence is obviously not a new one. It can be traced in the writings of the ancient Greek philosophers, in Cicero, and in many other authors through the succeeding 2000 years. There is, for example, a particularly interesting and well-known passage in the *Pensées* of Pascal that foreshadows much of the recent discussion about the difference between the intelligent and the creative person. But systematic empirical enquiry seems to have been suggested only about the middle of the nineteenth century, and to have been put into practice 50 years later when Charles Spearman and Alfred Binet made the first large pioneering ventures in the scientific and experimental analysis of intelligent performance.

In most fields of study it is certainly desirable to have a clear concept and definition of the phenomenon one is attempting to investigate. This has not always been the case in the study of 'intelligence', but the fault may not be so heinous as some critics have urged, since, to quote J. B. S. Haldane (Cattell 1971, p. 7), 'In science we are compelled to investigate before we know what we are investigating, and as our knowledge increases we must continually re-state our questions'. The questions raised by Binet and by Spearman just after 1900 were and still are crucial. Binet's main concern was with the question, 'What mental tasks can children of a certain age actually perform?' as distinct from popular belief about what they were supposed to be able to do. In this respect, in his determination to make his own observations and not to accept the popular stereotype, he was not unlike Galileo dropping objects of various weights and sizes from the top of the Tower of Pisa. Very soon after Binet's investigation, surprising results were found, notably that many children stigmatized as mentally deficient were merely retarded and could be benefited by remedial education. Binet's work thus had immediate practical results of importance, but it is fair to say that the work of Spearman was more significant in terms of psychological theory. The main question he attempted to answer was, 'How can intelligence (as conceptualized 50 years earlier by Herbert Spencer and Francis Galton) be defined in operational and behavioural terms?'. To obtain an answer, he made the first extensive use in psychology of the recently discovered statistical technique of correlation, and went far to develop the method of factor analysis, an extension of correlational technique. From his use of factor analysis, which aims to extract from the matrix of intercorrelations one or more common factors running through the various test performances, he believed—and to a large extent his belief was justified—that he had developed an objective means of isolating general intelligence. Furthermore, Spearman maintained that the statistical factor which he interpreted as general intelligence (but named 'g', to avoid many of the popular connotations of the term) entered into the performance of *every* mental task, and that apart from the contribution of general intelligence all such tasks entailed only a specific skill. Later he came to acknowledge that some more specialized abilities had to be taken into account, but he continued to maintain that such abilities were relatively unimportant.

Spearman's theory was elegant and convincing. In fact, it dominated the study of abilities for another 30 years, but (unfortunately for scientific parsimony) it proved too simple in at least two respects. It became apparent during the 1920's and 1930's that the relatively narrow abilities which Spearman had believed to be of little or no serious importance were quite pervasive and easily replicable. This modification of the accepted view was due in large degree to the work of Sir Cyril Burt, who was also responsible for propounding a view of the structure of abilities that is still as defensible as any. The core of Burt's theory was the proposition that abilities form a hierarchy, at the summit of which is the most general kind of ability, namely, Spearman's g. When, by elaborate statistical means, the contribution of g is removed from the set of test performances, group factors are still found, i.e. factors common to a subset of these performances, perhaps, for example, involving either numerical or spatial tasks. Further down the hierarchy again, narrower group factors may be found. For instance, if the test battery includes a large number of mathematical tests or problems, mathematical ability may be found to split into two or three subfactors representing a particular ability for arithmetic, geometry or algebra. It thus became apparent during the latter part of the period under consideration that the observed structure of abilities was dependent upon two crucial features of the sampling design. As we have already implied, the selection of performances to be analysed would clearly determine the observed structure, but so too would the sampling of individuals to be tested. It was a wider sampling of variables that caused later factorists to modify Spearman's views. But it is mainly divergent views about the sampling of people that account for much of the disagreement between present-day factorists (for instance between Vernon and Guilford) about the structure of abilities. Vernon has frequently argued that the structure as described by many American writers has been unduly influenced by an overnarrow selection of people to be tested. According to Vernon, the most general structure of abilities is clearly seen if an unselected sample of the whole population is employed. Guilford, however, adopts a contrasting philosophy and argues that even in principle an unselected sample of the kind favoured by Vernon would give misleading results, his own preference being for a sample homogeneous in terms of age, education and other salient variables.

The considerations already described made necessary a substantial modification of Spearman's so-called two-factor theory during the first 30 years of the period we are considering. A second discovery was made which had even more drastic effects upon the neat and simple picture drawn by the early factorists. The new realization was that neither on purely mathematical nor on purely psychological grounds could any one structure of abilities be said to be the most satisfactory. On every complex pattern of intercorrelations between a number of variables there can be imposed an infinite number of different factor solutions. Certainly, where the correlations happen to show a clear pattern that fits a psychological hypothesis or a mathematical model, there is little dispute. But the history of this field of study and the frequent disputes between psychologists of individual differences about the most desirable factor structure suggests that such clearcut patterns are the exception rather than the rule, and that the ultimate indeterminacy of the factorial method has played a large part in contributing to the persisting divergence of theories, which is, however, in many respects more apparent than real, as was shown by the technical innovations introduced some 20 years ago.

Beginning in the 1950's, advances were made in the technique of factor analysis that seemed likely to remove some of the subjectivity involved in the multiplicity of alternative solutions. These advances were of two main types. The first, depending upon the advent of electronic computers of large capacity, was the development of objective methods of rotation, usually of simple structure. Examples of such programs were those of Wrigley and Neuhaus, of Kaiser, and of Cattell and Muerle. The second development was the bringing into line of factor analysis with other more traditional methods of statistical reasoning. The maximum likelihood method of Lawley and Rao, for instance, enabled sampling error to be estimated in a much more satisfactory way than could be achieved in any earlier method. Subsequent developments on these lines are fully described in the book by Lawley and Maxwell (1963).

In spite of these considerable technical advances, the aims of those psychologists who desire to formulate a taxonomy of human abilities seem to have been gradually changing during the last 10 or 15 years. There has been a perceptible trend away from the somewhat blind empiricism evident in many of the earlier large-scale factor analytic studies towards a more rationalistic, theoretical and *a priori* approach. The work of J. P. Guilford has been influential in this direction. It seems fairly clear (Butcher 1970b, Merrifield 1970) that Guilford's far-reaching attempt to chart the map of abilities differed in this respect from the philosophy of earlier workers such as, for instance, Spearman, Burt and Thurstone. The implicit or explicit aim of these earlier workers was to sample the whole domain of human abilities by suitable tests, to intercorrelate these tests and to see without any specific hypotheses what factors or common influences would emerge. Guilford's aim, on the other hand, has been to delineate the categories in which abilities may logically be expected to fall, to draw up a logically convincing system of such categories and their cross-classification, and then to construct a test or tests for each cell in the resulting system. This is a facet approach, and perhaps the most detailed and useful discussion of the difference between factors, traits and facets and of their respective implications has been provided by Humphreys (1962). The general approach has been very influential, although probably few psychologists if any would give wholehearted support for Guilford's particular choice of facets and their elements. His choice has been criticized mainly on two distinct grounds. The first kind of criticism points to the arbitrariness of Guilford's threefold division of all mental abilities into categories called operations, contents and products. Thus a type of ability is uniquely defined by operating in a certain way on a certain type of material to produce a certain kind of product. Guilford defines five possible kinds of operation, four different types of content and six possible products, the cross-classification of these categories resulting in a theoretical scheme that allows for 120 different kinds of human ability. It is easy to point out that many different alternative schemes on this model are possible, and Eysenck (1967) in particular has criticized Guilford's third facet, that of product, as being weaker and more arbitrary than the other two. In the same paper he has outlined an alternative three-dimensional facet classification of his own, although it must be said that many psychologists would find this little more convincing.

The second line of criticism against Guilford has been that his 120 different human abilities operate at too specific and narrow a level. As a consequence say the critics, none of the specific abilities for which Guilford and his associates have constructed tests has been shown to have any very convincing real-life predictive value as compared with the broader factors formerly employed by other psychologists. Humphreys has pointed out that the logical conclusion, or perhaps the *reductio ad absurdum*, of this approach would be to have two tests so similar that they only just missed being parallel forms of the same test. If a number of such pairs were constructed, each pair would give rise to a factor, and these resulting factors would be even more 'primary' and basic according to this whole philosophy of analysis than Guilford's 120.

Very recently, R. B. Cattell has outlined a prospective taxonomy of abilities that has clearly been influenced by the trends just described and which is in some ways even more elaborate. It is again a threefold scheme, but at first sight it seems that his three main categories or facets, corresponding to Guilford's operation, content and product, may be more basic and more in line with general psychological concepts. Cattell's new and very interesting suggestion is to categorize abilities in terms of type of input, type of processing involved and type of output. This new scheme of Cattell's is described in his massive (1971) book *Abilities: their Structure, Growth and Action*, which summarizes perhaps 30 or 40 years' thinking about intelligence, specific abilities, their relationship and their development through human life.

Cattell begins by making some of the criticisms of Guilford's schema that we have already mentioned, although he recognizes its great value as a pioneering attempt to produce a systematic taxonomy of human abilities. His main criticisms are as follows: (a) he endorses Eysenck's view already quoted that the category of products is not essential or primary; (b) he suggests that the operations such as cognition, evaluation, convergent production and divergent production are not in fact mutually exclusive; (c) he maintains (and this is the most fundamental point of criticism) that the categories are in general chosen on too rational, philosophic and a prioristic a basis.

Cattell's new taxonomy, which so far has only been presented in a very condensed but highly suggestive outline, is based like Guilford's on three main facets or principles of classification. The first facet or domain, which deals with input, process and output, has already been briefly described. The general idea behind it is as follows: mental tasks clearly vary very considerably in the respective demands they impose on (a) perceptual processes, such as listening to verbal instructions for a test, reading a complex musical score, or scanning an array in a test such as a Raven's Matrices; (b) the processing in the central nervous system, which may vary on a dimension ranging from an almost instantaneous and quasi-reflex response to a long and complex chain of reasoning; (c) the actual physical response, which may vary on a dimension ranging from at one extreme pressing a button to select an alternative out of half a dozen to executing a complex drawing, writing a sentence or singing a tune.

One's immediate reaction to this first facet is that of its three dimensions the second, i.e. that of processes within the central nervous system, is of predominant importance, and this is obviously recognized by Cattell, who introduces this area again as his second domain or main facet (P). Thus, his first principle of classification depends upon the relative *extent* of demands placed by a particular ability on the respective input, process and output variables; a second main facet is based upon the *type* of central processing supposed to be taking place. In a sense, and from a rational and philosophical point of view, there is a hierarchical implication here in that the second facet is perhaps interpretable as logically subordinate to the first, but in practice Cattell is very likely correct in seeing them as empirically independent. His third facet or domain (C) (presented second by him, but given here in third place for ease of exposition) is concerned with content, but differs very considerably from Guilford's category of the same title. This content facet is divided into two subcategories, the one being concerned with the familiar distinction between type of material acted upon, for example verbal, numerical, spatial, etc., the other distinguishing the sense modality involved, for example oral, visual, kinesthetic, etc. This seems a valuable distinction and one that has frequently been obscured in previous studies, whether of rational classification or of empirical factor analytic results.

Cattell's own account of these new ideas is extremely succinct, and throws off so many sparks, so to speak, that it is almost impossible to précis. If therefore the reader is to form any proper idea of the density and complexity of his recent thinking, it will be convenient to reprint his own scheme for classifying abilities.

The Ability Dimension Analysis Chart (ADAC):
A Theoretical Schema

Domain or Panel A: Action Phases (In Ability Action)

1. *Involvement of Input* (largest in perceptual abilities). The value on this is the extent to which the ability score rests upon sensory input activity relative to the stimulus.
2. *Involvement of Internal Processing and Storage* (largest in memory measures). The value on this is the extent to which processing of resources of storage (committing, retention, retrieving, comparing) determines the score.
3. *Involvement of Output* (largest in executive performances). The value on this is the extent to which qualities of output determine the score.

Domain or Panel C: Content

1. *Involvement of Experiential–Cultural Dimensions.* This includes such separate subdimensions as verbal (semantic), numerical, social, spatial, mechanical knowledge, art, music, science.
2. *Involvement of Neural–Organizational Dimensions.* This includes subdimensions of visual, auditory, kinesthetic, tactile, motor, cerebellar, etc.

Domain or Panel P: Process Parameters

1. *Demand in Terms of Complexity Level of Relation Eduction.* This concerns the complexity of relations handled as relations, as well as the complexity implied in the eduction of correlates (fundaments) required in any process. This parameter defines level in a standard hierarchy of relations.
2. *Demand in Terms of Multiplexity of Sets.* This concerns the amount of complication in processing, independent of relational complexity in any one operation. It could be analysed into subsets covering (a) number of items handled, (b) number of simultaneously applied sets, e.g. belonging to class X, larger than a, beginning with letter B, etc., (c) number of sets in successive steps. A model for such an 'amount of processing' evaluation exists in logic and in the computer. It may be thought of insofar as it applies to the output phase, as degree of restriction and control of output. In human and animal behavior they are expressed by the operation of mental sets, in multiplex systems of various rank

levels, from the simplicity of a reaction time response, to the response of a diplomat at a UN committee.

3. *Amount of Committing to Memory* ('Gramming'). This may seem to apply as a dimension only of the storage phase, and so it does in an immediate sense. But inasmuch as perceptual and executive abilities are dependent on level of storage, and level of storage is dependent on effectiveness of committing to memory, a person's score on gramming (as we may call, for brevity, 'committing to memory') will affect *all* abilities. Conceivably, even when level of interest-motivation is set aside (as it is from all this cognitive analysis) a person's effectiveness in committing to memory (gramming) is dependent on more than one factor, e.g. a neural structure and a physiological efficiency factor. But for initial simplicity committing to memory is considered one dimension.

4. *Amount of Retentive Activity Involved.* Again this is a dimension obviously concerned with the storage phase but affecting all performances. In most memory abilities—other than immediate memory—level of success would depend substantially upon individual differences in whatever capacities enter into efficiency or retention. Again, as with gramming, the retaining of impressions may be found in the end to depend on more than one factor. As pointed out in Chapter 8, on physiology, this subject is at present in a highly speculative state.

5. *Amount of Retrieval Activity.* There is good reason to consider retrieval as an entirely distinct activity from retention. It may be affected in its result, of course, by the amount in storage, the nature of the content, the complexity of the relations, and the multiplexity of conditions requested in the retrieval. But by hypothesis there are individual differences in some general retrieval efficiency when all the above are held constant. In this case we have a dimension restricted, however, to a subspace, since the differences among abilities in the extent to which retrieval is involved can apply only to the executive panel, unless we assume that retrieval at a nondeliberate level applies also to perceptual recognition. Retrieval plays a major part in such abilities as fluency.

6. *Flexibility versus Firmness.* Every dimension or function so far discussed could vary on a dimension of flexibility versus firmness. Presumably flexibility would give advantages especially in trial and error learning but also in relational insight learning. Lack of firmness and freedom from fluctuation of response would also bring impairment of performances in other situations.

7. *Speed Demand.* Speed is an anomalous and extra dimension in the sense that, as pointed out above, it arises only for that form of measuring abilities in which a time limit is set. However, the latter is at least a widespread requirement both in tests and life performances. Consequently it is an important dimension in the classification of abilities to state to what extent they involve speed. The extent to which the individual is able to score well on a speeded test is, however, decided by a whole subset of cognitive and temperamental speed factors, as indicated in the text above. Speed is a dimension obviously responsible for distinguishing between an ability as a 'level' and as a 'power' ability, as discussed below in connection, for example, with intelligence tests.

(From *Abilities: Their Structure, Growth and Action*, by Raymond B. Cattell. Houghton Mifflin Company, Boston, USA, 1971. Reprinted by permission of the publishers)

This elaborate new formulation is by no means easy to evaluate. But without attempting to analyse its merits and demerits in detail, certain distinguishing characteristics are clearly evident. Firstly, there is a marked contrast between Guilford's conceptualization and Cattell's in that Guilford's is truly a facet system and contains no dimensions as such; Cattell has been influenced by the facet approach as already described, but each of the elements in his model remains a true dimension, ranging from high to low. The consequence is that Cattell's scheme, although containing only some 12 subfacets, will, if carried to its logical conclusion, result not in 120 different kinds of human ability but (in strict theory) in 2^{12}, or in effect some 4000. This would, however, assume that every cross-classification of the subfacets is viable. Cattell's own opinion, however, is that perhaps only one-eighth distinguish separable and important human abilities. Even so, there will thus, on his new system of classification, be some 500 distinguishable and identifiable types of ability.

Heredity and Environment

In the preceding section we have noted quite a marked change in direction of interest in classifying abilities, from a relatively undirected empirical approach to a more rationalistic and *a priori* method of classification.

In other related fields of cognitive psychology a similar change has been more dramatically evident. Stimulus-response theories of learning have been on the defensive for some 20 years, and only diehards now believe that *all* learning can in principle be accounted for on these lines. Chomsky's (1959) devastating, though perhaps overstated, criticism of Skinner's account of language acquisition was a major influence in this direction. What has proved astonishing, however, is not simply the swing against a *'tabula rasa'* behaviourism, but the extent to which a frankly rationalist and neo-Cartesian account of language acquisition and linguistic competence is now taken seriously by many experimental psychologists. The idea of a genetically determined, species-specific, 'pre-wired' language acquisition mechanism in the human brain is explicitly formulated by biological scientists such as Lenneberg (1964) and forms the implicit base of sophisticated empirical studies by psychologists such as McNeill (1970).

This conviction of a largely innate and predetermined cognitive structure forms an integral part of the position adopted by Chomsky and by Chomsky-influenced psychologists, and is clearly at the opposite end of a fundamental spectrum to Watsonian or Skinnerian behaviourism. It is also interesting to note in passing that a familiar stereotype is invalidated in this instance—the stereotype that conservatives emphasize hereditary factors and radicals environmental ones, since Chomsky is impeccably radical in the political sense.

It would be quite wrong to suggest, though, that in cognitive psychology generally, or even in the field of language study, psychologists predominantly adopt a hereditarian viewpoint. The main change has been that such questions are wide open again and an implicit extreme environmentalism is no longer uncritically accepted.

The division of opinion in regard to individual intelligence or ability is even more evident and, for obvious reasons, more related to social and ethical considerations. No one is going to become very upset on *social* grounds if it proves true that every human brain contains a genetically determined language acquisition device, although discomfort may be felt, as in any enforced change of attitude. But if it proves true that the gene pool of American blacks is, on average, less favourable to the development of intellectually gifted individuals than that of whites (or *vice versa*), such a finding is likely to produce intense social and political reactions, especially when oversimplified and misinterpreted. The genetic determination of human characteristics held in common is relatively undisturbing; but a similar determination of *differences* can be political dynamite. The result of all this has been that what seemed a moribund issue has had new life breathed into it and is again the subject of heated controversy. To make this change clearer it will be necessary to describe the position some six or seven years ago, when the issue seemed relatively settled or at least temporarily abandoned.

The highest common factor of agreement among psychologists at that period, say about 1967, was something as follows: it was widely agreed that general intelligence and also more specific human abilities were clearly influenced both by hereditary and environmental factors, but that it was a difficult and probably unrewarding task to attempt to disentangle them completely and to assign proportions of variance to the two influences. Where such attempts had been made, as for instance by Burt, by Holzinger and by Cattell, and where it had been suggested that, say, 70 to 80 per cent of the variance in human intelligence was due to heredity, it was generally agreed that such exercises were technically sound if one agreed with the initial assumptions, but that the results reported were dependent upon (a) the particular national or local population sampled and (b) the particular economic and social circumstances prevailing at that time in that population. This is a large qualification, since in the last half-century social and economic circumstances and possibilities of educational opportunity have been changing very rapidly in Western industrial societies, with obvious and generally acknowledged consequences for the relationship between these two main factors on individual differences in ability. A degree of paradox is evident—that the general trend in these Western societies has been towards equality of educational opportunity and levelling up of social and economic circumstances. This has been accompanied by an increasing emphasis upon environmental and social conditions affecting intelligence and ability in contrast to hereditary and genetic factors. Yet the greater such efforts towards economic and social equality, and the more effective they prove, the greater will inevitably be the influence exercised by hereditary and genetic differences.

Before the Jensen controversy many middle-of-the-road psychologists specializing in the study of human abilities, such as Vernon in Britain and Cronbach in the US, had clearly been strongly influenced by the prevailing climate of opinion and by the fairly convincing sociological findings about the effect of environment upon both ability and achievement, with the general result that to emphasize hereditary and genetic factors was becoming slightly unrespectable if not positively reactionary. The sole deviant in this respect was the aged and highly respected figure of Sir Cyril Burt, who remained firmly out of tune with the spirit of the age, and was perhaps the only psychologist to continue to *define* intelligence as *innate* ability. This definition was in principle perfectly acceptable, indeed probably more theoretically acceptable than any definition of intelligence as a kind of amalgam of hereditary and social influences, but the weakest point in Burt's case (Vernon 1970) was the assumption that this hereditary definition of intelligence was operationally supported by the use of current tests.

What put the cat among the pigeons was Arthur Jensen's celebrated, or in some quarters notorious, and exhaustive paper in the *Harvard Educational Review*. Understandably, this paper produced a great deal of emotional and almost hysterical reaction, so it may be as well to put on record what one sees as Jensen's intentions, technical qualifications and quality of argument. It is of considerable sociological and cultural interest that such comment is necessary. Nine-tenths of Jensen's long article is entirely defensible and on the whole reiterates, with some additional technical and statistical sophistication, what had previously been frequently stated and supported with evidence by psychologists of individual differences as eminent as Burt and Cattell. Nor does it stress race differences more than previously published books and papers by, for instance, Garrett and Shuey. The great intensity and stridency of reaction must be ascribed to two main factors. The first is contained in the *Zeitgeist*. At a time when it is offensive to any American of liberal sympathies to acknowledge innate differences in natural endowment, and at a time of American guilt about treatment of the blacks in the last century exacerbated by the rapid growth of Black Power movements, it inevitably appeared tactless in the extreme to suggest that on the average American blacks suffer from an hereditary handicap in powers of reasoning and logical analysis. A second possible reason for the intensity of reaction—and I advance this hypothesis more speculatively—was a feeling among psychologists generally that their own discipline had been too narrow, too rigid and perhaps in a sense too reactionary in the 20 or 30 years preceding the period of which we are speaking. They had received a good deal of criticism or at least of feedback from the general public and from academics of other disciplines to the effect that psychology was too ivory-tower, too confined to the laboratory, too unconcerned (unlike sociology) with real life and with current social trends.

Whether or not this analysis is correct, it is clear that the reaction to Jensen's long paper was disproportionate and distorted. It was an important paper, but not in the way one would suppose from reports in the popular press or even from the reactions of many of the psychologists and sociologists who commented upon it in the subsequent issue of the *Harvard Educational Review*. I call it important for the following reasons. Firstly and speaking at the most general level, it restated a point of view that was evidently novel to many of its readers in the current climate of opinion. Summarized very briefly, this view amounted to a statement of the possibility of behavioural genetics. While it has probably never been denied that a large selection of human qualities are principally genetically determined, for example physical and sexual characteristics, there has been the increasing tendency to deny or to forget that the principles of genetics apply just as much to psychological or mental characteristics as to physical. Within this latter field there has also been a particular reluctance except among psychometric specialists to accept that *individual differences* may very well be largely genetic. Jensen's long original paper, together with his reply to his critics also published in the *Harvard Educational Review*, and his two recent books (1972, 1973) provide the most scholarly and lucid account of genetic principles applied to individual differences in ability that is yet available. It is a pity that this fact has been obscured largely for non-psychological and non-scientific reasons. The difficulties of swimming against such a strong tide of fashionable opinion should not be underrated—especially for someone who is scrupulously careful to support his views with the best evidence available. The strength of the tide is illustrated by the reaction of Cronbach, a very distinguished figure in American educational psychology, who, in the issue of the *Harvard Educational Review* that contained criticisms of Jensen's original paper, wrote 'Unfortunately Dr Jensen has girded himself for holy war against environmentalists, and this has led him into over-statements and mis-statements'. Yet if one compares the tone and level of scientific discourse in Jensen's article with that in most of the articles by his critics, it is hard not to see Cronbach's own account as disproportionate and onesided almost to the point of mis-statement.

Up to this point we have been talking generally about the importance of Jensen's approach in terms of the applicability of genetics to the study of human abilities—and rightly so, because this is the main tenor of his argument. But what has attracted all the attention and generated all the heat has been his more specific suggestion that the almost universally observed difference in mean IQ between whites and blacks in the US contains a large or appreciable genetic component. In this issue I believe Jensen has been selective (as he is perfectly entitled to be) and my own views differ from his, as stated in more detail in a paper in *Educational Research* (Butcher 1970a). The main argument here has been whether, if one accepts that a certain quality has been shown to have a high heritability index within two separate subgroups, one can then conclude that a mean difference between the two groups contains a component of heritability. The answer, as stated by a number of geneticists and as acknowledged by Jensen himself, is simple. It cannot. Yet Jensen seems to have a strong case, as expressed in a footnote to his reply to critics' papers in the *Harvard Educational Review*, in which he suggests specifically to Dr Crowe (one of the geneticists commenting on his original paper) that in these circumstances it would be reasonable and analogous to procedures in more developed sciences to formulate a probability statement. In other words, given two subgroups differing quite markedly in mean score on some quality, and evidencing an acknowledged heritability index within the two subgroups, it seems inherently improbable that the between-groups' difference should be completely devoid of an heritability component.

These are touchy issues, and it is perfectly understandable that reactions should be fierce, because they basically arise from a generous and humane impulse—generous and humane, but uncritical and misguided. Suppose for a moment that Jensen is correct, and suppose further that the reasons suggested by Eysenck (1972) for the hypothetical lower mean IQ of negroes in the US are also correct, it suggests a far more damning indictment of white American policy towards the blacks in the US even than any put forward by those who insist that the observed differences are exclusively environmental.

There is a very great deal more one could say on these questions, but in these few paragraphs it has not been my aim to review the technical disputes— to my mind, they are inconclusive—but to air and clarify some of the *attitudes* involved. Even this latter, more modest enterprise really requires some thousand more words for which space in this context is not available.

Divergent Thinking and Creativity

Whereas the systematic study of intelligence clearly began around 1900, the equivalent study of creativity and originality only got under way some 50 years later. The year 1950 is commonly taken as a turning point because in that year J. P. Guilford delivered a celebrated address to the annual convention of the American Psychological Association. In his speech, he described how he had searched through *Psychological Abstracts*, the journal that summarizes articles in the whole range of psychological journals, and how from the reports of many thousands of psychological papers he had found only a sprinkling on the subject of originality. In addition, and this is what excited the interest of many psychologists attending the conference, he described an extensive programme in his own laboratory at the University of Southern California to produce new kinds of test to assess this elusive quality.

At about this time or very soon afterwards Mackinnon and Sanford also started a large research programme into originality, among other aspects of personality, also in California.

Although Guilford rightly complained of the paucity of research studies, quite a number of eminent psychologists had displayed interest in the topic, although they frequently used different terminology. In the late nineteenth century, Francis Galton, a pioneer in this area as in so many others, had written the book *Hereditary Genius* in which he traced the tendency of particular families to produce individuals of exceptional talent. Early in the history of mental testing, Chassell (1916) had devised psychological tests of originality and had correlated these with the existing tests of intelligence. Three of the most eminent British psychologists in the inter-war period—Spearman, Burt and Bartlett—all thought considerably about the subject and references to it are scattered among their writings. By and large, both Spearman and Burt came to the conclusion that any capacity for original thinking was not easily assessable as distinct from general intelligence, but Bartlett drew a clearer distinction, between 'adventurous thinking' and 'thinking in a closed system'. The work of the Gestalt psychologists is also relevant. Maier, Duncker and Wertheimer, for instance, were all primarily interested in the kind of imaginative leap that avoids a routine solution and cuts straight to the core of a cognitive problem. Wertheimer's book *Productive Thinking* (revised edition 1959) is still of very great interest, containing chapters on the long chain of mental processes that led to Einstein's discovery of relativity theory (which Wertheimer based on a series of interviews with Einstein), and others on the teaching of geometrical principles to schoolchildren by what are now called discovery methods. Yet another approach is exemplified by Catherine Cox, who contributed a volume to Terman's massive series of *Genetic Studies of Genius*. Terman, however, was primarily concerned with intelligence rather than with creativity as such, and Catherine Cox's book devoted enormous labour to estimating from biographical particulars the intelligence quotient of a wide range of geniuses during the last 500 years. All these researches and speculations, however, were in general isolated and sporadic, and before Guilford's programme there was no long-term and systematic attack upon the problem. Guilford's work in this area was based on his 'structure of intellect' approach to human cognition, which has been briefly referred to in an earlier section (for a fuller account see Guilford's 1967 book). This theory categorizes types of human ability in three main ways. They consist of the cognitive processes involved, the material upon which these cognitive processes are employed, and resulting classes of product. In Guilford's system, two of the basic cognitive processes are described as convergent production and divergent production. Convergent production refers to the analytical kind of thinking which is required when a problem has a definite, often predetermined, answer which the subject has to reach, as in a conventional intelligence test. Divergent production, on the other hand, represents a more open-ended kind of thinking, freer from constraints, which may be devoted to the kind of problem that has no simple answer and perhaps not even any answer at all, but a variety of equally acceptable or unacceptable near-answers. This is a valuable distinction, operationalizing and making more specific some of the ideas of earlier workers in this field, but it is still somewhat crude and would benefit from further logical analysis and probably finer distinctions. It is worth noting at this point in view of further developments that Guilford was by no means a unitary theorist of divergent production or creativity; on the contrary, his whole approach is a fragmenting and diversifying one, in that he is generally opposed to broad single traits such as creativity or intelligence; in his system there are 120 different kinds of ability and some 20 even within the category of divergent production.

Guilford's speech certainly made an impression, but after this for some 10 years there was a considerable incubation period in which this impression began to take effect in substantial researches. The first to arouse wide interest and controversy was that of Getzels and Jackson, as reported in their (1962) book. The subjects of their research were what normally would be called a group of very gifted children, who were pupils at a school attached to the University of Chicago, many of them being the sons and daughters of professors there, and whose average IQ was 132. But in fact one of the main aims of Getzels and Jackson's inquiry was to establish that giftedness is not equivalent to IQ but is multivariate and had for too long been identified with results on the conventional kind of intelligence test.

The central feature of their research therefore was to form two contrasting groups of these children, one exceptionally intelligent even within this intelligent group, the other markedly less intelligent in these terms but exceptionally high on the new tests of creativity or divergent thinking. The score on divergent thinking, on the basis of which these contrasting groups were formed, depended upon an aggregate or composite of five different measures, as follows. (1) Word association. Common words of multiple meanings were presented, for example 'bolt', 'sack'. Scores were allotted both according to number of definitions and to number of radically different meanings. (2) Uses for things. A number of different common objects were named such as 'brick' or 'paper-clip'. The number of uses reported within the given time and the variety or originality of such uses were scored separately. (3) Hidden figures (part of a test battery devised by R. B. Cattell). A simple geometrical shape was presented such as a triangle or a quadrilateral, and after that four more complex figures. The task here was to determine which of the more complex figures contained the original simpler shape. (4) Fables. Subjects were asked to read a number of uncompleted short stories and complete them in three or four different respects. They were asked, for instance, to provide a moralistic, a humorous and a sad ending to each of the stories. (5) Make up problems. A number of complete paragraphs, containing numerical statements, were presented, as for instance about income tax situations. The subjects were required not to solve any particular problems but to make up questions; here again the scoring was multivariate, being based on the number, complexity, appropriateness and originality of the questions that the subjects devised.

Getzels and Jackson claim two main kinds of new finding from this experiment, as follows. Firstly, they found that the two traits of creativity and intelligence could be fairly readily separated; secondly, that the two contrasting groups of children they had formed, one exceptionally highly intelligent and the other exceptionally highly creative, differed in various biographical features and in terms of personality and performance.

When Getzels and Jackson examined the performance and characteristics of the two contrasting groups they had formed, they found a number of interesting differences. The highly intelligent children differed from the highly creative principally in terms of academic performance, popularity with teachers, values (especially in terms of conformity) and sense of humour. The children who had scored especially high on tests of divergent thinking were scholastically overachievers in that, although on average scoring 20 points lower on an IQ test, they were equal in scholastic performance in this school. On the other hand, they were less popular with teachers, although as Getzels and Jackson reasonably pointed out they might have been expected to be more popular, since in this sense they were overachieving in terms of scholastic performance as related to IQ. The 'creative' children were also found to have a more developed sense of humour and to be less conformist in the following sense. Questionnaires were administered to both groups asking (a) what character qualities they thought the teacher would value, (b) what character qualities they would value in themselves, (c) what qualities would be likely to make for success in general in adult life. In the highly intelligent group the values they held themselves corresponded very closely with those they thought would be held by the teacher and valued by society. In the 'creative' group this correspondence was much less marked.

The account by Getzels and Jackson of their research was widely criticized on technical grounds, especially the following. Firstly, the pattern of correlations among their data did not suggest that they had adequately succeeded in separating intelligence from creativity. Secondly, they omitted to provide any information about those children who had scored high on both kinds of test or about those who had scored low on both.

The next important research of this type in the US was conducted by Wallach and Kogan (1965), who agreed with the criticisms of Getzels and Jackson's study and attempted to remedy the points just described. They also claimed that in all earlier researches the way the tests of divergent thinking had been administered had been unsatisfactory, tending to restrict performance. Divergent thinking, they suggested, was not likely to flourish in a competitive test situation with strict time limits imposed. Accordingly, in their study with fifth-grade children, they attempted to provide conditions conducive to creative production. The tasks were presented to children not as tests but rather as games, orally, without any time limit and by people well known to them. The results appeared to justify Wallach and Kogan's procedure. For the first time, fairly satisfactory correlations were found among the various tests of divergent thinking, enabling a reasonable composite justifiably to be made, but correlations between the aggregate of these tests and a similar aggregate of intelligence tests were negligible.

In the United Kingdom, research in this field has been scattered rather than systematic, the chief exception being the work of Liam Hudson (and also that of P. E. Vernon, to be described later). Hudson started from a rather similar viewpoint to that of Getzels and Jackson. Like them, he was impatient with what he saw as over-reliance on the traditional IQ measure, pointing out that it would not discriminate in a classroom of clever boys although other differences were undoubtedly of importance. Moreover, he has used tests of divergent thinking very similar to theirs, which he has adapted for the use of English public and grammar schoolboys. Unlike Getzels and Jackson, however, and unlike perhaps the majority of American psychologists working in this field, Hudson does not believe that tests of divergent thinking are indicators of 'creativity'. His own researches have led him to believe that they are strongly associated with subject choice in children and adolescents; also that predominantly divergent thinkers are using a different and contrasting ego defence mechanism from that employed by 'convergers'.

Hudson's work, particularly that described in his (1966) book *Contrary Imaginations*, has been criticized (e.g. Butcher 1972a) on rather similar grounds to that of Getzels and Jackson, that is to say as claiming a sharper distinction than can be fully justified between 'convergent' and 'divergent' thinking and between 'convergers' and 'divergers'. But his 'arts-diverger, science-converger hypothesis' has proved fruitful and has generated a great deal more research—which is usually accepted as one criterion of a good theory. The results have been mixed. Hudson's original work was with boys, and it now seems fairly generally agreed that any such relationship is less well established in girls (Haddon and Lytton 1971, Nuttall 1973). Some support for the Hudson hypothesis was reported by Child (1967), but the most recent researches have been negative, for example Christie (1970) and Duckworth (1972). Duckworth, whose main aim was to provide a new evaluation of the supposed 'swing from science' in recent years (and concluded that it was mainly a 'swing from rigour'), included among his measures the familiar 'Uses of objects' test. The actual objects named were taken from Hudson's account. In three separate age-groups, ranging from second to sixth year in secondary schools, boys showing scientific inclination or specializing in science subjects scored *more* highly than non-scientists. In the sixth form, especially, the difference reached a high degree of statistical significance.

Another large-scale research by a British psychologist that involved the use of tests of divergent thinking was that of P. E. Vernon (1969). It is not possible here to do more than mention the nature and scope of this cross-cultural study, since its main aim was not primarily concerned with divergent thinking or creativity, but with the effect of cultural environment on the whole pattern of abilities. Vernon and his wife tested groups of boys in Southern England, the Hebrides, the West Indies, parts of Canada (including Eskimo and Indian communities) and Uganda. They administered a varied battery of tests, including conventional intelligence tests, Piaget-type problems and divergent thinking tests. The broad pattern of abilities in each culture appeared in general to reflect environmental circumstances, and this applied also to the main divergent thinking test, 'Uses of a tin can'. Eskimo boys did remarkably well on this, a finding which Vernon ascribed in part to their early training in self-reliance.

The most recent survey of British work is that of Nuttall (1973) (but see also Butcher 1971, 1972b). Nuttall reviews research under five headings, corresponding to the following issues: (1) Is divergent thinking a unitary trait? (2) The relationship between divergent and convergent thinking abilities. (3) The validity of divergent thinking tests. (4) The influence of environmental and educational conditions. (5) Factors affecting the reliability of divergent thinking tests.

In the following few paragraphs I shall summarize some relevant research of the last few years under Nuttall's first three headings, although not necessarily referring to the same studies that he includes.

It is still debatable whether there is a broad general factor or unitary trait of divergent thinking somewhat parallel to Spearman's g, or a group factor of lesser generality, or a congerie of rather specific factors. In a sense, correlations have often proved high when one might have wished them to be low and *vice versa*. Many of the tests we have referred to are scored separately for fluency, flexibility and originality; on a Guilfordian model one would hope for low correlations and the emergence of separate factors. Without exception to my knowledge these three measures have proved to be highly correlated and, in any factor analysis including a fair range of other material, to load on the same factor. In fact, for most purposes it hardly matters which score you use. On the other hand, correlations between different tests of divergent thinking have typically been fairly low, often hardly high enough to justify combining them into a composite. Verbal and non-verbal tests, in particular, seem to be relatively independent and to load separate factors (Butcher 1972b, p. 88). Foster (1969), in a factorial study of children's performance, found a pattern of several, rather specific, divergent thinking factors; and Nuttall, summarizing a considerable number of studies, concludes, 'Divergent thinking therefore appears to be far from a unitary trait and is better considered as a number of distinct abilities. These abilities seem to depend largely upon the stimulus material; that is, there is evidence for a verbal divergent thinking factor, a diagrammatic factor, a numerical factor and so on'.

If this is the case, one might expect conflicting findings about the relationship between convergent and divergent thinking, and these have not been lacking. Results vary from zero or negligible correlations, as in some of the studies we have described and in Christie's (1970) research with students, to correlations of $+0.7$ or higher, which (especially when corrected for attenuation, to adjust for the relatively low reliability of the divergent thinking tests) suggests virtual identity of the two kinds of measure. Hasan and Butcher (1966) found high correlations with a group of Scottish children unselected for ability and suggested that the 'threshold' or 'triangular scatterplot' theory might account in part for the discrepant results in the literature; that is, the two kinds of ability might correlate highly in the whole population, but might diverge at the higher levels of intelligence. There is some evidence confirming this hypothesis (e.g. Yamamoto 1965, Haddon and Lytton 1968, Ogilvie 1970, Nuttall 1971), but it is far from solid.

Bennett (1972) has carried out what is probably the most thorough study in the UK of the relation between divergent and convergent thinking in children. He tested 1000 children, about equally divided among three age-groups (third-year primary, fourth-year primary and first-year secondary); each of these three samples was quite closely representative of the whole range of ability. His main findings were that (a) most of the intercorrelations of the separate tests of divergent thinking were somewhat higher than the correlations of these measures with IQ; (b) when a creativity aggregate was formed, this correlated very consistently between 0.5 and 0.6 with IQ in all groups and subgroups but there was some indication of a slight decrease with increasing age; (c) when the average of these latter was corrected for attenuation it became 0.87; (d) as expected, IQ was a much better predictor than divergent thinking aggregate of performance in a conventional examination in English literature; (e) as less expected, when 'creative writing' was the criterion, IQ remained slightly more predictive.

Bennett's comprehensive research contained other findings of interest. He looked for a 'threshold' effect, inspecting the scattergrams of correlations between convergent and divergent measures, but found little sign of it. But he found more confirmation of the Haddon and Lytton (1968) findings—that divergent thinking abilities flourish better in an informal than in a formal primary school—while pointing out that neither in his own study, nor for that matter in Haddon and Lytton's, was the crucial variable of formality-informality very satisfactorily isolated. The schools concerned may have differed also in other relevant respects, for example social class composition. Bennett's research included personality questionnaires as well as measures of ability and attainment, and these too yielded interesting results. Rather little relation was found between the personality measure and those of divergent thinking. In the prediction of attainment, the CPQ (A+, C+, G+, O−) accounted for far more variance than the JEPI, and there was some evidence for the 'cross-over' effect, whereby the second-order factors that favour attainment in primary school apparently become a handicap in secondary school and later.

The validity of tests of divergent thinking involves questions that are difficult enough to frame satisfactorily—let alone to answer. Insofar as such tests claim to tap abilities that can be consistently measured and that are different from abilities assessed by older types of instrument, they have had a modest success, though not a spectacular one. We have already examined much of the available evidence on this point. But insofar as they are supposed to be measures of 'creativity' and to correlate with originality and productiveness in the arts and sciences, or even with ratings and estimates of creative potential, there is still a long way to go before their value in this crucial respect is satisfactorily demonstrated. The typical result of studies employing ratings is a low positive correlation (e.g. Clarke 1968, Dewing 1970, Haddon and Lytton 1971). The extent to which tests of divergent thinking can predict real-life creative performance is still highly uncertain, and likely to remain so until large-scale longitudinal studies have been carried out.

In the context of this chapter, most of the research reviewed has necessarily been concerned with the cognitive aspects of originality and creativity. I think it quite likely, though, that this is not the most profitable or promising approach. It has proved difficult to demonstrate convincingly that the new tests add very much to what was achieved by the traditional type of ability-testing. Cronbach (1968) has urged the use of techniques such as multiple regression to determine more rigorously how much predictive power (against any criterion) is added. In the few studies where this has been attempted (e.g. Nuttall 1971), the results have not been very impressive.

It may well be that, within the psychometric context, tests of personality and motivation will account for more additional variance than tests of divergent thinking. Among others, Roe, Eiduson, Mackinnon, Barron, Cattell, Drevdahl, Cross and Taft have achieved decidedly promising results in view of the relative novelty and thinness of research on these lines. This work is very fairly and capably summarized in a recent book by Gilchrist (1972, Chap. 6). Outside the psychometric context, there is enormous scope for 'process' studies, that is for studies of the kind pioneered by Wertheimer, as already mentioned, but preferably longitudinal rather than retrospective.

References

Bennett, S. M. (1972), 'The relationship between personality, divergent abilities and academic attainment in ten-to-twelve-year-old children', Ph.D. Thesis, University of Lancaster.

Boyle, D. G. (1971), *Language and Thinking in Human Development*, London, Hutchinson.

Butcher, H. J. (1970a), 'Comments on Arthur R. Jensen's "Do schools cheat minority children?"', *Educational Research*, **14**, 92–5.

Butcher, H. J. (1970b), 'Summary of discussions at the Toronto Conference on Intelligence', in W. B. Dockrell (Ed.), *On Intelligence*, London, Methuen.

Butcher, H. J. (1971), 'Recent research into creativity and divergent thinking in Great Britain', *Journal of Research and Development in Education*, **4**, 109–12.

Butcher, H. J. (1972a), 'Creativity', in R. Dreger (Ed.), *Multivariate Personality Research*, Baton Rouge, Claitor.

Butcher, H. J. (1972b), 'Divergent thinking and creativity', in W. D. Wall and V. P. Varma (Eds.), *Advances in Educational Psychology 1*, University of London Press.

Cattell, R. B. (1971), *Abilities: their Structure, Growth and Action*, New York, Houghton Mifflin.

Chassell, L. M. (1916), 'Tests for originality', *Journal of Educational Psychology*, **7**, 317–28.

Child, D. (1967), 'A study of some aspects of divergent thinking and their relation to arts or science preferences in average and above-average secondary school children', M.Ed. Thesis, University of Leeds.

Chomsky, N. (1959), 'Review of Skinner's "Verbal Behaviour"', *Language*, **35**, 26–58.

Christie, T. (1970), 'Cognitive bias, university faculty and degree of success', Abstracts of the British Psychological Society Education Section Annual Conference, 1970.

Clarke, D. F. (1968), 'Some aspects of creative thinking abilities in British schoolchildren', Ph.D. Thesis, University of Reading.

Cronbach, L. J. (1968), 'Intelligence? Creativity? A parsimonious reinterpretation of the Wallach–Kogan data', *American Educational Research Journal*, **5**, 491–511.

Cronbach, L. J. (1969), 'Heredity, environment and educational policy', *Harvard Educational Review*, **39**, 338–47.

Dewing, K. (1970), 'The reliability and validity of selected tests of creative thinking in a sample of seventh-grade West Australian children', *British Journal of Educational Psychology*, **40**, 1, 35–42.

Duckworth, D. (1972), 'The choice of science subjects by grammar school pupils', Ph.D. Thesis, University of Lancaster.

Foster, J. (1969), 'A factorial study of creativity in junior school children', M. Ed. Thesis, University of Manchester.

Getzels, J. W., and Jackson, P. W. (1962), *Creativity and Intelligence*, New York, Wiley.

Gilchrist, M. (1972), *The Psychology of Creativity*, Melbourne, Melbourne University Press.

Guilford, J. P. (1967), *The Nature of Human Intelligence*, New York, McGraw-Hill.

Haddon, F. A., and Lytton, H. (1968), 'Teaching approach and the development of divergent thinking abilities in primary schools', *British Journal of Educational Psychology*, **38**, 171–80.

Haddon, F. A., and Lytton, H. (1971), 'Primary education and divergent thinking abilities—four years on', *British Journal of Educational Psychology*, **41**, 136–47.

Hasan, P., and Butcher, H. J. (1966), 'Creativity and intelligence: a partial replication with Scottish children of Getzels and Jackson's study', *British Journal of Psychology*, **57**, 129–35.

Heim, A. (1970), *Intelligence and Personality*, London, Penguin.

Hudson, L. (1966), *Contrary Imaginations*, London, Methuen.

Jensen, A. R. (1969), 'How much can we boost IQ and scholastic achievement?', *Harvard Educational Review*, **39**, 1–122.

Jensen, A. R. (1971), 'Do schools cheat minority children?', *Educational Research*, **14**, 3–28.

Jensen, A. R. (1972), *Genetics and Education*, London, Methuen.

Jensen, A. R. (1973), *Educability and Group Differences*, London, Methuen.

Kuhn, T. S. (1962), *The Structure of Scientific Revolutions*, Chicago, Chicago University Press.

Lawley, D. N., and Maxwell, A. E. (1963), *Factor Analysis as a Statistical Method*, London, Butterworth.

Lenneberg, E. H. (1964), 'A biological perspective of language', in R. C. Oldfield and J. C. Marshall (Eds.), *Language*, London, Penguin.

McNeill, D. (1970), *The Acquisition of Language*, New York, Harper and Row.

Merrifield, P. R. (1970), 'Structuring mental acts', in W. B. Dockrell (Ed.), *On Intelligence*, London, Methuen.

Nuttall, D. L. (1971), 'Modes of thinking and their measurement', Unpublished Ph.D. Thesis, University of Cambridge.

Nuttall, D. L. (1973), 'Convergent and divergent thinking', in H. J. Butcher and H. B. Pont (Eds.), *Educational Research in Britain 3*, London, University of London Press.

Ogilvie, E. (1970), 'Creativity, intelligence and concept development', Doctoral Dissertation, University of Southampton.

Vernon, P. E. (1969), *Intelligence and Cultural Environment*, London, Methuen.

Vernon, P. E. (1970), 'Intelligence', in W. B. Dockrell (Ed.), *On Intelligence*, London, Methuen.

Wallach, M. A., and Kogan, N. (1965), *Modes of Thinking in Young Children*, New York, Holt, Rinehart and Winston.

Wertheimer, M. (1959), *Productive Thinking*, New York, Harper.

Yamamoto, K. (1965), 'Effect of restriction of range and test unreliability on correlation between measures of intelligence and creative thinking', *British Journal of Educational Psychology*, **35**, 300–5.

3

THE MEASUREMENT OF PERSONALITY BY OBJECTIVE TESTS

John D. Hundleby

University of Guelph

Introduction

THE WORD 'objective' has had many uses in psychology. It can refer to the use of multiple-choice or true–false tests, to a test that has clear, unambiguous scoring instructions, or to a measure that avoids any hint or flavour of the subjective or mental in content and interpretation. The present use of the word 'objective', or the rather more clumsy but descriptive 'objective-performance', refers to a particular group of tests within a comprehensive classification of personality measures. Objectivity in scoring is assumed to be a necessary characteristic of all sophisticated scientific measures in psychology, and will not be discussed as such.

In this chapter we shall attempt to define the class of measures known as 'objective', to show that it can be differentiated from other classes, such as questionnaires, and that it can be subdivided into various subclasses. Examples will be given. The usefulness of a 'structured' or 'construct' orientation will be stressed, and some major objective test traits described. Finally, practical considerations and possible future developments will be discussed. Special attention is given to the measurement of stable traits of personality, though much material will be relevant to the study of human motivation and temporary states and moods.

The Classification of Measures of Personality

A measure of personality is a procedure that eventuates in a set of individual difference scores relevant to the study of personality. Such procedures clearly embrace much more than paper-and-pencil tests. They include such data as peer-ratings, summary evaluations given on the basis of case-history files, delinquency records, EEG tracings, rate of conditioning, and so on. It is convenient for many purposes to regard personality measures as falling into a set of relatively distinct classes. The need for a descriptive classification is shown in most texts covering personality measurement, the chapter headings indicating what the author regards, at least in some sense, as being relatively distinct groups of tests or methods. Guilford (1959), for example, lists under separate chapters: morphological and physiological methods; observational methods, ratings, interviews; personality inventories, interest and attitude measurement; behaviour tests; expressive methods; projective techniques; other clinical methods (such as Kelly's (1956) REP test).

In an ideal sense, a classification system should represent a set of classes that have viability on logical, theoretical, empirical and perhaps practical grounds. We need a classification system that maximizes the unique and independent character of each class and minimizes differences between measures within a class. However, this is not as simple as it appears. What do we mean by the unique character of a class? More specifically, what attributes should be considered in the search for uniqueness?

There are attractive features to a system that has been developed on logical and rational grounds, leading to classes that could be designated prior to any empirical work. Psychology is perhaps too empirical a science, however, for purely rational grounds to be widely used, as can be illustrated by the search for clinical classification and diagnostic systems. A theoretically oriented system would be excellent if we had a theory of personality with clear divisional properties among all the measures we could use. There are certainly examples of sets of measures that are grouped together on a theoretical basis. One example is the 'projective' test. Such a test considers the responses made to a set of ambiguous stimuli, and is usually interpreted in terms of the influences of various motivational and attitudinal constructs upon perception. Not all psychologists are agreed upon the unique character of projective tests, and this is true for most theoretical classes. Most importantly, there is no single generally agreed upon personality theory with explicit reference to classes of measurement. Suppose we turn to practical considerations—whether the test is group or individually administrable, whether it involves complex apparatus, paper and pencil, short or long term duration. Practical considerations tend to spawn many different classifications, depending upon the purpose of the assessment. The non-fundamental aspect of such classes, compared with their many overlapping versions, makes them unacceptable for much beyond the immediate practical demands of assessment programmes.

The final consideration—empirical—appears to have long-term potential. The variance of any measure can be thought of as being composed of a reliable and an unreliable part. Presumably, a large proportion of the reliable variance will be associated with a single trait—the trait the test is supposed to measure. Another part of this variance will be due to other traits or abilities than that upon which the test is focused (for example, verbal comprehension of instructions may enter into performance on a test of spatial relations). However, with this we are not concerned. A further part of reliable test variance of particular importance to empirical classification is the set of dimensions or factors associated with methods of measurement (Fiske 1971, Campbell and Fiske 1959). It is here that we may find useful clusterings of tests and measures. Thus high similarity between tests within a domain and low similarity between tests in different domains would be assessed in terms of dimensions of method or instrument variance. The biasing characteristics of one domain should be different from those for another domain.

At present there are insufficient data to achieve a completely satisfactory solution to the problem of classification. Attempts involve some compromise among the considerations given above and this is probably reasonable at this stage. Most solutions show considerable similarity, however, and we are not in the position of trying to reconcile radically different systems.

Domains of Personality Measurement

The classification system I should like to suggest divides personality measures into eight separate domains:

(1) *Self-description*. Data come usually from interviews or questionnaires, and are scored for the *content* of what is said. Statements concern current feelings, beliefs and opinions, and often involve direct self-reference (e.g. 'I feel shy at parties').

(2) *Ratings, judgments and reports by others*. Includes such measures as verbal reports from letters or case-histories and systematic ratings under controlled conditions.

(3) *Life history*. Factual information on previous behaviour.

(4) *Morphology*. Body build.

(5) *Expressive movement*. Measures here concern habitual style of everyday behaviours such as talking, walking, writing.

(6) *Simulated real-life situations*. An attempt is made to simulate one or more situations that are regarded as crucial for some long-term prediction. The total procedure is often long and complex.

(7) *Physiological variables*. Includes the full range of physiological measures, including biochemistry.

(8) *Motor-perceptual and performance measures*. This large group of tests is of major importance in any discussion of objective tests, and is often described as performance tests of personality.

Domain 1 is what Cattell (1946) describes as Q-data (Self-report) and seems close to Fiske's (1971) Mode 1: (Subject describes his past behaviour). Domains 2 and 3 combine into Cattell's L-data (Summary evaluations and ratings) which seem close to Fiske's Mode 4: (Prior behaviour). Domains 5, 6, 7 and 8 would come under Cattell's T-data (Objective tests), and these again are close to Fiske's Mode 2: (Current experiencing), Mode 3: (Capabilities), Mode 5: (Observations of behaviour) and Mode 6: (Psychophysiological measurement).

Objective Tests

It is with objective tests that we are concerned in this chapter. Having given some indication of their place within a total stratification of personality data, it is time to look for clear definitions. An objective test is a procedure for obtaining an individual difference score, based on the responses to a specific set of stimuli or sequences of stimuli, such that either the correct implication of the response in question is unknown to the subject or the nature of the response is such that the subject cannot readily modify his response in some desired direction. Objective tests are thus separated from Domain 2 (Ratings, judgments and reports by others) and Domain 3 (Life history) in that the individual being tested must be present, and a score is usually assigned to one or more of his responses; and from Domain 1 (Self-description) in that self-evaluation and self-report, scored for the content of such introspection, are not involved. Domain 4 (Morphology) is not included because no response, as such, is involved, though there is a definite link with certain objective test domains (e.g. physiological data). Present use of the term objective test (Domains 5, 6, 7 and 8) derives directly from Cattell's (1946) definition and is close to what Eysenck (1960a, 1960b) has called 'objective behaviour' tests, Cronbach (1970) has called 'performance' tests and Scheier (1958) has called 'objective' tests.

There is an issue that must be faced at this point in that it has direct implications for the above definition. Although a subject may not know the precise implication of his response, he is still likely to have *some* interpretation, and this in turn can bias his response in a manner unknown to the tester. For example, in a test of drawing completion, scored for the number of identifiable object completions *versus* the number of simple, but meaningless, completions, the subject may by some obscure means derive his own unique personal *idée fixe* that the test is measuring dominance and that this will be assessed by the number of solid, heavy, pencil completions. If this should happen then the final score might well be distorted by the use of such a strong but irrelevant set. It is certainly true that some sorts of irrelevant sets and expectancies are, at least theoretically, capable of entering and distorting the pattern of scores. In practice, however, (i) the effect of such sets appears to be minimal, (ii) steps should be taken to minimize this damage during the process of test construction, and (iii) in most cases the manifest purpose is sufficient as a guideline for the subject.

Domains of Objective Tests: Description and Examples

Domain 5: Expressive Movement

This domain has a long history in personality description (Allport and Vernon 1933), but has played a decreasing role in personality research as time has gone on. Tests in this domain cover such behaviours as talking, walking, eating, writing, and stylistic hand and body movements. In most cases the response has been emitted many times before and often is recognizable as being a stable aspect of an individual's behaviour. Many such responses have been tied to particular dimensions of personality or to personality types. Thus the limp handshake, the inability to look someone in the eye, the bouncing walk, the florid handwriting, are familiar ways of telling us not only how someone behaves but, through implication, quite a lot about his personality as well. Needless to say, the actual evidence linking such mannerisms to broader personality constructs has not been particularly encouraging, as the history of graphology well illustrates. In spite of the generally meagre results of such research, there remains enough interest to retain the area in the study of personality. The results of research suggest that expressive movement can tap only a small portion of total personality variance. At best, it may provide some measures that, in consort with others, produce a test composite that is an effective trait estimate. Thus if we took this domain *alone* our measures of personality—and thus our research—would be woefully inadequate. It remains a subdivision of what we are calling objective tests, but one of limited and specialized appeal.

Domain 6: Simulated Real-Life Situations

The growth of occupational psychology, coupled with increasing sophistication and ingenuity in personality measurement, led to the development of simulated real-life situations as testing instruments. Such tests usually focus on the prediction of success in some area of human endeavour. If there are certain situations critical for the success of an enterprise, then it is clearly desirable to select individuals who will perform effectively in such situations. The best predictive device may well be response to some *simulation* of the eventual task, making the simulation as close as possible to the target situation. There were attempts along these lines prior to 1939, but it was during and immediately after World War II that some of the more interesting attempts were made. Well-known examples are the Office of Strategic Services (OSS) branch of the US Army and the British War Office Selection Boards (WOSB).

It must be realized at the outset that most of these tests—and we can call them tests even though they are more complex and more time-consuming than the usual psychological test—fall within our notion of objective tests.

An exception would be measures derived from ratings by observers of behaviour in the simulated task situation; this would fall within Domain 2.

Placing these large-scale simulations in perspective, it is clear that they play a minor role as a data source. This is probably due to three main reasons. The first is that the specificity of response and situation works against their use as estimations of broad, general, personality traits that should have some impact on a fair range of human problems; nor do they attempt to cover the full range of personality structure. Second, the evidence on their predictive validity, relative to some particular criterion, is limited and usually lacking firm confirmation. Third, they are very expensive in terms of time, money, facilities and support personnel. For these reasons, measures derived from large-scale simulations cover a very limited part of the total field of objective measures.

Domain 7: Physiological Variables

That there should be considerable information relevant to an individual's personality from physiological sources scarcely needs saying. However, in spite of the research, increasing in volume, that is appearing, the precise nature of the links between physiological variables and personality measures from other domains remains largely obscure. This lack of clarity is also to be found in many of the relations *between* physiological measures, these being of particular concern as it may well be the *patterns* of such relations that turn out to be most important (Kleinmuntz 1967). Early attempts (e.g. Wenger 1948) to obtain dimensions among physiological variables did not lead to the setting up of established traits, and clearly multivariate research using such measures has much domain-specific complexity (Mefferd 1966).

Particular note may be made of measures involved in the study of arousal, of biochemical correlates of the behaviour disorders (such as schizophrenia and anxiety), and of indices used in the study of individual differences in learning.

It seems unlikely that physiological measures—at least as presently used in research—will, either singly or in a battery of physiological measures, be able to constitute feasible and practical measures of personality, with a range of generality for applied and research problems. It is likely, however, that they may be of considerable use as part of a trait composite composed otherwise than from Domain 7, and in addition they provide a rich source of data for experimental purposes when theory-testing work is being carried out.

Domain 8: Motor-Perceptual and Performance Tests

This is the last of the domains falling under the objective test umbrella, and is probably the most important from a practical point of view. A major consideration is that the variety and range of measures come closer than any other of the objective test domains to not only providing feasible measurement for most research and applied purposes but having sufficient coverage across the universe of measures and constructs that interest the personality researcher.

The relation of this domain to the others is quite important. Of the data sources considered under the various domains, it is from Domain 8: Motor-perceptual and performance tests that the vast majority of measures used in research and applied batteries will come. It is with this domain, therefore, that we shall be mainly concerned in this chapter.

The initial use of perceptual-motor and performance tests in psychology is associated largely with J. McKeen Cattell and Sir Francis Galton. Although Cattell and Galton were interested in individual difference measures in terms of cognitive functions, many of their tests were the forerunners of measures of temperament and motivation that were to appear in the 1920's and 1930's in Europe and America (DuBois 1970).

The diversity of these tests makes a simple description of this kind of measure very difficult. A considerable number of measures from recognizable and familiar sources do appear, of course. Among these would be projective tests, measures of preference, response styles and sets, maximum performance measures, response to various forms of interference in performing some assigned task, response to various forms of suggestion, and many other classes of response. For an account of such measures the reader should turn to Cattell and Warburton (1967), Hundleby, Pawlik and Cattell (1965), Eysenck (1960a, 1960b) and Santostefano (1968).

In order to give some clearer notion of the tests in this domain certain examples have been chosen. These illustrate not only the ingenuity needed in test conceptualization and construction, but also some of the advantages and disadvantages of their use.

Body Sway. In this test the subject is blindfolded and asked to stand still for a period of time (usually for a relatively short period, say, two to four minutes). A record is then kept of the extent to which the subject sways backwards and forwards.

Tapes are available for both sway-forward and sway-backward suggestion in the form:

'You are falling. You are falling forward. Falling forward. You are falling forward.', etc.

The main scores that can be obtained include the extent of sway, both forwards and backwards, (a) under the different suggestion conditions, and (b) without the suggestion condition (i.e. silence).

Although research using this test does not give very clear results with normal adults and young children, there is a consistent correlation between the amount of sway and diagnosis of neurosis in mixed neurotic and normal subjects. Both Eysenck and Cattell have used this test and associate it with their respective personality dimensions of neuroticism (Eysenck 1960b) and U.I. 23: Mobilization vs. neurotic regressive debility (Cattell 1957, Hundleby, Pawlik and Cattell 1965).

This measure illustrates many of the features of an objective test. The precise implications are most unlikely to occur to the subject, and minor variations of set or expectancy appear to have little or no influence on scores. *Acquiescence.* The various response styles and response sets form a cluster of measures within this domain. Most of the very extensive literature on this topic has concentrated on sets and styles associated with the multiple-choice or true–false format of many questionnaires and achievement measures (Cronbach 1950, Jackson and Messick 1958) and involves such variables as acquiescence, social desirability, and preference for extreme responses among response alternatives.

Acquiescence may be measured by the extent to which a subject endorses the *agree strongly* or *agree* alternatives of the typical Likert multiple-choice answer. There are other, related, ways of scoring for acquiescence but they are all likely to imply that the high scorer on a measure of acquiescence is a person who characteristically endorses agreement in answering questionnaire items regardless of item content. There are many possible sets of item stimuli that are appropriate for such a measure, and if no specifically constructed acquiescence measure is available, then the extent of agreement on a set of items may be used if (a) the number of items is large (say, definitely greater than 100 and preferably greater than 300), and (b) the subscale items, in terms of content keys, are appropriately balanced in terms of agree/disagree endorsement on the one or more content sources of item variance.

Acquiescence, as so defined, does not appear to be a pure measure but to bear a moderate relation to several personality traits (Couch and Kenniston 1960, Hundleby, Pawlik and Cattell 1965).

Thus, although a questionnaire format is being used, acquiescence becomes an objective test measure due to its reliance not upon item content but on a stable style of responding to questionnaire items in general. In this case we have an often unwanted source of variance in one domain of measurement being used as a useful individual difference measure in another.

Hidden Figures/Embedded Figures. Many objective tests appear in a maximum performance guise, and the group of tests that we can label 'hidden figures' is an example. Early work on such a test was carried out by Gottschaldt (1926) and more recent versions are associated with Witkin *et al.* (1962), Jackson, Messick and Myers (1964) and Cattell and Warburton (1967). In general, the subject is presented with some relatively simple figure and then has to locate it in a rather more complex figure. The item shown in Figure 1 (from Hundleby and Cattell 1973) is a fairly typical example. The subject has to circle the letters either on the test or on the separate answer sheet corresponding to the more camplex diagrams within which the smaller diagram is concealed.

The personality trait associated with this measure is U.I. 19: Independence (Hundleby, Pawlik and Cattell 1965) or field independence (Witkin *et al.* 1962).

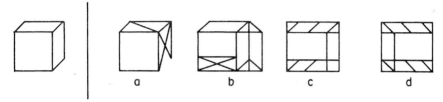

F I G U R E 1.

The subject is not likely to anticipate the psychologist's meaning from his score, but accepts the sets and motivations associated with the taking of an ability test. He is likely to regard the successful location of many diagrams as preferable to the location of few diagrams. The test is group administrable, although there are individually administered versions.

Annoyances and Irritations. One of the characteristics associated with anxiety, conflict and maladjustment of a neurotic type is increased reaction to the minor irritants of everyday living. This can be assessed in several ways, both questionnaire and ratings being feasible, of course. An objective test version, for example T38 Common annoyances (Cattell and Warburton 1967), gives lists of such minor irritants and asks the subject to indicate the extent of his annoyance. An example from T38, appropriate for children, is as follows.

People who borrow your things and never return them.

(a) Very annoyed and mad
(b) A little bit annoyed and mad
(c) Not annoyed and mad

The subject either underlines an alternative or responds on a separate answer sheet.

This test is closer to the twilight zone between the objective tests of Domain 8 and the questionnaires of Domain 1 than the previous measures we have considered. Although it is more 'objective', in the sense we are using here, than the usual self-report test, it is still likely to have some of the distorting features common to questionnaires. Nevertheless, the implications of endorsing many or few annoyances are not likely to be clear to the subject, and indeed there is no simple interpretation of such scores, the test, like acquiescence, being associated with more than one factor although the main source of variance appears to come from an objective test trait of anxiety.

Unstructured Drawings. The use of ambiguous visual material as stimuli has been a common feature among many projective tests, notably the Rorschach and Thematic Apperception Test (TAT). There is no reason why such test vehicles should not be included among our objective tests as long as (1) the implications of the responses (in terms either of kind or frequency) are not known to the subject, and thus he cannot readily manipulate his response in some desired direction, (2) the test administration is standardized, and (3) the scoring is objective and does not depend upon individual subjective interpretations by the scorer. Let us take an example (Figure 2) from T20 (Cattell and Warburton 1967, Hundleby and Cattell 1973). The test has a strict time limit per drawing, and there are four to six drawings depending upon the version of the test. The subject is instructed that the test is one of imagination, that he will be shown different drawings which are not very clear in interpretation, and that he is to write down all the things that he can imagine seeing.

FIGURE 2.

Among the different scores that could be obtained from this test, two may be used for illustrative purposes. These are (a) the total number of responses given, and (b) the number, or proportion, of threatening objects seen in the drawings (according to a key of such responses provided the scorer). Analyses of the first score suggest that it may be due to two correlated factors, one named U.I. 21: Exuberance, and the other involving a broad factor of imaginative fluency (Hundleby 1972b). The second score is associated with a factor of timidity (U.I. 17), though this last result needs further confirmation (Hundleby, Pawlik and Cattell 1965).

Tracking and Aiming. This test derives from some of the measures used by Hartshorne and May (1928) and Brogden (1940) in the study of character. In brief, this test, and others like it, sets a plausible task for the subject which is either extremely difficult or impossible to accomplish. A highly successful score thus carries with it the implication that the subject is using a response procedure different from that suggested in the instructions. It is an over-simplification to say that in many such tests this different procedure may be regarded as 'cheating'. Again we have a measure that appears to be more complex, factorially, than was first supposed. Impulsiveness, desire to please the test administrator, high competitiveness, and a general lack of respect for the rules of testing as laid down by the test administrator, may all be involved.

In one version of the measure, Tracking and aiming (Hundleby 1972b) (see Figure 3), the subject is asked to move a pencil line from an initial starting

FIGURE 3.

position ① to fall within a second circle ②. This must be done on a command from the tester: first to put a pencil point in ①; then to close his eyes; to move to ② as best he may; and finally to open his eyes after some five seconds have elapsed. If the subject's pencil point touches or cuts the black rectangle, then 1 is subtracted from his score. Total score is the number of successful lines that fall within the prescribed circles. There are twelve circles.

Rod-and-Frame. Some years ago Witkin and his associates (Witkin *et al.* 1962, Witkin and Oltman 1967) developed a number of objective tests related to a personality trait (or, as it has been described, cognitive style) of *field independence*. Among such measures were the Rotating-Room test, the Body-Adjustment test, and the Rod-and-Frame test. A central feature of these tests is that the spatial orientation of the subject is manipulated by the experimenter at the same time as the subject is required to make judgments in terms of the vertical.

There are several versions of the Rod-and-Frame test, but the general principles of testing remain the same. The subject is presented with an off-vertical rod at a distance and is instructed to adjust the rod to a vertical position, using a control device. The frame is a square set on an angle to the vertical, and appears to act in a manner such that the direction of angle of the frame induces the subject to adjust the rod to a position somewhere between the true vertical and the angle of the frame. Over several trials the angle of adjustment of the rod is recorded. Field dependence is associated with responses closer to the angle of the frame, while field independence is associated with greater proximity to the true vertical.

Paper-and-Pencil Maze Performance. There has been a very small but relatively steady flow of researchers on human individual differences in maze performance since the time of World War I. The most consistent researcher has been Porteus (1959), who developed a series of graded-difficulty pencil-and-paper mazes suitable for different age levels. Relevant to our present purpose is the Q score, which derives from errors and failures to follow instructions. This score has been associated particularly with delinquency in children, among a wide range of criteria. In general, maze-tracing by delinquents appears to involve a more careless style than that of non-delinquents.

Group administrable mazes, using a strict time limit (Cattell and Warburton 1967), have been used and show links to other personality measures and criteria. Not surprisingly, an important score is the extent of error performance relative to the distance travelled.

What do Objective Tests Measure?

The Theoretical Construct Versus Predictive Orientations

There are two main orientations in personality measurement, the theoretical construct and the non-theoretical predictive. In the former case concern is with measuring a theoretical construct; in the latter with producing a set of tests which maximally predict a real-life criterion (such as success in medical school training). The predictive argument leads to a plethora of tests and predictive batteries; but for very narrow purposes, such as selection for specific trades and professional institutes, a plausible case can be presented. For broad areas of psychology, notably fundamental research in the personality, social and abnormal areas, our need is for adequate theory, and theory-based research. This inevitably leads to the measurement of constructs, the attempt to account for behaviour in terms of a relatively small number of theoretical variables. It is also assumed that such constructs will be maximally useful in the majority of applied predictive situations, and that as soon as any criterion generality is desired—perhaps over time, over different related criterion measures, or over different subject populations—that a construct-oriented approach will prove preferable to one which avoids theory in developing predictive systems. The construct-oriented approach is thus also an empirical approach, but it involves the intermediary steps required of theory and science. The present chapter favours the construct-oriented approach, and this follows the general historical line from Spearman through to Guilford, R. B. Cattell, Eysenck, Jackson, Nunnally, and many others. Thus our answer to the question, 'What do objective tests measure?' is that they measure theoretical constructs, traits, abilities, hypothetical variables, and, indeed, all manner of variables that are not directly observable yet which can be used in models to account for the variation in the personality measures falling into the various domains.

Criteria for Assessing the Viability of Objective Test Traits

A large number of constructs is too indigestible a fare for most personologists. The majority of theoretical systems, after all, can only handle with ease a small number of fundamental variables and many researchers have been content with studying a single trait, such as need achievement (n ach) or anxiety. It is now time to consider the manner in which we choose our major traits in order that future research may concentrate on a few variables rather than indulge in a blind striking out in all directions. The rationale is straightforward. It is desirable, in terms of theory, research and practice, to view personality in terms of a small number of theoretical variables. There are many tenders, both in terms of single traits and of systems of traits, for this fundamental status. Therefore we need criteria to aid us in judging the viability and usefulness of a trait. When we turn to empirical evidence of the viability of a trait then it is the trait *measure* that concerns us.

On what basis does one make such a judgment? Elsewhere (Hundleby 1972a) four criteria have been suggested. These are: (1) *Fidelity*, the extent to which the variance of a measure can be associated with a given trait; (2) *Consistency*, the degree to which the fidelity of the measure remains constant over different populations and changes in administration circumstances; (3) *Circumstantial relations*, the extent of demonstrable and known relations to measures of other theoretical constructs; (4) *Relevance*, the extent to which a measure has been shown to have associations with the full range of personality criteria (defined here in a very broad sense and including traditional clinical, educational and industrial measures along with more unusual criteria such as likelihood of adopting leadership roles, affection for others, involvement in community activities, adjustment to death, adjustment to major permanent physical injury, and so on). Many of these measures will come from Domains 2 and 3 discussed on page 68. These four criteria are suggesting that a trait measure is viable if it is internally, psychometrically sound and if it has something to offer as a source of variance among the theoretical and empirical variables that concern the personologist. Other criteria of adequacy are given by Fiske (1971). There may be differences between writers in terms of the importance assigned to certain of the criteria of judgment, but there can surely be no argument against an attempt to clear house among our major theoretical constructs.

Major Source Traits Deriving from Objective Tests

It would be incorrect to suggest that there is complete agreement on the major traits to be found in objective tests. Nor do most of our trait measures appear satisfactory in terms of the criteria suggested in the previous paragraph. There is probably no trait that shows a satisfactory high level in terms of all four criteria. Where there is a fairly high level of competence in developing the measure from a psychometric point of view, there is often little or no evidence as to external relations. When external relations are emphasized these often turn out to be a single criterion or narrow band of criteria, and our measure has little additional meaning than that of an alternate and perhaps rather inadequate measure of this criterion.

The most systematic and extensive attempt to cover a wide sampling of tests, and at the same time provide data that are generalizable in the sense used in the previous section, has come from R. B. Cattell and his associates (Cattell and Warburton 1967, Hundleby, Pawlik and Cattell 1965). The general research strategy has been to obtain data on a large number of variables (more than 60 variables per study is not uncommon) on a wide range of populations (students, mental hospital inmates, military personnel, adolescents, children in the middle-childhood years, even preschoolers and criminals). Each study is a link in a chain of studies as information on the major traits, and on different sets of variables, becomes clearer. The majority of studies have been factor analyses, and effort has been made to relate or match the factors from different researches.

In order to simplify the cataloguing of factors from so many studies, a special indexing was devised such that each trait, when it appeared to have been replicated sufficiently in independent studies as a source of covariation among objective tests, was given a Universal Index (U.I.) number (Cattell and Warburton 1967). The numbers range from U.I. 16 to U.I. 36, the first sixteen U.I. factors being given to abilities. The various U.I. factors, however, are not equal in terms of their candidacy as the building blocks of a strong empirically based theory of personality. There is a need for further evidence, and for considerably more research. These U.I. traits do represent, however, a starting position on the difficult path of establishing and confirming objective test personality dimensions.

Four Major Objective Test Dimensions of Personality

A complete list and description of objective test traits is beyond the scope of this chapter. In lieu of this, four traits will be discussed: U.I. 16, U.I. 19, U.I. 23 and U.I. 24. These objective test traits appear to be important, particularly in the clinical area, and to suggest links between Cattell's system and those of Eysenck and Witkin.

U.I. 16: Assertiveness. This trait has been identified in a large number of factor analytic studies (Hundleby, Pawlik and Cattell 1965). Among the tests that are associated with this factor, and which could be used to obtain a trait score, are:

Preference for 'unquestionable' and socially acceptable book titles rather than 'questionable' book titles.

Faster speed of tapping (using a simple stylus and electrical recorder).

Faster tempo of arm and leg circling.

Faster speed of reading under instructions to read at one's usual rate.

Higher score on a complex maze task (cursive miniature situation).

Higher ideomotor tempo (reading poetry and copying simple stick-figure drawings).

Greater preference for objects or activities that appear sophisticated or 'highbrow'.

Both educational and cultural sophistication and a generally high tempo of bodily movement and performance on simple tasks enter into many of these tests. Positive correlations between U.I. 16: Assertiveness and achievement are usually to be found. There are rather consistent relations with clinical criteria, the person having a low score on assertiveness being rather more likely to fall into a psychotic or neurotic group (Hundleby 1972a).

U.I. 19: Independence. Like U.I. 16, the objective test trait of independence has emerged from a long series of factor analytic studies. Among the tests that are associated with this factor are the following:

Greater accuracy in pictorial gestalt closure (scored as the percentage correct out of 20 incomplete drawings).

Greater accuracy in Gottschaldt figures (see page 72).

Greater criticism of others relative to self (assessed by fluency on a range of personal attributes).

Higher score in a task involving the careful following of rather complex instructions in a relatively simple perceptual task.

Higher score in a task involving the crossing points of imaginary lines from different points of a complex diagram.

Greater severity of judgment in assessing the performance of others on a series of tasks.

A feature common to many of these tests is an ability to cope with a task in a manner independent of the environment in which the task is placed. As to whether or not the rather self-centred and critical aspects of this trait are indeed central or are an outgrowth of the development of this trait in childhood, it is impossible to tell at the moment. Assuming that U.I. 19: Independence and Witkin's field independence are very similar, if not identical, then considerable information on the trait may be obtained from Cattell (1955), Hundleby, Pawlik and Cattell (1965) and Witkin *et al.* (1962). Clinical evidence suggests that the individual with a high score on independence is likely to be relatively free from psychiatric problems, though the relationship is probably complex.

U.I. 23: Neural Reserves. This trait has been identified in many studies, but rather clearer results are probably obtainable from groups containing a number of neurotic subjects. Measures associated with the trait include:

High accuracy in a test of two-hand coordination (the apparatus involving two wired metal discs with a recording device for registering correct placements of a stylus).

Lower perceptual-motor rigidity (scored on a measure involving the usual and reversed version of such overlearned tasks as writing a common word or number).

High ratio of accuracy to speed in a range of perceptual-motor tasks.

Less body sway under suggestion of sway, while blindfolded.

Greater accuracy in performing simple numerical addition and multiplication problems (without the aid of paper and pencil).

Like U. I. 16 and U.I. 19, the two previous traits described, U.I. 23: Neural reserves is a predictor of neurosis. There is a suggestion that U.I. 23 may be rather central to a theoretical model for neurosis, and it must be closely related to Eysenck's rather broader factor of neuroticism (N) as this appears in objective tests (Eysenck 1960b). The relation between N and U.I. 23 brings forward the difference in research strategy between Eysenck and Cattell. In the case of N, tests tend to be selected on the basis of known association to neurosis and little attempt is made to move beyond a one-dimensional predictive framework for these measures. With Cattell's strategy, a rough picture of personality attributes as derivable from objective tests was first attempted and *later* an association between the attributes (one of which was U.I. 23) and neurosis was examined—thus favouring a multidimensional framework for the prediction of neurosis.

U.I. 24: Anxiety. Variables associated with this objective test trait in previous studies (Hundleby, Pawlik and Cattell 1965) include:

Greater number of admissions of minor wrongdoing or frailties.

Greater acquiescence in the answering of questionnaires.

Higher score on a checklist of annoyances.

Little self-confidence that good performance could be reached in a range of untried skills.

There appears to be a link between U.I. 24 and diagnosis of neurosis, but magnitude of association is not as great as might be expected (Hundleby 1972a).

It is interesting to note that many of the scores that correlate consistently with U.I. 24 are obtained from paper-and-pencil, verbal tests. Indeed, this trait is one of the few emerging from analyses of objective tests that show this rather definite trend. There is, of course, no hard-and-fast line dividing objective tests from the self-report, questionnaire, domain, and here we do find tests which are somewhat closer to the self-report form than is usual, or desirable. However, our criteria of an objective test are satisified, though it may well be that some of the sources of errors of measurement that appear in questionnaire data will also be present here to some degree.

An issue of considerable importance is the extent to which anxiety, as the construct has been discussed and described in numerous clinical settings, can be usefully assessed by ratings, questionnaires and objective test measures. The extent of the literature on anxiety (see Levitt 1967, Spielberger 1966) is such that sound measures of the construct would be expected to be found with relative ease among different domains of measures, and any two such trait scores would be expected to correlate in the $+0.70$'s or higher. Unhappily, the empirical evidence is not as confirmatory on this point as would be hoped. The number of studies using a broadly conceived multivariate analysis of anxiety measures from objective test and other domains is very small, and the results have not given unequivocal support to one central dimension determining most of the variance of the different sets of measures. It may be that anxiety is a more complex notion than perhaps our rather simplistic indices can presently handle. Be that as it may, it is most likely that U.I. 24 will play an important part in the development of research on this aspect of behaviour (Cattell and Scheier 1961).

Considerations in the Use of Objective Tests

The Need for a Multitest Battery for each Trait

An objective test, as such, should not be directly compared in terms of psychometric properties with the typical questionnaire scale. The typical objective test has rather high specificity in the sense that a rather larger proportion of its reliable variance is likely to be unique to the test than would be expected with, say, a reasonably efficient 30-item questionnaire scale. This places the objective test, in comparison with such a questionnaire, at some point between an average item and total scale score in terms of indices of reliability and validity. These considerations, with others, suggest that traits measured by objective tests should be assessed by a composite of some 6–10 tests. The tests in such a composite may be given either unit weights or different weights according to some estimation procedure, such as the traditional regression weights for factor scores (Harman 1967). The use of a composite reduces the degree to which irrelevant but systematic variance can enter into a trait score. To the extent that the tests are chosen to minimize any possibility of instrument variance (Campbell and Fiske 1959), the composite score should give a relatively unbiased and accurate score.

The notion of having to administer several tests, rather than one, is disturbing to some test-users. In the objective test area this is largely due to a carryover from the influence of earlier multipurpose tests such as the Rorschach. It was hoped that a relatively comprehensive and presumably reliable set of personality scores would emerge from the one-test vehicle. However, surely by now we must be convinced that no single measure can perform this function, no matter its apparent plausibility. The argument is indeed much stronger. Where objective tests are concerned, one trait or dimension of personality should be measured by a composite of several measures, and if several aspects of personality are under investigation then this means the use of several such composites! Alarming though this may seem, the writer is convinced that no other course is really useful. If indeed we need several objective tests in order to get a satisfactory measure of a trait, and the evidence certainly suggests this, then there is little choice for the investigator.

Individual versus Group Administrable Tests

Objective tests may be either group or individually administered. Psychogalvanic skin response (PGR), as it is customarily measured, can scarcely be a group test, whereas a test of gestalt closure, based on a booklet of incomplete drawings, clearly can be group administered. Most of the measures falling within the objective test domains discussed by Eysenck (1960b) and Guilford (1959) are individually administrable, whereas many of those described in Cattell and Warburton (1967) can be handled very well in groups.

Apart from the obvious economic advantages of group testing, there are two important points to bear in mind:

(a) All other things being equal, an individual test is likely to be more valid than a group test. Put rather loosely, a five-minute individual test with special apparatus is probably better than a five-minute group pencil-and-paper test.

(b) Personality traits differ in terms of the extent to which individual or group administrable tests are found amongst their best measures. Some traits are so dependent upon individual tests that a useful composite of group tests would be very difficult to put together.

In many cases there is no real choice for a group test cannot be found for use as a substitute for an individual test. Tests to measure the different traits are not yet plentiful enough to give the researcher much room in selection.

The Importance of Standardizing the Total Situation in the Administration of Objective Tests

An aspect of testing that has received little attention has been the effects of different aspects of the total situation upon the subject while taking an objective test.

There are many examples of objective tests where the administrator, by verbal or non-verbal means, directly or by suggestion, can influence test score. The administrator is, however, just one part of the total testing situation. Take, for example, the 'peeping' test described on page 75. The verbal instructions, if given by different administrators, can vary in terms of firmness and implied strictness in adhering to rules, among several other facets, without any change in wording. If we put the words on tape, then one source of variance is eliminated. Yet others remain. The testing may be of children in a classroom, and the general level of activity in classrooms can vary considerably. In some classrooms the noise level will be low with an established pattern of obedience to the teacher; other classrooms will differ. It would not be unreasonable to suppose that a test which depends upon adherence to rules may show somewhat different results when tested on groups with different established habits of responding to verbal instructions. The 'peeping' test is, actually, fairly robust in this regard, but the point being made is that some objective tests appear to be prone to certain error influences that are of less concern with questionnaires or achievement measures. An objective test assessment procedure is a very novel experience for most subjects. This being so, they have much less in terms of established test-taking attitudes and habits to fall back upon. It is, after all, customary to keep quiet during achievement tests and to attempt to work at a fairly constant level of performance (per person). The required responses are clear, as are the implications of carrying out the 'correct' response. Questionnaires are becoming familiar in most school systems, and from then onwards rather well-established test-taking attitudes and expectancies are likely to prevail. Objective tests present a far more unstructured situation to the subject, a situation in which chance cues may be seized upon as guides to behaviour. The problem concerns both group and individually administered tests.

What are the implications of this? It is not unlikely that some of the variation in observed correlations between objective tests, and thus in later factor loadings if such an analysis be carried out, may be due to variation in circumstances surrounding the testing—the administrator, the testing room, the purpose of the testing session, even the seriousness of intent that surrounds and flavours the testing. These influence most personality tests to some degree, but almost certainly influence some objective tests more than others. It may be that the evidence for specificity in these measures (e.g. typically low intercorrelations) is due in part to a degree of non-standardization in the testing circumstances.

It is therefore important for the user of objective tests to pay particular attention to all details of administration instructions, and to note any rather unusual features of his own administration procedures. For the test constructor there is a definite need for more comprehensive administration instructions and for more research on potential sources of error variance.

Test-Taking Motivation and Morale

The time for completion of sufficient objective tests to yield an adequate measure of, say, four or five traits could well be two to two and a half hours. A question that comes naturally to mind concerns the extent to which test-taking motivation and interest can be sustained and remain constant over such a period, or longer. Observation of groups, both children and adults, suggests that objective tests are far more palatable to subjects than are either ability or questionnaire measures. This would appear to be due to at least two main reasons. First, the tests are usually novel and intriguing experiences and not what the subject expects when he reports for psychological or educational testing. Resentments over past achievement examinations and learned boredom are less easy to associate with such measures. Many of the tests have a game-like quality that tends to sustain effort over several hours. Second, if the tests are relatively short, as is usually the case, with 10 minutes being the period for a fairly long test and many being of two to three minutes in duration, the constantly changing format and task retain the subject's interest.

Objective tests have been used with a wide variety of subjects, including clinical and delinquent groups, and from preschool to advanced adulthood, and have been found to be acceptable and interesting. Such findings are important in work with children or with educationally below-average groups, for not only is interest kept relatively high but the influence of linguistic skills tends to be reduced.

Availability

The choice of standardized batteries of objective tests is in no way as extensive as is found with questionnaires, interest inventories, aptitudes and achievement tests, and the measures that are found in the *Mental Measurements Yearbooks*. What published batteries there are tend to be rather experimental in nature. The problem is largely a practical one. It is an enormous undertaking to develop, validate and standardize, with appropriate norms, a set of measures for a series of objective test traits. Recently a battery of tests, group administrable, was published by IPAT (Schuerger and Cattell 1971) for girls and boys of an adolescent age. A clinical battery at the adult level is at present nearing completion (Hundleby and Cattell 1973).

The Future Development of Objective Tests of Personality

It is hazardous to attempt to predict future trends in psychology. However, taking the area of objective tests of personality, and dealing with the next decade or so, certain issues and developments seem highly likely.

The Measurement of Constructs. It would appear inevitable that the single test, with its hope of solving a multitude of predictive and theoretical problems, will disappear from the scientific study of personality. So many hopes have not been fulfilled that such overoptimism is bound to give way to a more reasoned approach combining quantitative and psychometric expertise with predictive importance and salience. In other words, we may hope for research using sounder personality measures.

Integrative Research. As psychologists realize the need for multiple-test batteries, so too is there likely to be a move towards integrating research findings around a relatively small set of traits. Much more emphasis must be placed on studies comparing and integrating different trait systems and measures. It is of fundamental importance that the traits used in personality theory be acceptable to the majority of workers in the field, and such agreement will only be reached by gathering pertinent empirical evidence.

The Relationship Between Objective Tests and Self-Report Measures. For a long time now the main thrust of structured testing has involved questionnaires. Our most sophisticated models have used self-report measures because there is a large pool of information on their interrelations, their relation to practical criteria is becoming established, and lastly but importantly, they are easy to administer and score. However, questionnaire measures have come under some fairly heavy criticism in terms of (a) the appropriateness and occasions for their use, and the decisions based upon such scores, and (b) our growing technical knowledge of the biases and limitations of self-report measures. Particularly relevant is the increasing body of information that suggests that though there is a relation between self-report and a range of applied criteria, this relation is often not as high or as extensive as would be hoped. Such reasons suggest that in some areas—certainly in the assessment of children and adolescents for educational or adjustment problems, for adult clinical purposes, and perhaps for rather specific purposes such as the prediction of behaviour in small groups—researchers will turn more towards objective tests.

Cross-Domain Matching of Traits. Implicit in much earlier discussion is the need to establish the extent to which a given trait can be found in all, or only one or two, domains. This has practical relevance since objective tests can be rather demanding in terms of personnel and equipment. More important, though, is a theoretical issue concerning the nature and characteristics of personality constructs. Mischel (1968) and others have suggested that the absence of firm confirmatory evidence on the cross-domain matching of traits (and there is indeed relatively little evidence on this) has negative implications for the trait approach in general. Such arguments are of most concern to theorists who propose either complete or nearly complete isomorphism of traits. For such arguments the absence of clear evidence of transfer from one domain to another is doubtless a vexing issue. However, there is no *necessity* for an isomorphic view, as such, within the trait approach. Indeed, what little evidence there is seems to favour a limited degree of cross-domain matching as well as some uniqueness. Clearly, it is important that we examine the extent of the appearance of objective test traits in other domains. These are empirical matters that need to be explored as we derive workable models of personality.

References

Allport, G. W., and Vernon, P. E. (1933), *Studies in Expressive Movement*, New York, Macmillan.

Brogden, H. E. (1940), 'A factor analysis of forty character tests', *Psychological Monographs*, **234**, 39–55.

Campbell, D. T., and Fiske, D. W. (1959), 'Convergent and discriminant validation by the multitrait–multimethod matrix', *Psychological Bulletin*, **56**, 81–105.

Cattell, R. B. (1946), *The Description and Measurement of Personality*, Yonkers, New York, World Book Company.

Cattell, R. B. (1957), *Description and Measurement of Personality and Motivation*, Yonkers, New York, World Book Company.

Cattell, R. B., and Scheier, I. H. (1961), *The Meaning and Measurement of Neuroticism and Anxiety*, New York, Ronald Press.

Cattell, R. B., and Warburton, F. W. (1967), *Objective Personality and Motivation Tests*, Champaign, Illinois, University of Illinois Press.

Couch, A., and Keniston, K. (1960), 'Yeasayers and Naysayers: Agreeing response set as a personality variable', *Journal of Abnormal and Social Psychology*, **60**, 151–74.

Cronbach, L. J. (1950), 'Further evidence on response sets and test design', *Educational and Psychological Measurement*, **10**, 3–31.

Cronbach, L. J. (1970), *Essentials of Psychological Testing*, Third edition, New York, Harper and Row.

DuBois, P. H. (1970), *A History of Psychological Testing*, Boston, Massachusetts, Allyn and Bacon.

Eysenck, H. J. (Ed.) (1960a), *Experiments in Personality. Volume II. Psychodiagnostics and Psychodynamics*, London, Routledge and Kegan Paul.

Eysenck, H. J. (1960b), *The Structure of Human Personality*, Second edition, London, Methuen.

Fiske, D. W. (1971), *Measuring the Concepts of Personality*, Chicago, Aldine-Atherton.

Gottschaldt, K. (1926), 'Über den Einfluss der Erfahrung auf die Wahrnehmung von Figuren I: Über den Einfluss gehaufter Einprägung von Figuren auf ihne Sichtbarkeit in umfassenden Konfigurationen', *Psychologische Forschung*, **8**, 261–317.

Guilford, J. P. (1959), *Personality*, New York, McGraw-Hill.

Harman, H. M. (1967), *Modern Factor Analysis*, Chicago, University of Chicago Press.

Hartshorne, H., and May, M. A. (1928), *Studies in Deceit*, New York, Macmillan.

Hundleby, J. D. (1972a), 'The structure of personality: surface and source traits', in R. M. Dreger (Ed.), *Multivariate Approaches to Personality*, Baton Rouge, Louisiana, Claitor Press.

Hundleby, J. D. (1972b), Personality Constructs and Adjustment in the Middle-Childhood Years, Unpublished Manuscript.

Hundleby, J. D., and Cattell, R. B. (1973), *A Battery of Objective Tests for Clinical Purposes*, Champaign, Illinois, Institute for Personality and Ability Testing.

Hundleby, J. D., Pawlik, K., and Cattell, R. B. (1965), *Personality Factors in Objective Test Devices*, San Diego, California, Knapp.

Jackson, D. N., and Messick, S. (1958), 'Content and style in personality assessment', *Psychological Bulletin*, **55**, 243–52.

Jackson, D. N., Messick, S. J., and Myers, C. T. (1964), 'The role of memory and color in group and individual embedded-figures measures of field independence', *Educational and Psychological Measurement*, **24**, 177–92.

Kelly, G. A. (1956), *The Psychology of Personal Constructs*, New York, Norton.

Kleinmuntz, B. (1967), *Personality Measurement*, Homewood, Illinois, Dorsey.

Levitt, E. E. (1967), *The Psychology of Anxiety*, New York, Bobbs-Merrill.

Mefferd, R. B. (1966), 'Structuring physiological correlates of mental processes and states: The study of biological correlates of mental processes', in R. B. Cattell (Ed.), *Handbook of Multivariate Experimental Psychology*, Chapter 22, Chicago, Rand McNally, pp. 684–710.

Mischel, W. (1968), *Personality and Assessment*, New York, Wiley.

Nunnally, J. (1967), *Psychometric Theory*, New York, McGraw-Hill.

Porteus, S. D. (1959), *The Maze Test and Clinical Psychology*, Palo Alto, California, Pacific Books.

Santostefano, S. (1968), 'Situational testing in personality assessment', in D. L. Sills (Ed.), *International Encyclopedia of Social Science*, Vol. XII, New York, Macmillan and Free Press, pp. 48–55.

Scheier, I. H. (1958), 'What is an "Objective" Test?', *Psychological Reports*, **4**, 147–57.

Schuerger, J. M., and Cattell, R. B. (1971), *The High School Objective–Analytic Battery* (*HSOA*), Champaign, Illinois, Institute for Personality and Ability Testing.

Spielberger, C. D. (1966), *Anxiety and Behavior*, New York, Academic Press.

Wenger, M. A. (1948), 'Studies of autonomic balance in Army Air Force personnel', *Comparative Psychological Monographs*, **101**, 1–111.

Witkin, H. A., Dyk, Ruth B., Faterson, Hanna F., Goodenough, D. R., and Karp, S. A. (1962), *Psychological Differentiation*, New York, Wiley.

Witkin, H. A., and Oltman, P. K. (1967), 'Cognitive style', *International Journal of Neurology*, **VI**, 2, 119–37.

4

NEW DEVELOPMENTS IN PROJECTIVE TESTING

Boris Semeonoff

University of Edinburgh

THE INCLUSION in this book of an account of what is new in projective psychology would appear to presuppose validity, in the most general sense, of the projective hypothesis. Consequently, it is not proposed to examine here the question of whether projectivists are wasting their time and that of their subjects. The term 'new' has been interpreted in the sense of 'novel', and that, in its turn, more in the sense of 'unfamiliar' than that of 'recent'. However, considerations of recency are relevant insofar as they allow the present position to be assessed in the context of the history and development of the projective approach to personality study.

Various events have been identified as marking the beginning of projective psychology. The actual techniques are, mostly, older than their projective applications. Inasmuch as their interest is predominantly idiographic they may be said always to have had projective implications; it is probably the intention underlying their use that defines their status as 'projective' as that term is now commonly understood. Such 'intention' is not, of course, uniform: it usually implies a therapeutic aim, or guidance or selection in an occupational setting. Quasi-projective techniques have also been used or devised for purposes of theory-testing and the like. Such uses have been considered to be largely outside the scope of the present discussion. Accordingly, such landmarks as Galton's earliest self-administered 'psychometric experiments' in free association (Galton 1879) and the still earlier 'discovery' of ink-blots by Justinius Kerner (1857) are prehistory for projective psychology even more than for psychology in general.

Projective use of word association may be said to date from the almost simultaneous publication, in 1910, of papers by Jung and by Kent and Rosanoff. It is interesting to note that these two papers represent exemplars of contrasted approaches in projective psychology—the holistic or global 'clinical' approach in Jung's work, and the more strictly psychometric,

89

diagnostic or 'actuarial' in that of Kent and Rosanoff. Word association no longer holds its premier position among projective methods, and no widely used application of its principles is discussed in this chapter. If, however, one thinks of a stimulus word and the response given as fused in a single sentence, one has an approximation to a sentence completion technique, many varieties of which have been formulated and put on the market since it was first proposed for clinical use by Payne in 1928. Some are of comparatively recent date, but the approach cannot be said to be 'novel', and is therefore only briefly treated here.

Very often a completed sentence obtained in one or other of these tests reads rather like the kernel or 'import' of a TAT story. The TAT (Thematic Apperception Test) was first described by Morgan and Murray in 1935; this too is therefore a key date, particularly as the TAT stands second, among projective techniques, to the Rorschach in status and frequency of use. The writer's briefing from the editor of this volume referred to 'anything other than the Rorschach and the TAT'; these two major techniques are therefore excluded from this chapter.* However, the TAT has served as a prototype or template for a wide variety of derivative techniques, some of them showing highly original features; a selection of these will be seen to have been included.

Much of the same may be said of the Rorschach. Rorschach's *Psychodiagnostik* was first published in 1921, and thus had nearly fifteen years' start over the TAT. Even allowing for this, however, it has generated more than twice as much research, but—perhaps not altogether surprisingly—considerably fewer variants and adaptations. These are included here only where they represent significant departures in approach or treatment.

As already noted, the emergence of the techniques just mentioned antedated the use of the term 'projection' in the sense of—to quote English and English (1958)—'the process of perceiving objective stimuli in line with personal interests, desires, fears, or expectations'. Some reference will be made later to the possible relevance of the other main use of the term, in the sense of a *defence mechanism*. Meantime, it may be noted that whereas credit for the first use of the word in the sense that concerns this discussion should probably go to Henry Murray, the first systematic treatment of the concept, along with its relevance to personality study, was that of Frank (1939), whose paper in the *Journal of Psychology* also presented the first attempt at a taxonomy within the projective field. Frank's classification is often quoted, but his is essentially a taxonomy of response, and therefore his categories are, inevitably, not mutually exclusive. Nevertheless, it calls attention to modes of projective response other than verbal interpretation of ambiguous stimuli, under which thematic apperception, word association and ink-blot techniques

---

* Along with the Blacky Pictures, the Rosenzweig Picture-Frustration Study and the Bender-Gestalt, all long-established tests, and on the whole unamenable to 'developments', although 'Blacky the Cat' has taken a tentative bow.

may all be subsumed. Manipulation of materials, or other forms of what in classical psychophysical terminology used to be called 'the method of expression', presents a wide range of possibilities, including some which have formed the basis of well-established techniques. Outstanding examples are, first, fantasy production with play materials and, second, drawing techniques which range from a similarly free fantasy-based activity to drawing or copying specified objects or designs. Some of the latter would seem to be only marginally projective. From this observation one is tempted to pass to consideration of whether there is indeed a hard-and-fast distinction to be drawn between projective methods of personality assessment and others. We shall return to this topic later.

Systematic surveys of projective methods in book form began to appear approximately a decade after the publication of Frank's article. Three such books, those of Bell (1948), Anderson and Anderson (1951) and Abt and Bellak (1952), are noted in the References. With them projective psychology may be said to have 'arrived', and, as if to clinch the issue, the *Fourth* (1953) *Mental Measurements Yearbook* saw a division, for the first time, of the Character and Personality section of the book into 'Nonprojective' and 'Projective'.

The foregoing brief sketch of the history of projective literature would seem to suggest that somewhere around the mid-fifties may be taken as the point later than which developments in projective practice may be said to be 'recent'.

Other things happened during the early and middle fifties which either certainly or probably were influential in determining the direction of those developments. A full discussion of Meehl's provocative and balanced book *Clinical Versus Statistical Prediction* (1954) is outside the scope of this chapter, but some of the issues it raises will be touched upon later. Uncompromising criticism of projective psychology, notably by Eysenck (1957), also dates from about this time. Whether attempts to put projective practice on a firmer psychometric footing were influenced by these events is a question to which there is probably no single or simple answer. Equally, it is uncertain whether thoroughgoing psychometricization (if so ugly a neologism may be permitted!) is possible or even desirable. Many projectivists would answer 'no' to both of the implied questions.

In order to provide a framework within which to examine recent developments, it is perhaps desirable to suggest an alternative to Frank's classification of projective response. Since the application of a projective technique—and indeed the process of projection itself—is something in which the nature of the stimulus is as important as the variability of the response, no unidimensional system of classification would seem to be possible. Let us therefore consider the possibilities, first in relation to the stimulus situation, then in terms of mode of overt response, ending with a word or two about function, or what was earlier (see p. 89) referred to as 'intention'.

Projective stimuli have from the start always been predominantly visual, the outstanding exception being word association techniques using oral presentation. There is, however, an essential difference between the pictorial representation of an object and its conventional symbolization in terms of language, and word association (or sentence completion) stimuli do not become 'visual' if they are 'shown' instead of 'spoken' to the subject. Visual projective stimuli, as already hinted, are normally pictorial, but actual 'concrete' objects have also been used; ink-blots would seem to occupy an intermediate position, but their use, principally, of course, in the Rorschach, has been so widespread that they should probably be given separate status. Other sense modalities the possibilities of which have been tentatively explored are hearing and touch. 'Concrete' objects can, of course, be handled, or their sound-producing potential may contribute to their connotative 'meaning'; accordingly, although they are usually apprehended visually, they clearly form a separate category.

A working classification of projective stimuli might therefore be:
(1) Verbal
(2) Visual
(3) Other sense modalities
(4) Concrete.

Passing to response, what one can do in a projective situation of course depends on the nature and arrangement of the stimulus material. In a sense, *all* projective response can be subsumed under the term 'apperception', i.e. the perception of the qualities of an object and the relating of these to one's previous experience. Insofar as this perception is selective, the process may be thought of as a model of projective experience in general. Nevertheless, the varieties of overt response required by the structure of the various projective techniques are sufficiently clearcut to make classification worthwhile.

Rorschach response is sometimes described (particularly in shorter accounts) as consisting of 'association to ink-blots'. This is not strictly correct, since it implies the question 'What does this make you think of?' rather than 'What do you see?'. However, *association*, thus defined, *is* called for in some techniques, and is different from *interpretation*, which is the basis of the TAT and all its derivatives.

If the subject, in addition to assessing the material, is required to *do* something, one arrives at behaviour for which Murray thought it worthwhile to coin the term 'motone', to distinguish it from the 'verbone', an instance of purely verbal behaviour. Writing one's responses in group presentation of, say, the TAT would not, of course, constitute a motone, unless the speed of the actual process of writing, or something similar, was considered to be of interest. Some projective techniques require the arrangement of picture or concrete material, possibly amounting to the creation of a new object, or the reproduction or copying of some sort of model. All these, although they are somewhat diverse activities, may be grouped together as *manipulation*.

A further variation in response, which to some extent cuts across the other categories, may be distinguished where the subject is required to make some sort of value judgment. This may be to rank or rate stimuli according to 'liking' or preference, or to choose the 'most appropriate' from a specified range of alternative interpretations.

Projective response may, therefore, be classified as:

(1) Association
(2) Interpretation
(3) Manipulation (possibly with subvarieties: (a) creation, (b) arrangement, (c) reproduction)
(4) Choice.

Finally, a few words about what has already been referred to as 'function' or 'intention' (neither term by itself quite covers the point at issue). Elsewhere (Semeonoff 1969) the writer has attempted to draw a distinction between two functions of personality assessment, *description* and *prediction*, and to show that these aims can be reconciled or synthesized. How one sees the function of personality assessment will depend on one's theoretical orientation as well as on the immediate purpose of the investigation in hand. In a sense, *all* psychological testing is concerned with prediction, and perhaps it might have been better to think in terms of *diagnosis*, the allocation of an individual to a usually but not necessarily nosological category, as being the process that can usefully be contrasted with *description*, the building up of a picture of a total personality reacting with its environment. While the former of these aims and functions is not, of course, ruled out, it is the latter that is more characteristic of—as it is indeed exclusive to—the projective approach.

Mention has already been made of therapy as an objective of the assessment process. Viewed from a slightly different angle, it may also be seen as one function of the *application* of a projective technique. The most obvious instance is to be found in the broadly defined area of 'play therapy', but the increasing recognition of the application of a psychological test as an inter-person situation carries further implications.

The function of projective techniques can then perhaps be classified as follows:

(1) Description
(2) Classification (or diagnosis)
(3) Therapy.

This rather crudely formulated analysis provides the basis for a three-dimensional ($4 \times 4 \times 3$) classification, in which some combinations are unlikely to be encountered. In the selective survey that follows, it has been used as a frame of reference rather than as a guide to be closely followed.

No attempt has been made to survey all projective methods which have appeared during a given period. To do so would have been a formidable task, but one made considerably lighter by the existence of the *Mental Measurement*

Yearbooks (MMY) and their associated publications. Furthermore, in spite of what has frequently been said about the proliferation of projective techniques (proliferation being used in its inevitably pejorative connotation), published projective techniques are by no means as numerous as one might be led to suppose. *Personality Tests and Reviews* (PTR) (Buros 1970), an MMY publication complete to the end of 1968, lists just under 100 projective tests, in print and out of print, in a total of just over 500. Since the coverage of the *Yearbooks* is limited to 'standardized tests published in English-speaking countries', and since tests originating elsewhere have not been similarly documented, it is difficult to estimate just how many projective techniques can be said to exist or to have existed. However, since the best-known European tests have in fact been published in English, and since the 100 include many instances of what can best be described as duplications or minor variations, it is probably safe to say that about 100 projective techniques have been devised, and that these represent about 20 per cent of all personality instruments.

'Proliferation' is thus clearly not something confined to projective techniques. Further, it is possible to take issue with the view, often vehemently expressed, that the publication of new tests, particularly if imperfectly standardized, should not be encouraged until 'the wheat is separated from the chaff of those already in print' (Segal 1965). It is not proposed to argue the case, from either side, at this point, but if the harvest of this survey contains a proportion of unwinnowed chaff, extenuation may be sought in the reflection that 'new approaches', being new, do not always reach their destination. Excluded, however, are those instances where the wayfarer gives little indication of knowing where he is going.

It is probably true to say that techniques based on verbal stimuli are less 'projective', in the sense most commonly understood, than those in the other stimulus groups defined above. Since at least the denotative meaning of most words is relatively constant and unambiguous, the implications of a word association stimulus, or still more clearly a sentence completion stem, cannot but be obvious, to an extent varying with the circumstances of the application of the test and with the sophistication of the subject.

The decline of word association as a projective instrument has already been remarked. Nevertheless, a trickle of work keeps coming in (for the Kent–Rosanoff test PTR notes three references in 1968). More relevant to the present purpose, however, is the publication in 1959 of an *Association Adjustment Inventory* (AAI) (Bruce 1959), in which the words of the Kent–Rosanoff list are presented, along with alternative choice responses. This device, it might be held, takes the technique out of the area of association proper, and the fact that the protocols are used to provide scores on empirically derived scales makes it still less typical of its genre. As the title implies, the test is intended to measure 'adjustment', in either a clinical or a vocational sense.

The only other association test of recent origin would seem to be the *Brook*

Reaction Test (Heim and Watts 1966). Whereas techniques deriving from the Kent–Rosanoff make use mainly of unambiguous works with little affective content, 'the Brook' (as it is referred to by its authors) is explicitly based on the many words with double or multiple meanings—or indeed homonyms— occurring in the English language. Originally designed as an instrument for the study of interests, vocational and avocational, and as such as an adjunct to vocational guidance, the possibilities of the Brook are now being explored in relation to the study of 'temperament'. No pertinent data are as yet available, but if the hoped-for potential is realized, the status of the Brook as a *projective* technique will have been established. At present it is doubtful whether its authors wish it to be regarded as such. One rather uncomfortable feature it shares with the typical 'projective' is that the responses have to be evaluated— i.e. not all contingencies can be covered in a 'scoring' guide.

In some respects, what has been said here about the doubtful status of word association as a projective applies even more strongly to sentence completion. Indeed, P. A. Goldberg (1965) in a survey of sentence completion methods goes so far as to suggest that 'the relevance of the projective hypothesis to the sentence completion seems questionable . . .'. This follows a favourable evaluation of the method, in that it 'works', although, as he adds, 'how it works [is] not clear'. Many writers have remarked that sentence completion may be said to stand midway between a projective technique and an inventory, and indeed a sentence completion stem can be compared not only to an in-complete TAT 'import' (see p. 90), but also to an open-ended inventory item. The degree to which some stems are 'structured', of course, varies, as does the explicit personal reference, but unless a sentence completion test is framed so as to measure some construct or constructs rather than to delineate attitudes, there is little scope for treatment of the data in a characteristically 'projective' manner. Prior to Goldberg's article, reviews of sentence completion had appeared in the books by Anderson and Anderson and Abt and Bellak already mentioned. Among more recently published variants of the method, the majority would seem to be specifically directed towards occupational and similar aims; thus, an *Industrial Sentence Completion Form* (Bruce 1963) and a *Marriage Adjustment Sentence Completion Survey* (Manson and Lerner 1962–5) have appeared. Few of these have been the subject of published work, except, in isolated cases, by their authors.

Reference has already been made to the predominance of visual material in projective practice. Since the potential range of visual stimulus material is obviously extremely wide, this is perhaps an appropriate point at which to discuss the concept of *structure* in relation to projective stimuli. The term is used (often in its adjectival form as 'structured') in a variety of ways, some-times loosely or incorrectly. In the projective context it occurs more frequently in its negative form, as 'unstructured', the connotation going little beyond 'ambiguity' or absence of unequivocal meaning. In order to make projective response possible at all, picture material must, of course, carry some element of ambiguity. Structure, in the sense of 'articulation of parts to form a relatively stable system or whole' (English and English 1958), and ambiguity are not necessarily inversely related to one another, nor does either bear a definable relation to realism of pictorial representation. Thus, a Rorschach inkblot is commonly said to be unstructured: it certainly cannot be said to represent any real 'thing'; nevertheless, Rorschach blots are highly structured in the proper sense of the word, even though the relations of the parts to one another may be variously interpreted. In relation to the TAT and its derivatives the relevance of the concept of structure, however defined, is less open to debate, since picture material can range between photographic realism (as in TAT card 13B) and extreme diffusion or vagueness of outline, as in some of the cards of the ORT (Object Relations Technique, see p. 98 below), or 'stick figures', as in the *Group Personality Projective Test* (Cassel and Kahn 1961). (A *Stick Figures Test* (Sarbin and Hardyck 1955), based on interpretation purely of posture, has not been made generally available.)

If by 'structure' one is to understand 'meaningfulness' (and, still more, if 'universality of meaning'), it would seem that attempts to measure structure in a given stimulus, irrespective of specific content, are foredoomed to failure. It may be argued that structure, as commonly understood, is imposed upon a stimulus, and not inherent in it, and further that it is itself something that varies projectively, so to speak, as in Form Level Rating in Rorschach. Even sentence completion stems, which may perhaps be unequivocally defined in terms of the number of content words they contain, are not entirely free from this contamination.

These considerations are relevant insofar as they affect the choice of picture material for projective tests. Although standard TAT is, as has already been stated, outside the scope of this chapter, it is worth noting that there appears to be a trend in the variants of TAT that have appeared towards verisimilitude, or appropriateness of the human (or other) figures depicted to the circumstances in which the test is to be applied.

The best-known example of this aim is to be seen in the attempts that have been made to adapt the TAT method for use with children. Murray's own series, of course, includes pictures (those numbered 12BG, 13B and 13G) which are to be substituted for the corresponding 'adult' pictures. This, however, represents only a very small departure from the series of 20 cards for use with adults, and it was not until 1954 that the first series designed specifically for children—Bellak's *Children's Apperception Test* (CAT) (Bellak 1954) —appeared. The main innovation was that animal rather than human figures were used throughout, albeit heavily anthropomorphized in all but two of the 10 pictures. Research findings have cast serious doubt on the basic premise, that children will relate more readily to animal figures; indeed, the Bellaks themselves have developed an equivalent 'human' form (CAT-H) (Bellak and

Hurvich 1966). This rare instance of the reversal of a development seems to have passed almost unnoticed.

To illustrate further, one may consider the various attempts to produce TAT material suitable for use with African subjects. The Thompson modification of the TAT (Thompson 1949), cited in MMY as designed for 'negroes ages 4 and over', does little more than substitute figures with dark skin colour and negroid features for those in the original TAT; seven cards (admittedly including two or three not containing human figures) are indeed left unchanged. This material was claimed to have advantages over the standard TAT in a study based on negro college students, but similar success was not achieved with other groups of coloured subjects. Closer attention to cultural as distinct from personal characteristics of a racial group is evident in Lee's *Thematic Apperception Test for African Subjects* (Lee 1953), although critics have pointed out that such details as the type and amount of clothing worn by the people depicted would make vastly different impressions in different African cultures. An *African TAT* published in 1960 (De Ridder 1961) was stated to be designed for 'urban [South] African adults'. Finally, the *South African Picture Analysis Test* (SAPAT) of Nel and Pelser (1960). The authors of this children's test questioned their subjects (presumably white South African children) about their preferences in the way of stories, as a guide to their choice of stimulus material. The resulting pictures include three (arguably only two) showing ordinary human figures; of the rest, two show anthropomorphized animals, while seven are of 'pixies', or some such fairy-like beings equipped with pointed ears, wings or the like. The only item suggestive of the South African scene is the presence, in one of the pictures, of a sjambok.

Mention may also be made, in passing, of attempts to adapt the CAT to other cultures. Rabin and Haworth (1960) illustrate Indian and Japanese adaptations; the changes would seem to be minimal. Since the CAT, and to a lesser extent its supplement, the CAT-S, are rather specifically designed to elicit themes relating to basic psychodynamic problems, one cannot but be a little sceptical of the universality of the symbolism in many of the pictures, in whatever version. This, of course, applies also to modifications of the TAT, and to the original TAT itself.

Special mention must be made of a variant of the TAT which has, at least in Britain, established itself as an independent technique. Phillipson's (1955) *Object Relations Technique* may be described as an attempt to introduce some features of the Rorschach method into both the stimulus material and the analysis and interpretation of data obtained from an essentially TAT-type technique. There are three sets each containing four cards presenting, respectively, one-person, two-person, three-person and 'group' situations. The three series are characterized by the use of (a) light shading, producing an effect of vagueness and diffusion; (b) dark shading, with clearly defined outlines and maximum contrast; (c) colour—although this is applied sparingly, and at times apparently almost at random. Cards from the three series are intermingled in a standard order of presentation; there is also a blank card, as in the TAT.

Space does not allow close examination of the rationale of the ORT, nor of the relation of its stimulus variables to Rorschach determinants. The important thing to note is that the technique was explicitly designed as an adjunct to clinical practice based on the 'object relations' psychoanalytic theory developed through the work of Klein and Fairbairn. It is intended to serve both as an aid to 'diagnosis'—or perhaps, rather, 'understanding'—and, through the inter-person relationship existing between patient and clinician, as an instrument of therapy.

Rather similar, in general approach, is the *Pickford Projective Pictures* (PPP) (Pickford 1963). Unlike the ORT, however, which is probably most suitable for work with adults (it was developed in the context of the Adult Department of the Tavistock Clinic), Pickford's technique is specifically intended for use with children. The material consists of 120 line drawings of children in various situations, mostly realistic and fairly clearly defined; a few, however, contain 'monsters' or other fantasy figures. It is recommended that the pictures should be used six at a time, 'thus providing material which will occupy about twenty therapeutic sessions'. Fixed rules for choice of pictures or for method of administration are not prescribed. Interpretation is not seen as a crucial part of the process; when used, it is in the psychoanalytic sense, as providing guidance for the patient rather than, in a diagnostic sense, for the clinician, although frequent reference is in fact made to the 'diagnostic value' of individual pictures. The therapist is seen by Pickford as 'a person upon whom [the child] may test out in the transference his inner and seemingly dangerous fantasies . . .'. The existence of such is clearly assumed to be axiomatic; their nature is similarly assumed to be in accordance with more or less orthodox Freudian theory. Lest it be thought that the PPP does little more than provide a framework within which the therapist can give rein to his own fantasies—an imputation sometimes laid at the door of *all* projective techniques—it should be added that the method does not entirely lack normative data. Frequency tables are provided showing the incidence of thematic and content variables, for each picture separately, in a sample of about 100 children. The data are derived mostly, but not exclusively, from child guidance clinics in Glasgow; there are indications of a slight culture bias. We shall return later to the possible implications.

Two other techniques having some affinities with the PPP call for some comment. They are Lydia Jackson's *Test of Family Attitudes* (TFA) (Jackson 1950), now again in print after a lapse of some years, and the much more recent *Family Relations Indicator* (FRI) of Howells and Lickorish (1963). Each consists of a set of pictures (seven in TFA, 24 in FRI) depicting family situations. In both cases some pictures occur in alternative forms appropriate to the sex of the respondent or (in the case of the FRI) to the structure of his family. The TFA is designed for use with children only; the FRI also allows for the parents' attitudes to be investigated. Indeed, the test having been conceived within the framework of the 'family psychiatry' movement, it is considered essential to test parents as well as children. A scoring system is offered, and the test is intended to be 'free from any marked theoretical or psychoanalytic bias'. 'Story-telling' is not asked for; simple questions such as 'What do you think they are doing?' are asked, but the tester is free to supplement these in any way he thinks fit. In contrast, the TFA does ask the child to tell a story, but a list of 'standard' questions, covering points on which it is felt information *must* be obtained, is appended for use if necessary.

An apparently similar but basically different approach to the study of relationships within the family is to be found in the *Family Relations Test* (Anthony and Bene 1957). This is commonly thought of as a projective test, but is correctly classified in MMY as 'Nonprojective'. It is being taken still further 'out of turn' here, since its 'stimuli' are as much verbal as visual, if not more so, and its mode of response places it in the 'choice' category within the classification set out on p. 93. Designed originally for use with children, it has now been produced in a slightly modified form for adults. It should be noted, however, that even in the latter case it is attitudes obtaining at some point in the respondent's childhood that are the subject of investigation. Statements relating to relationships within the family, etc., printed on cards, are 'posted' in boxes each of which carries an outline drawing of a human figure. From the wide range provided, the subject himself chooses appropriate figures to represent members of his family, although no significance is attached to the actual choices made. If a statement does not apply to anyone in the family, the card goes to a figure called 'Nobody'. The bulk of the statements are classifiable as 'positive' (indicating favourable attitudes) or 'negative' (unfavourable); as 'strong' or 'mild'; and as 'outgoing' (the subject's attitudes to members of his family) or 'incoming' (attitudes of members of the family to him). A small additional group of statements is concerned with overprotection, overindulgence and competence or strength of personality. It will be seen that the test is in effect only a disguised inventory, but the format and the play element involved give it the 'feeling' as well as the 'distancing' effect of a projective technique. Interesting and suggestive research findings, particularly in relation to homosexuality, have been published (Bene 1965).

With the exception of the Bene–Anthony test, all the techniques just described are clearly recognizable as rooted in TAT methodology. An example of a marginal case is the *Hand Test* (Bricklin, Piotrowski and Wagner 1962) in which the pictures used are drawings of hands—together with the inevitable 'blank card'. The subject is asked to say what the hand might be doing. The subtitle of the manual indicates 'special reference to the prediction of overt aggressive behaviour', but other traits and attitudes can also be scored. A feature deriving from the Rorschach rather than from the TAT is that attention is paid to the turning of the cards. A plea by a reviewer for the addition of two-hand cards, to allow for the study of affectional relationships, was met by Zucker and Jordan (1968) with a *Paired Hands Test*, using colour photographs rather than drawings. Some degree of concurrent validity, deduced from correlations of measured 'friendliness' with reported 'popularity', is claimed.

Two fairly well-known techniques, both making some use of 'choice', as defined on p. 93, have features which call for comment. The *Four Picture Test* (FPT) of Van Lennep (Anderson and Anderson 1951) is one of the oldest projective instruments still in use. A single story has to be told, covering all four pictures, which the subject has previously arranged in the order which seems to him most appropriate. The pictures are executed in dull shades of watercolour. In a second edition of the test, published in 1958, no attempt has been made to update the pictures, which according to one reviewer (Lee 1965) 'carry a definite atmosphere of the 1920's'. An odd feature is that normative data, etc., contained in the first edition of the manual are now omitted, along with most of the discussion of the rationale, while 'extensive' research findings, promised for publication, have not, to the writer's knowledge, been made available.

Arrangement in order is also the basic idea in the *Tomkins–Horn Picture Arrangement Test* (PAT) (Tomkins and Miner 1957). This consists of 25 'plates', each containing three rather crudely drawn outline pictures, printed in a sort of 'Y' form, at an angle of 120 degrees to one another. In contrast to the Van Lennep test, there is in all cases a fairly obvious connection between the three pictures. The subject indicates what he considers the best order, and then tells a story, using one sentence for each picture. An extremely elaborate scoring system is provided; interpretation is based mostly on a consideration of 'rare' responses, i.e. rare *sequences*, rather than the content of the stories. The test has had a mixed reception, dependent—as is wellnigh inevitable—on the critic's view of what a projective technique ought to do.

Other techniques based on visual–pictorial material, but using different modes of response, are noted later. Others again have been omitted because they seemed to lack 'novelty', or simply because they have not been accessible to the writer.

Although, as already stated, standard Rorschach has been ruled to be outside the scope of this chapter, a brief discussion of derivatives of the Rorschach, corresponding to the foregoing account of variants of the TAT, is perhaps not out of place.

For reasons which are understandable at various levels, Rorschach has aroused hostility on a scale possibly unprecedented in any branch of science. Nevertheless, the basic idea of using ink-blots as a means of studying thought processes or personality or whatever else seems to have an irresistible attraction, even where least expected. Mention will be made of three attempts to 'adapt' Rorschach in such a way as to eliminate one or other of its 'undesirable' characteristics.

The time taken to administer the Rorschach and to analyse the resulting protocol has often been quoted as a serious handicap. The most obvious remedy is to reduce the number of cards. This was done in the development of the *Zulliger Test* (Zulliger 1969) which, although it goes back to 1948, has only recently begun to become known in English-speaking countries. The Zulliger material consists of three cards: one black and white, one 'coloured' and one black and red. Since the balance between monochrome and colour is different from that of the Rorschach, as well as for other reasons, one cannot expect to obtain a closely comparable distribution of determinants, etc. Zulliger was a pupil and associate of Hermann Rorschach, and his own account of his technique is in the continental tradition of Rorschach's time, and lacks normative and other validatory data. Nevertheless, there is a slowly-growing body of evidence to suggest that a shortened version of Rorschach can 'work' in the same way as the original.

A second criticism of Rorschach is that many of the measures for which validity is claimed are confounded by the total number of responses. An attempt to control for this is one of the main features of the *Holtzman Inkblot Technique* (HIT) (Holtzman *et al.* 1961), namely, that responses are limited to one per card. Other features that have received commendation are that two 'excellently matched' forms of the test (each comprising 45 cards) are available, and that both scoring and interpretation are fully objective. In other words, the HIT measures up well to strict psychometric standards. Nevertheless, evidence of the value of the test in personality study has been described, for example by Cronbach (1970), as 'unconvincing'. Test–retest reliabilities tend to be low, and certain scores seem to be uncorrelated with corresponding inventory measures or interview ratings. Superior validity cannot, of course, be claimed for either of these latter, but this raises fundamental questions for personality assessment which cannot be dealt with here. That the HIT should have been greeted with little enthusiasm by users of normal Rorschach is not surprising, partly perhaps because it is seen to inhibit the subject's spontaneous response, and to make less than full use of the potential stimulus value of the cards. Whether the technique allows for a saving of time, as compared with the orthodox Rorschach method, is doubtful. Relationships between factor scores are not calculated—this too may be thought to lead to loss of information—but each of 45 responses has to be assessed on each of 22 variables, and that is a lot of scoring.

A further degree of departure from normal Rorschach procedure occurs in the *Structured-Objective Rorschach Test* (SORT) (Stone 1958), which applies a forced-choice technique, with 10 triads per card, to the standard Rorschach blots. Scoring is objective, but may in a very real sense be erroneous, since it is *assumed* that, for example, a particular choice will represent a 'W' (whole blot area) response, or that a given determinant, such as shading or perceived movement, will have been 'used'. Ratings on 26 attributes are derived, in some cases from single 'factors', in others from combinations of factors. There are two instances of pairs of separately named traits being derived from exactly the same single factor score; admittedly, however, in each case one trait comes under the heading of 'Intellectual Functioning' and the other under that of 'Temperament'. Good concurrent validity in relation to vocational requirements is claimed: the test was, in fact, designed 'to appraise and analyze vocationally significant temperament traits . . .'. One cannot help feeling that if it succeeds in doing so it is in spite of the construct validity claimed for but not apparent in the various measures. Although it makes use of standard Rorschach material and scoring categories, the SORT would seem to be even further removed than the HIT from the Rorschach ethos.

Finally, corresponding to the cross-cultural adaptations of the TAT described above (see pp. 96–97), brief mention may be made of the *Ka–Ro Inkblot Test*, a Japanese version of the Rorschach devised by Yasufumi Kataguchi (1970). Most of the plates bear a very close resemblance to the standard Rorschach—indeed probably too close to make them a practicable parallel series—and are certainly more similar to the original in general perceptual impact than any of the better-known Western alternatives. The author suggests the term 'psychopsy', on the analogy of *biopsy*, to denote the projective approach to personality study, and claims to have made a re-evaluation of projective methods in general. However, the manual for the test adheres very closely to the Klopfer treatment of Rorschach, from which it shows only very minor deviations.

Techniques using visual material and what was described earlier (p. 92) as the 'manipulative' mode of response are more conveniently considered along with those using 'concrete' material. Those based on 'choice' form a small but markedly heterogeneous group. Some, indeed, have rather little in the way of clearly recognizable 'projective' quality.

One such is the *Faces Test* of Liggett (1959) (listed in MMY as *Self-Evaluation Test*, and marketed as such). The material consists of 'destructured' faces, i.e. portraits so distorted in the photographic process used as almost to lose the semblance of faces. These are presented to the subject two at a time, in all possible combinations, with the instruction to say which of the two would be taken to be, for example, the more dominant person. Finally, the subject is asked: 'Which of these two is probably most like you *as a person*?'. Inferences are drawn regarding the subject's perception of himself, with adequate statistical checks on the significance of the various concordances, etc. The method can, of course, be adapted to other purposes in the field of personality study. It would seem to have anticipated and to approximate rather closely to certain aspects of the grid methodology associated with construct theory. Indeed, it is a little difficult to understand why the Faces

Test is classified as a projective technique whereas the Bannister–Fransella (1966) *Grid Test of Schizophrenic Thought Disorder* is not, since in both cases the subject is asked to make personality judgments on the basis of inspection of photographs of faces. Both, furthermore, show points of similarity to the now almost universally discredited Szondi Test and the relatively little-known *Picture Identification Test* (Chambers 1957), in both of which diagnosis or classification is based on expressed preferences within a range of comparable stimuli, namely faces.

Probably the most obvious stimulus material for a test based on preferences is colour, and just such a test was widely publicized in Britain in 1970. This was the *Lüscher Colour Test*, hitherto virtually unknown in English-speaking countries, but allegedly in wide use in Europe, following its presentation at the 1947 International Congress of Psychology and its publication (in German) in 1949. The full test makes use of 73 colours presented in a variety of ways, but the publicized version was an abbreviated one, calling merely for two successive rankings of eight standard colours. A manual, published in the same year (Lüscher 1970), contains a small amount of normative data, together with 'interpretation tables' from which a ready-made personality description covering a number of areas of behaviour is derived. Perhaps because of the method of publicity employed, the test received little serious attention, and indeed the underlying theory is sketchily—and dogmatically—presented. Nevertheless, the Dutch psychologist de Zeeuw (1957), while rejecting the theory 'for the greater part', contends that 'Lüscher is to be honoured as a pioneer'. Further reference to the Lüscher Test appears later in this chapter.

Consideration of visual techniques calling for expressive or 'manipulative' response leads into a topic which might well have merited entirely separate treatment, although not, perhaps, within the context of this book. This topic touches upon what at one time was broadly and loosely referred to as 'play therapy', the reference being to the cathartic effect believed to be produced through the opportunity to work out one's fantasies through the medium of play. It may be—and has been—held that *all* play has this function; when such play occurs in a specially structured situation one has what amounts to a projective technique of a sort, particularly if an observer formulates his inferences within a theoretical or a clinically-oriented framework. An example conforming more or less to this model has already been seen in the Pickford Projective Pictures, where story-telling takes the place of overt play.

A further example, making use of material which may be described as borderline between visual and concrete, is *Ten Silhouettes*, a technique devised by Dockar-Drysdale on the basis of her work with maladjusted children, and mainly developed by Babington Smith (1959). The material consists of 10 cards bearing silhouette photographs of human figures on both sides, the one silhouette being a mirror image of the other. This device permits of the cards being turned over and placed in meaningful juxtaposition with one another. In the first part of the test responses to the question '... What can you tell me about this one?' are obtained for each card, presented singly. In the second part the subject is invited to pick out pairs of cards, place them in relation to one another and respond to the instruction '... Tell me about the people'. A third stage gives an opportunity for making and telling about larger groups. Little seems to have been done with the test later than the publication of the original group of papers describing it. Apart from considerations of validity, etc., it would seem to have fairly obvious merits and disadvantages. Ten Silhouettes is typical of the many lesser-known projective techniques which may or may not appeal to the inclinations of the individual clinician.

A similar and much better-known technique, making use of more fully 'concrete' material, is *Make-A-Picture-Story* (MAPS) (Shneidman 1947). This makes use of a large number of cut-out figures and backgrounds against which the figures can be arranged, much in the manner of a toy theatre. At one time popular (it is one of the tests rating a 'Name Index' in PTR), MAPS seems to have fallen from favour, perhaps because of its being overelaborate and presenting an incompatible blend of its play function with TAT methodology.

Very much the same may be said of Lynn's *Structured Doll Play Test* (SDPT) (Lynn and Lynn 1959), which comes more within the time span of this survey. Compared with MAPS, the main difference in method is the substitution of a standard set of questions for free fantasy production; the child, however—and the technique seems suited mainly to very young children—is encouraged to carry out play activities, such as putting the little boy or girl doll to bed. The material itself is also rather different in scope: an 'ego' doll of each sex is provided, with which the child is expected to identify, together with 'visiting' and unclothed child figures, father and mother figures, and a number of 'objects', all connected with food. A second series adds a baby, a doctor, a nurse, medical equipment, a teacher and a 'bad animal'. All these are not really 'dolls' in the commonly accepted sense, but flat 'press-outs'; the author points out that the test is intended to cover only situations (bed, toilet) where an approximately horizontal position and 'flat' figures are appropriate. To this end 'flats' showing beds and toilet equipment are provided. Also available are sets of figures with negroid and oriental features, but identical with the standard figures in all other respects, including details of clothing. (In contrast, MAPS is definitely white-oriented, in that 'minority' figures are included but number only 11 out of a total of 67.)

A higher level of realism, together with wider scope, is achieved in Moore's *London Doll-Play Technique* (Moore and Ucko 1961). Work on this has been in progress since the middle fifties, but the material has not been made commercially available; indeed, the author would appear to be of the opinion (in which the present writer would concur—see below, p. 112) that absolute specification of such material is irrelevant. The technique requires the provision of four 'wire' dolls (father, mother and two children), a naked baby doll, an open-topped dolls' house and certain articles of furniture, etc., at least approximating to what would be described in theatrical parlance as 'practicable'. Some plasticine is also required. Using the doll family, the clinician takes the child through a number of situations (e.g. mealtime, naughtiness), in which the child is invited to indicate what happens next, in answer to questions, or through acting out, or in a combination of both. The emphasis, as in the case of SDPT, is on the projective function of the technique, and therefore on its value for the understanding of the child, rather than for therapy. It is realized that the child may want to indulge in what Moore calls 'tangential' play. It is recommended that if this occurs the child should, if possible, be tactfully steered back to the situation in hand. If, on the other hand, it becomes clear that the child is bent on evasion, 'the child's individual way of avoiding difficulties can be a valuable personality indicator'.

Doll play, particularly when the emphasis is on its therapeutic function, may be thought of as a specialized and limited variant of structured play methodology, which in its earliest forms antedates the broader development of projective personality study. Typical equipment consists of a sand-tray (sometimes water is also provided) and a varying selection, usually standardized, of minature objects—people, animals, trees, vehicles, etc. The history of the method is outlined by Ruth Bowyer (1970) in her book *The Lowenfeld World Technique*, which also gives an account of forms of the technique, notably those of Mucchielli (1960) and of Von Staabs (1964), well known on the Continent, but not listed in MMY. Much has been written, particularly in the earlier treatments, about the symbolic value of this kind of play and its material, but there does seem to be a current trend to try, at least, to apply psychometric standards, and Bowyer reports a number of research findings. Lowenfeld herself, however, is at pains to point out that her own method is to be regarded as a technique, and not a test.

The same is partly true of the *Lowenfeld Mosaic Test*, with which its author's name is most commonly associated. The Mosaic Test (Lowenfeld 1954) goes back to 1930, so that it cannot in any sense be described as 'new'; indeed, it was familiar in Britain considerably earlier than the Rorschach. For a time it was in eclipse, but of recent years it has aroused a measure of renewed interest. As regards material, it is perhaps the most elegant of all projective techniques. Small pieces or 'tiles' (originally in turned beechwood; now, alas, plastic is substituted) are presented in five simple geometric shapes, all of which 'fit into' each other easily, and six colours. The subject is invited to 'make something' with these pieces within the tray provided. An additional constraint formerly imposed—that the subject should be satisfied with his production— seems now to have been abandoned. Clearly, there is scope for exhaustive and objective analysis of the productions, making use of categories comparable to those of the Rorschach while avoiding many of the pitfalls of Rorschach scoring. Dr Lowenfeld herself provides an elaborate scoring sheet, but her interpretations are for the most part intuitive; indeed, following a line of reasoning very similar to her own one can sometimes come to an opposite conclusion. Recent work, however, has been increasingly more in accordance with psychometric practice. Thus, a study by Ames and Ilg (1962) of the Gesell Institute of Child Development bears all the marks of its origin: a very careful developmental study is reported, and there is discussion with reference to problems of diagnosis, cross-cultural differences, etc. However, for a technique of such high potential merit the general picture is disappointingly inconclusive.

A much more recent and as yet very little-known test devised by Margaret Lowenfeld is the *Lowenfeld Kaleidoblocs* (Ames and Learned 1954). In contrast to the Mosaic material, the kaleidoblocs are surprisingly unattractive, at least on casual inspection. These are 29 variously shaped wooden blocks, painted in four colours and white, with no clearly discernible basis for the choice of shapes, relative proportions, or distribution of colours. The test is in several parts, the first requiring the subject to make something with the blocks, as in the Mosaic Test, except that the kaleidobloc material is more suitable for three-dimensional constructions. The subsequent parts of the test consist of problems mainly involving space perception; in others, the blocks have to be used to make common objects. In short, the test would seem to be intended for use as a multipurpose instrument. Since well-established tests exist for all these purposes, one feels that here we have an example of a test that was not obviously 'needed'.

Superficially similar to the Lowenfeld Mosaic, but also showing affinities with the Lüscher Test, is the *Colour Pyramid Test* (CPT) (Schaie and Heiss 1964). The material consists of inch-square 'chips' (although it is said that squares of coloured paper may be used instead) in 24 colours, including black, white and grey, accurately specified in terms of their Munsell values. The task is to construct, successively, three 'pretty' and three 'ugly' pyramids, on a blank consisting of 15 squares arranged in the form of a stepped triangle. The scoring system is elaborate, difficult to grasp, and almost impossible to describe adequately in a short compass. Use is made of such variables as relative frequencies of the colours (grouping the various hues of the basic colours together), form characteristics, symmetry, etc.; particular interpretive significance is attributed to certain colour combinations known as 'colour syndromes'. The underlying conceptual model is more acceptable, at least on *a priori* grounds, than one has come to expect in discussions of the 'meaning' of colours, in that it makes use of such concepts as excitation potential and arousal value, and of distinctions between mood state, affect and emotion. Similarly, the authors show awareness of all relevant problems of validity.

Evaluation is even more elaborate than scoring, but it may be noted that the statistical techniques used appear sophisticated, and the populations studied based on adequate sampling. The aim of the CPT as a projective instrument is to provide actuarial personality description in terms of 42 of Cattell's bipolar trait scales. Whether the cumbersomeness of the method is too formidable an obstacle to the attainment of such a goal is an open question; one feels that the answer is likely to remain in the affirmative.

Sharply contrasted from the point of view of standardization, etc., is the Twitchell–Allen *Three-Dimensional Personality Test* (3-DPT) (Fein 1960), which may be thought of as a destructured 'World' technique on which a TAT-type task has been superimposed. The material consists of 28 'forms'— small plastic objects, some of which have definable geometric properties while others show varying degrees of similarity, mostly minimal, to real objects. The task is to choose some of the forms, arrange them on a table, and tell a story about the production. This is done twice; interpolated between the two trials is a 'naming test', in which the forms are presented one at a time in a standard order, with the question 'What does this remind you of?'. There is also a limits procedure, on the analogy of Rorschach practice, and a fairly complex system of analysis. Once again we have an 'interesting' technique which seems to have progressed little, if at all, beyond its development stage, with very meagre underpinning for either its rationale or its demonstrable usefulness.

Finally, among the group of techniques broadly classifiable as concrete/ manipulative, the *Kahn Test of Symbol Arrangement* (KTSA) (Kahn 1956, 1957) will be seen to have points of resemblance to both the 3-DPT (with which it was roughly contemporaneous) and the Lowenfeld Kaleidoblocs, from both of which, however, it differs in that it has generated a fair amount of research. The material consists of 16 'culturally structured object symbols'. These range from 'real' objects (butterflies, dogs, an anchor) through stars, a cross and a circle to a 'green amorphous phallic symbol'. Variations in colour, size, etc., occur; an unusual additional variable introduced is that of translucency. The subject is required to arrange these objects, five times, on a felt strip with numbered spaces. The first two and the last of these arrangements are 'free'; the third calls for a reproduction, from memory, of the second, and the fourth is a ranking in order of liking. Additional tasks involve naming, 'symbolizing' (saying what the objects 'could stand for') and sorting in terms of categories rather like those commonly used in the semantic differential.

The main purpose of the test is diagnosis or prediction in terms of conventional psychiatric classification, brain damage, etc., but the technique is also offered as an instrument for developmental studies. From the point of view of conformity with psychometric standards, and, to a less extent, from that of proven validity, the test has on the whole been accorded favourable comment. The rationale, however, is less convincing, and there is an uncomfortable feeling of miscellaneity about the material. As with the Lowenfeld

Kaleidoblocs, one feels that the author has tried to do too much with too little.

What has been said above (p. 93) about the projective and therapeutic functions of play applies also to drawing. Drawing may be thought of as an activity intermediate between play and story-telling, and 'free' drawing, at least, partakes of the nature of both. However, insofar as drawing may also be from a model, projective techniques based on drawing may, in terms of the response classification offered on p. 93, belong to either the 'creation' or the 'reproduction' subgroups of the 'manipulation' category.* In addition, variations in the quality of line, and in short what may broadly be called 'style', add a further dimension, summed up in the term 'graphomotor', which has sometimes been applied to drawing and allied techniques.

By far the most popular projective use of drawing is in relation to the human figure. PTR contains an entry [442A] 'Human Figure Drawing Techniques' which is explained as follows: 'This is a dummy entry to act as a catchall for references on the use of human figure drawings in general'. The appended list contains 181 entries, while six specific tests muster 515 references among them. The grand total of just under 700 would put human figure drawing in third place among projective techniques, although it should be noted that not all the entries refer to projective use of figure-drawing. The two variants in most frequent use are '*H-T-P*' (Buck 1949), the *House–Tree–Person Projective Technique* (1947), and the *Machover Draw A Person Test* (MDAP) (Machover 1949), which appeared two years later but has now overhauled H-T-P in popularity, although it would seem to be less satisfactory by psychometric standards. MDAP calls for drawings of two persons, the second being of the opposite sex to the first. An optional 'inquiry' allows for a story to be told about each of the figures, supplemented by questions. H-T-P starts, as the initials imply, with a request for a picture of a house, which should be 'as good as possible', followed by a tree and a person. Here, too, an inquiry follows. There is no reason, as one reviewer has suggested (Haworth 1965), why features from both techniques should not be combined in a single test. The respective authors' theoretical positions, although not too well defined, are not in serious conflict and concentration of research resources might yield a better and possibly simpler approach to the undoubtedly rich potential of figure-drawing as a projective method. It might also be interesting to discover whether elements from the *Tree Test* (Koch 1952), a drawing technique which apparently has a considerable vogue on the Continent, might be compatible with such an enterprise. It must be stated, however, that figure-drawing is an area in which perhaps more often than in others the validity of 'obvious' or 'symbolic' inferences tends to be taken for granted.

---

* As it happens, the latter type is not represented in this survey. The best-known test based on copying of visual material is the *Bender-Gestalt*, excluded (see footnote, p. 90) mainly on grounds of 'age' and familiarity.

A number of additional drawing techniques merit some attention, either because they present individual or novel features, or because they are frequently mentioned in psychological literature. None is of very recent date.

Originating from an Art Aptitude Inventory (Horn 1939), the *Horn–Hellersberg Test* (HHT) (Hellersberg 1950) makes use of a principle long familiar in the form of a children's pastime. Lines representing the basic compositional structure of a well-known picture are presented enclosed in a rectangle, and the subject is invited to use these as the basis of a drawing. A similar principle is used in the *Wartegg Test* (Wartegg 1939) and its derivative the Drawing-Completion Test (DCT) (Kinget 1952) except that in this case the stimuli more closely resemble the 'circles', etc., now widely used in tests of 'creativity'. Still further variations on this theme are seen in the *Franck Drawing Completion Test* (FDCT) (Franck and Rosen 1949), which is specifically concerned with the assessment of masculinity–femininity, and in the *Symbol Elaboration Test* (SET) (Krout 1950), an ambitiously framed technique which was the subject of a 'Whole Number' in the *Psychological Monographs* series.

Myokinetic Psychodiagnosis (Mira 1940) is the rather puzzling name given to a drawing technique which becomes less puzzling when one realizes that the tasks prescribed might have made the technique more properly classifiable under 'other modalities'. The drawing required is very simple—nothing more elaborate than lines and very simple geometric figures. Both hands are used, sometimes together, and the forearm has to be kept raised above the table. Interest can thus be seen to lie less in the drawings themselves than in the record they provide of the movement involved. The test is listed in PTR as out of print, and has never been popular in English-speaking countries. An extensive literature, however, has appeared in Latin America.

Movement is also the basis of an out-of-print test of American origin—the *Graphomotor Projection Technique* of Kutash and Gehl (1954). In this the subject (who is blindfolded) has to scribble freely on paper for five minutes, after which he is invited to identify meaningful areas in his production and to trace them on 'onionskin'. Comments by reviewers have tended to be facetious, or at best sceptical.

Finally, a drawing technique which contains elements of the Rorschach as well as the Horn–Hellersberg and Kutash and Gehl approaches is the *Visual Apperception Test* '60 (VAT-60) of Rafi Z. Khan (1960). Its basic interpretive principle, however, rests on the emotional or mood connotations of colour, and in this respect it has affinities with the Lüscher Test and the Lowenfeld Mosaic. In spite of these numerous points of contact the method is notably original, and, superficially at least, uncomplicated. The test material consists of 12 'plates' which at first sight suggest the product of a short session with the Graphomotor Technique—in other words, a tangle of lines, or a single line reentering upon itself indefinitely. The last plate differs from the others in that the lines are mainly straight. The subject is given a set of eight coloured crayons (including black), with which he has to '*colour* whatever . . . he sees' in each plate, and then to name the product. Interpretation is based on weighted totals of the colours used in each plate, ignoring those beyond the second, on the criterion of area covered. Some validation data in relation to psychiatric classification are offered, but it should be noted that the 'meanings' attached to colours are at variance with those attributed by other theorists in this field; the actual hues of the crayons to be used are not specified. And although the author stresses the importance of 'form-recognition', as indicated in the 'naming' procedure, no guidance is given on this point in the manual or other published material. In an informal self-administration of the test, the present writer noted that when he set about colouring the objects perceived their outlines seemed no longer so appropriate, an observation which raises interesting questions regarding the difference, for projective psychology, between perception of an object and attempts to represent it graphically.

Reference has already been made, more than once, to the predominance of visual stimulus material in projective personality study. This is, of course, in line with the paramount importance of visual experience in most people's lives. Exceptions, however, include not only the sightless, but also persons who, in relation to a field of enquiry no longer fashionable, are known as 'audiles', i.e. those whose preferred mode of imagery is auditory and in general are what English and English (1958) call 'ear-minded'. Rather similarly, it has been suggested, notably by Viktor Löwenfeld in a study of the art production of the blind (Löwenfeld 1939), that even seeing individuals may be by nature 'haptic', i.e. disposed to interpret their experience in terms of touch. It is perhaps surprising that in the 'proliferation' of projective techniques no-one appears to have made use of this concept: the nearest among published techniques is the 3-DPT, in which—as indeed in Löwenfeld's work—emphasis would seem to be more on the 'handling' than on the 'texture' aspect of tactual experience. Tactile perception of the latter kind was studied by Audubon and Van Buskirk (1965) in a brave attempt to discover whether the use of Rorschach determinants 'remained unchanged across modalities'. The material they devised might well be developed into a 'Rorschach for the blind'.

Existing auditory projective tests are few in number; three are relatively well known, of which two are by no means recent.

The *Auditory Apperception Test* (AAT) (Stone 1950) is an attempt to transfer TAT methodology direct to auditory situations. The stimuli are mainly of the 'sound effects' type, and by all accounts mostly of unconvincing quality. This, and the fact that the manual and statistical data are rather inadequate, have no doubt caused the test to have been largely superseded by the Braverman–Chevigny *Auditory Projective Test* (APT), published in 1955, which also adds to the range of stimulus material. Of particular interest are a series of enactments of interpersonal situations spoken by professional actors, and a second series in which the same conversations are spoken in a nonsense language using the same variations in intonation and rhythm. Some of these are such as to allow a direct matching with standard TAT cards. A study by Abramson (1963) suggested that TAT methods could indeed be applied to auditory material, but that the need and press patterns evoked were to some extent different.

A reversion to realism is seen in part of the *Sound Apperception Test* (SAT) of K. L. Bean (1965). Sixteen sound situations are presented for TAT treatment, each consisting of sounds which are for the most part easily recognizable, although the connotations may be quite varied. Considerations of structure are clearly as relevant to auditory as to visual stimuli, and, as Bean points out (or implies), sound patterns which are always interpreted in the same way are as useless for projective purposes as unrealistic sounds, where guessing may have to take over from interpretation. The sounds in the main part (actually 'Series 2') of the SAT are in fact intended to be 'semi-structured', i.e. each item contains several fairly easily recognizable sounds combined in a plausible way. Series 1 consists of single sounds doctored in various ways—for example, 'cat purring, amplified and speeded up two octaves'. Series 1 is intended to correspond to ink-blots in the same way as Series 2 corresponds to TAT pictures. Nevertheless, it is stressed that the SAT is not intended as a substitute for visual techniques. Among specific suggestions made is that auditory material is more relevant to the study of ideas of reference.

Other sound apperception techniques are mainly unpublished, for example that of Wilmer and Husni (1953), which uses stimuli intermediate between those of the AAT and the SAT. Work using this material has examined the relation between sight deprivation and field dependency. Since imposition of structure is a more difficult task with auditory than with visual material, it may well be that auditory projective techniques have a special research role to play in this area.

An alternative source of stimulus material for auditory projection is, obviously, music. On the other hand, both associative and recognition factors play a very large part in listening to music, and, in general, control of extraneous variables presents serious problems. However, a small-scale exploratory study of a 'Music Projective Technique' by Van den Daele (1967) made use of short excerpts of largely familiar music and claimed to have demonstrated some degree of relationship between severity of schizophrenic disorder and 'appropriateness' of stories, as measured by deviation from commonality of response. One doubts, of course, whether this represents something that could not have been demonstrated more easily by other means. Much the same applies to such questions as whether known (or alleged) relationships between preferences in musical style and, say, introversion/extraversion do in fact exist. These are clearly matters which come within the scope of projective enquiry, but as far as the writer knows no techniques, as such, have been devised for their study.

Summing up on auditory projective techniques, one can say that although they have not gone far, the study seems promising. Obsolescence of methods of recording and of reproduction, however, make for impermanence of available materials.

The foregoing rather lengthy survey has been kept relatively free of comment or evaluation, partly because the majority of the techniques mentioned have not been tried out by the writer, except casually. Even disinterested critics often come to different conclusions from the same data—and, it must be conceded, 'hard' data are woefully absent from too many projective test manuals. If such absence had been noted wherever it occurred, the result would have made monotonous reading. Reviewers, particularly in MMY, frequently castigate authors of new tests for having put on the market an instrument not yet ready for routine use. Is it improper to suggest that there is another side to this question—one to which the phrase 'on the market' provides the key? Standardized test materials are expensive to produce, and manufacturers and sponsors of research are understandably unwilling to sink money in something that is unlikely to find acceptance. This writer inclines to the view that accurate specification, especially of 'concrete' material, especially, in turn, when that material is or represents 'real' objects, constitutes spurious precision—rather like reporting mean squares in analysis of variance of behavioural data to the fourth decimal place. The implication is that publication of at least the *method* of a projective technique, together with its rationale, before the time is ripe for marketing the materials (if, indeed, they need to be marketed) may stimulate research, and even clinical trials, if appropriate, using that technique.

An allied and still more fundamental question is what standardization data *should* (or can) be supplied with a projective technique? Normative data in the form of frequency tables setting out what in Rorschach terminology would be called content variables are usually necessary. Two points, however, must be made. First, that in most projective techniques aspects of response that go beyond what is readily classifiable are often more informative than an array of frequencies. Second, that incidence of responses of a given kind is bound to vary with the culture and the general circumstances within which a technique is being applied. If one is prepared to accept this fact, including the need to accumulate one's own 'norms', perhaps fewer manuals would have to be branded as inadequate.

Next, reliability. It is a commonplace to say that if a test doesn't give the same measurements at all times it doesn't measure anything at all. This is, of course, true if one is trying to measure an enduring function, but there is very little in human behaviour—or even in personality 'structure'—that is indeed enduring. Even along well-defined dimensions such as introversion–extraversion, one has to admit that people behave in a more extravert fashion on some occasions and in some circumstances than others. Neither split-half nor test–retest reliability estimation entirely handles these difficulties, which are related to the item content of a test as well as to considerations of context. An analogy may be found in the well-known Hartshorne and May finding that honesty is situation-specific (Hartshorne and May 1928). It is not, of course, being claimed that reliability is irrelevant to projective testing: due regard *must* be paid to reliability, an obligation which some projectivists observe in terms of lip-service only.

Finally, validity. This is not the place to enter into discussion of the various conceptions of validity and their applicability to projective techniques. The subject has already been touched upon earlier in this chapter, particularly in the section dealing with 'function' or 'intention'. If a projective technique aims at diagnosis, using that term in its widest sense, it should measure up to psychometric standards, including correlation with a stable and unequivocal criterion. Does such a criterion always exist? The question is thrown out for the reader to consider for himself. At a different level one may ask: if what projective techniques are doing is to sample behaviour, what relation do the obtained samples bear to the subject's behaviour and experience outside the test situation? This, too, is perhaps too large a question to consider here, but it may not be too much to hope that projective literature of the future, including test manuals, may present more corroborative evidence for the validity of the inferences drawn. Case material is probably more appropriate for this purpose than an experimental approach. Such material is indeed sometimes presented, but it should be possible by this means to give a more definite answer to such questions as to what extent a TAT subject does indeed attribute his own experience and attitudes to his focal figure or 'hero'. The 'opposite' possibility, that projective response is related to *rejected* tendencies, i.e. to projection in the psychoanalytic sense, would be more difficult either to substantiate or disprove. It is probably safe to say that few projectivists now hold to this belief, and indeed that it is no longer considered a real issue.

It may appear that the writer is advocating some degree of latitude in the evaluation of projective techniques. This is to some extent true. The question which it is suggested one should ask oneself is not whether a particular technique is scientifically respectable, but whether it is something from which valuable—and in the broadest sense valid—information can be derived. Further, in the face of sometimes derisory comment about the 'so-called art of projective testing', the writer is prepared to maintain that not all projective methods are equally suited to all clinicians or others who may employ them. This may perhaps explain why some long-established techniques have attracted little attention. On the other hand, a sifting-out process does take place, and it is possible to discern trends underlying the rise and fall of certain examples, as follows.

Respecting the constraints imposed by the editor, all that will be said about the Rorschach is that it survives, and that there has been an increasing tendency to stress the inter-personal aspects of the Rorschach test situation. In the TAT and its derivatives there has been, as already noted, a trend towards specialization, in respect both of material and of function. In word association there has been a slight resurgence, mainly in research, possibly related to increased interest in the psychology of language. Sentence completion shows a lull. Expressive, manipulative—or, if one may at this stage suggest an alternative name—'activity' techniques seem to be on the upgrade. It is possible to see here some connection with increased interest in ethology, perhaps even with the 'experiential' approach. Drawing and play techniques are both included, often with considerations of therapy as an essential element. Frequently a theoretical orientation plays a large part. This is a feature noted sometimes with approval, sometimes the reverse. A specific minor trend would seem to be increased interest in responsiveness to colour as a personality variable. Unfortunately, this is just the field which above all others seems open to the influence of ill-formulated theory, or of *a priori* assumptions.

Reverting, finally, to the question of 'proliferation': many will endorse the view that too much unproductive effort has been expended. How then might this energy best be deployed? Even the well-established techniques could do with strengthening, and other approaches, as already hinted, might be amenable to a process of synthesis. The remark was made in relation to human figure drawing, but might equally have been applied to 'World' and doll play techniques, and possibly to sentence completion. Where the emphasis is on therapy the need is mainly in relation to the validation of clinical inference in general, rather than anything in the nature of a 'merger': there seems to be no reason, if one is in agreement with the general principles propounded above, to impose uniformity to an extent that could be stultifying. Among individual techniques one would like to see, for reasons already indicated, more research on the Lowenfeld Mosaic, which might well develop, even so late in its history, into a worthwhile multipurpose instrument, yielding information on creativity and cognitive functioning generally, along with its uses in diagnosis and therapy. Other approaches to this possibility have been discussed in the main survey. Technological progress in sound recording and videotape techniques and in facilities for the use and control of colour combine to make the way open for cross-modality study. All these considerations would seem to favour and facilitate a global approach. Whether refinements in mathematical techniques and other indications are equally favourable for increased precision in the identification and definition of dimensions of personality is a topic which cannot be dealt with here.

References

Wherever possible and appropriate, a reference has been given to a book or a journal article rather than to a manual or other test material. Full information about most tests will be found in *Personality Tests and Reviews* (Buros 1970).

Abramson, L. S. (1963), 'A comparison of an auditory and a visual projective technique', *Journal of Projective Techniques*, 27, 3–11.
Abt, L. E., and Bellak, L. (Eds.) (1952), *Projective Psychology: Clinical Approaches to the Total Personality*, New York, Knopf.
Ames, L. B., and Ilg, F. L. (1962), *Mosaic Patterns of American Children*, New York, Harper.
Ames, L. B., and Learned, J. (1954), 'Developmental trends in child Kaleidoblock responses', *Journal of Genetic Psychology*, 24, 237–70.
Anderson, H. H., and Anderson, G. L. (1951), *An Introduction to Projective Techniques and Other Devices for Understanding the Dynamics of Human Behaviour*, Englewood Cliffs, N.J., Prentice-Hall.
Anthony, E. J., and Bene, Eva (1957), 'A technique for the objective assessment of the child's family relationships', *Journal of Mental Science*, 103, 541–55.
Audubon, J. J., and Van Buskirk, C. (1965), 'Projection across sensory modalities', *Journal of Projective Techniques*, 29, 140–50.
Bannister, D., and Fransella, Fay (1966), 'A Grid test of schizophrenic thought disorder', *British Journal of Social and Clinical Psychology*, 5, 95–102.
Bean, K. L. (1965), 'The Sound-Apperception-Test: Origin, purpose, standardization, scoring and use', *Journal of Psychology*, 59, 371–412.
Bell, J. E. (1948), *Projective Techniques*, New York, London, Longmans.
Bellak, L. (1954), *The Thematic Apperception Test and the Children's Apperception Test in Clinical Use*, New York, Grune & Stratton.
Bellak, L., and Hurvich, M. S. (1966), 'A Human modification of the Children's Apperception Test (CAT-H)', *Journal of Projective Techniques*, 30, 228–42.
Bene, Eva (1965), 'On the genesis of male homosexuality', *British Journal of Psychology*, 111, 803–13; 'On the genesis of female homosexuality', ibid, 815–21.
Bowyer, L. R. (1970), *The Lowenfeld World Technique*, Oxford, London, Pergamon.
Bricklin, B., Piotrowski, Z. A., and Wagner, E. E. (1962), *The Hand Test: A New Projective Test with Special Reference to the Prediction of Overt Aggressive Behaviour*, Springfield, Ill., Thomas.
Bruce, M. M. (1959), Association Adjustment Inventory.
Bruce, M. M. (1963), The Industrial Sentence Completion Form.
Buck, J. N. (1949), 'The H-T-P Technique', *Journal of Clinical Psychology*, 5, 37–74.
Buros, O. K. (Ed.) (1970), *Personality Tests and Reviews*, Highland Park, N.J., Gryphon.
Cassel, R. N., and Kahn, T. C. (1961), 'The Group Personality Projective Test (GPPT)', *Psychological Reports*, 8, 23–41.
Chambers, J. L. (1957), 'Identification with photographs of people', *Journal of Consulting Psychology*, 21, 232–4.
Cronbach, L. J. (1970), *Essentials of Psychological Testing*, 3rd edition, New York, London, Harper & Row.
English, H. B., and English, C. A. (1958), *A Comprehensive Dictionary of Psychological and Psychoanalytical Terms*, New York, London, Longmans.
Eysenck, H. J. (1957), *Sense and Nonsense in Psychology*, Harmondsworth, Penguin.

Fein, L. Gold (1960), *The Three-Dimensional Personality Test*, New York, International Universities Press.

Franck, Kate, and Rosen, E. (1949), 'A projective test of masculinity–femininity', *Journal of Consulting Psychology*, 13, 247–56.

Frank, L. K. (1939), 'Projective methods for the study of personality', *Journal of Psychology*, 8, 389–413.

Galton, F. (1879), 'Psychometric experiments', *Brain*, 2, 149–62.

Goldberg, P. A. (1965), 'A review of sentence completion methods in personality assessment', *Journal of Projective Techniques*, 29, 12–45.

Hartshorne, H., and May, M. A. (1928), *Studies in Deceit*, London, Macmillan.

Haworth, Mary R. (1965), 'Review of *The H-T-P Technique*', *Sixth Mental Measurements Yearbook*, 1240–1.

Heim, A. W., and Watts, K. P. (1966), 'The Brook Reaction Test of interests', *British Journal of Psychology*, 57, 171–185.

Hellersberg, E. F. (1950), *The Individual's Relation to Reality in Our Culture*, Springfield, Ill., Thomas.

Holtzman, W. H., Thorpe, J. S., Swartz, J. D., and Henon, E. W. (1961), *Inkblot Perception and Personality: Holtzman Inkblot Technique*, Austin, Texas, University of Texas Press.

Horn, C. C. (1939), *Horn Art Aptitude Inventory*, Chicago, Stoelting.

Howells, J. G., and Lickorish, J. R. (1963), 'The Family Relations Indicator: a projective technique for investigating intra-family relations', *British Journal of Educational Psychology*, 33, 286–96.

Jackson, Lydia (1950), 'Emotional attitudes towards the family of normal, neurotic and delinquent children. I, II', *British Journal of Psychology*, 41, 35–51; 173–85.

Jung, C. G. (1910), 'The association method', *American Journal of Psychology*, 21, 219–69.

Kahn, T. C. (1956), 'Kahn Test of Symbol Arrangement: administration and scoring', *Perceptual Motor Skills.*, 6, 299–334.

Kahn, T. C. (1957), 'Clinical Manual', *Perceptual Motor Skills*, 7, 97–168.

Kataguchi, Y. (1970), *Psychopsy—Manual for the Ka–Ro Test*, Tokyo, Kaneko Shobo.

Kent, Grace H., and Rosanoff, A. J. (1910), 'A study of association in insanity', *American Journal of Insanity*, 67, 37–96; 317–90.

Kerner, J. (1857), *Die Klecksographie*, Tübingen.

Khan, R. Z. (1960), *Visual Apperception Test '60*, Minneapolis, Midwest Psychological Services.

Kinget, G. M. (1952), *The Drawing Completion Test: a Projective Technique for the Investigation of Personality based on the Wartegg Test Blank*, New York, Grune & Stratton.

Koch, C. (1952), *The Tree Test: The Tree-Drawing Test as an Aid in Psychodiagnosis*, New York, Grune & Stratton.

Krout, Johanna (1950), 'Symbol Elaboration Test (SET): The reliability and validity of a new projective technique', *Psychological Monographs*, 64, Whole No. 310.

Kutash, S. B., and Gehl, R. H. (1954), *The Graphomotor Projection Technique: Clinical Use and Standardization*, Springfield, Ill., Thomas.

Lee, S. G. (1953), *Manual of a Thematic Apperception Test for African Subjects*, Pietermaritzburg, University of Natal Press.

Lee, S. G. (1965), 'Review of Van Lennep—*The Four Picture Test*', *Sixth Mental Measurements Yearbook*, 432–3.

Liggett, J. (1959), 'The paired use of projective stimuli', *British Journal of Psychology*, **50**, 269–75.

Löwenfeld, V. (1939), *The Nature of Creative Activity*, London, Kegan Paul.

Lowenfeld, Margaret (1954), *The Lowenfeld Mosaic Test*, London, Newman Neame.

Lüscher, M. (tr. and ed. Scott, I. A.) (1970), *The Lüscher Colour Test*, London, Cape.

Lynn, D. B., and Lynn, Rosalie (1959), 'The Structured Doll Play Test as a projective technique for use with children', *Journal of Projective Techniques*, **23**, 335–44.

Machover, Kate (1949), *Personality Projection in the Drawing of the Human Figure*, Springfield, Ill., Thomas.

Manson, M. P., and Lerner, A. (1962–5), *The Marriage Adjustment Sentence Completion Survey*, Los Angeles, Western Psychological Services.

Meehl, P. E. (1954), *Clinical versus Statistical Prediction: A Theoretical Analysis and a Review of the Evidence*, Minneapolis, Minnesota University Press.

Mira y Lopez, E. (1940), 'Myokinetic psychodiagnosis: a new technique for exploring the conative trends of personality', *Proceedings of the Royal Society of Medicine*, **33**, 173–94.

Moore, T., and Ucko, L. E. (1961), 'Four to six: Constructiveness and conflict in meeting doll play problems', *Journal of Child Psychology and Psychiatry*, **2**, 21–47.

Morgan, C. D. and Murray, H. A. (1935), 'A method for investigating fantasies: the Thematic Apperception Test', *Archives of Neurology and Psychiatry*, **34**, 289–94.

Mucchielli, R. (1960), *Le Jeu du Monde et le Test du Village Imaginaire*, Paris, Presses Universitaires de France.

Nel, P. F., and Pelser, A. J. K. (1960), *The South African Picture Analysis Test*, Amsterdam, Swets & Zeitlinger.

Phillipson, H. (1955), *The Object Relations Technique*, London, Tavistock.

Pickford, R. W. (1963), *Pickford Projective Pictures*, London, Tavistock.

Rabin, A. I., and Haworth, Mary R. (Eds.) (1960), *Projective Techniques with Children*, New York, London, Grune & Stratton.

De Ridder, J. C. (1961), *The Personality of the Urban African in South Africa: a Thematic Apperception Test Study*, London, Routledge & Kegan Paul.

Sarbin, T. R., and Hardyck, C. D. (1955), 'Conformity in role perception as a personality variable', *Journal of Consulting Psychology*, **19**, 109–11.

Schaie, K. W., and Heiss, R. (1964), *Colour and Personality*, Bern, Stuttgart, Huber.

Segal, S. J. (1965), 'Review of Khan. *Visual Apperception Test '60'*, *Sixth Mental Measurements Yearbook*, 539–40.

Semeonoff, B. (1969), 'Personality assessment: prediction or description?', *Advancement of Science*, **26**, 161–71.

Shneidman, E. S. (1947), 'The Make-a-Picture-Story (Maps) projective personality test: a preliminary report', *Journal of Consulting Psychology*, **11**, 315–25.

Smith, B. Babington (1959), 'Ten Silhouettes: an account of perceptual and procedural problems encountered in the development of a fresh projective technique', *Acta Psychologia*, **16**, 165–77.

Von Staabs, G. (1964), *Der Sceno-Test*, Bern, Huber.

Stone, D. R. (1950), 'A recorded auditory apperception test as a new projective technique', *Journal of Psychology*, **29**, 349–53.

Stone, J. B. (1958), *Structured-Objective Rorschach Test. Preliminary Edition*, Hacienda Heights, California, S-O Publishers.

Thompson, C. E. (1949), 'The Thompson modification of the Thematic Apperception Test', *Rorschach Research Exchange and Journal of Projective Techniques*, **13**, 469–78.

Tomkins, S. S., and Miner, J. B. (1957), *The Tomkins–Horn Picture Arrangement Test*, New York, Springer.

Van den Daele, L. A. (1967), 'A music projective technique', *Journal of Projective Techniques*, **31**(5), 47–57.

Wartegg, E. (1939), 'Gestaltung und Charakter', *Zeitschrift für angewandte Psychologie und Charakterkunde*, Beiheft No. 84.

Wilmer, H., and Husni, M. (1953), 'Use of sounds in a projective test', *Journal of Consulting Psychology*, **5**, 377–83.

De Zeeuw, J. (1957), *Colour Preferences in Psychodiagnosis*, The Hague, University Press.

Zucker, K. B., and Jordan, D. C. (1968), 'The paired hands test: a technique for measuring friendliness', *Journal of Projective Techniques*, **32**, 522–9.

Zulliger, H. (Ed. Salomon, F., tr. Dubrovsky, Dusya T.) (1969), *The Zulliger Individual and Group Test*, New York, International Universities Press.

5

RORSCHACH ANALYSIS

Jasper Wilson Holley

University of Lund, Sweden

IT IS a matter of common knowledge that attempts to validate the Rorschach test have been characterized by failure. Criticism of the test, with respect to its metric inadequacy, has been harsh. In his summary of the literature, Eysenck (1959), for example, has pointed out that most of the postulated relationships between projective test indicators and personality traits have no empirical support whatsoever. In addition, he has reported that evidence is lacking with respect to any marked relationship between Rorschach scoring categories, properly combined into a scale, and diagnostic groupings, when tested on a population other than that from which the scale was derived. Other references consistent with such criticism can be cited.

In discussing the difficulties met in the validation of projective tests in general, MacFarlane and Tudderham (Anderson and Anderson 1951) have commented: 'A clinician using projective techniques soon develops a strong conviction that they, or at least the ones with which he has had rich experience, present important data about persons and personality dynamics. Yet many workers with such strong convictions, who also have the equipment of disciplined scientific methods at their disposal, have, to their dismay, found little in their own research findings or in those of others to justify their present enthusiasm. Why this ambiguity? Have we been so wrong clinically? Are our present research tools of validation inadequate for the task?'

In spite of such negative reports, this writer, in collaboration with his co-workers, conducted several studies on Rorschach validity which yielded encouraging results.

The present writer's involvement with the Rorschach problem, it should be pointed out, was not intentional. The circumstances under which his initial study was carried out, on the contrary, might be described as chance. Having been properly taught as a university student that the Rorschach test was of questionable value, this writer had, ever since, avoided its use. In connection with a theoretical problem, however, data were required for the purpose of

119

providing an empirical demonstration. The only available material was from Rorschach protocols—the reason explaining its use in the research to be described.

To the surprise of all of the investigators, the clinical groupings obtained from the first analysis of the records gave an unusually distinct pattern. As a result of such clearcut findings, it was decided that a validity coefficient as high as 0.30 correlational points might reasonably be expected for a second population sample—a profitable goal for the investment of a small amount of additional effort. When, to their complete astonishment, placement accuracy of greater than 90% was actually obtained, it seemed, to the investigators at least, that the controversy over the validity of the Rorschach test—and with respect to other clinical measures as well—was by no means settled. There appeared to be some hope, after all, of demonstrating the validities of the measures on an acceptably high level.

It should be stressed, however, that questions of test validity are not to be resolved in so simple a manner—and certainly not on the basis of a few small studies such as those described here. Opponents of the hypothesis of Rorschach validity can properly be expected to demand more convincing evidence before their judgments can be reversed. It would seem likely, therefore, that additional studies will be required if sufficient interest is rekindled in the controversy.

For those researchers who might wish to enter the fray, some support is given here. Empirical studies on Rorschach validity, and the statistical operations which were applied in them, have been described in detail. In addition, some theoretical discussion relevant to the methodology of the research has been included.

A Factorial Theory of Clinical Subgroups

It will be alleged here that the various clinical categories, generally treated statistically as homogeneous variables, are, in fact, heterogeneous.

Furthermore, it will be posited, as a theory, that every clinical category such as 'schizophrenia', 'depression', 'epilepsy', etc., can be described in terms of a set of subclasses unique to each.

An essential task of empirical research in the clinical area, then, would be to determine in a systematic way the factorial composition of the clinical groups.

The Choice of a Factoring Method

If the clinical domain is, in fact, heterogeneous, some type of factor analysis, or its equivalent, will be required to unravel its complexities. Since there are two principal forms of factor analysis, Q factor analysis and R technique, a further selection must be made. As the reader may know, the R, or regular, form of factoring analyses a matrix containing the intercorrelations of tests, and is based on the responses of many persons to a relatively few tests. The Q method of factor analysis, on the other hand, analyses a matrix in which persons are the variables—a technique which requires many items but relatively few persons.

Now, a clarification of terms should be noted. The definition of Q technique, as used in the present discussion, refers to that type of factoring in which the variables of the matrix of correlation which is analysed are persons rather than tests. Stephenson (1953), on the other hand, has defined Q in a more restrictive manner so that it refers to those factor analyses based upon measures which are completely subjective. Stephenson's 'Q sort' is a psychometric method which he recommends for obtaining such measures.

This writer has used the G index, and not the Q sort urged—a preference not without reason. While Stephenson's approach would be highly esteemed by this writer, the application of his Q sort in the construction of objective tests, a prime objective of G methodology, would not be possible. Factor solutions based on Q sorts, in contrast to those obtained from the application of the G index, cannot be linked to the R factor systems—a requirement in the task of constructing tests in the clinical domain.

Thus the G index has been chosen in preference to the Q sort. Q factor analysis, too, has been used instead of R technique, primarily because Q provides a more direct method for determining the factorial composition of clinical categories. By way of illustration, consider the factor solutions of Figures 1 and 2.

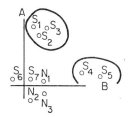 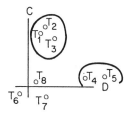

FIGURE 1. Q factors.   FIGURE 2. R factors. T, tests.
S, schizophrenics; N, normals.

Let us observe the clusters containing the variables descriptive of factors A and B, as shown in Figure 1. All of the persons in each of the clusters are schizophrenic. Factor A, then, would indicate one type of schizophrenic reaction, while Factor B would represent another—a reaction quite different from the first. Thus, the groupings of persons, as in clusters A and B, define the clinical subclasses called for by our theoretical model—isolates which can be obtained directly from the application of Q factor analysis.

In contrast to the results of the Q analysis, it may be noted that the variables of each of the two factors of Figure 2 represent tests rather than persons.

Such measures, it should be stressed, cannot be expected to represent the clinical subgroups required by the theoretical scheme.

It should be pointed out that once the clinical subclasses have been isolated using Q analysis, the remaining task of constructing tests of Q factors becomes routine. The Q isolates can be converted into R factors so that a separate test can be constructed for each of the clinical subgroups. Such tests can be expected to yield validation coefficients of respectably high magnitudes. In contrast with Q analysis, however, there can be no assurance that tests obtained from R factor procedures will result in discriminatory validities of appreciable magnitudes.

But there are other reasons for avoiding the use of R technique in the analysis of clinical data. The requirement of a general, or reference, population—as stipulated by Thurstone (1953)—cannot be met, since such a population does not exist in the clinical domain. Unlike such an area as that of mental abilities, differences in performance levels found in clinical studies are extreme. As a consequence, results can be chaotic, as pointed out in a previous paper (Holley and Sjöberg 1968). Consider as an example the scores of Table 1, typical of normal persons, with respect to two Rorschach items.

TABLE 1. Normal Responses

Person	Item 1	Item 2
1	1	1
2	1	1
3	1	1
4	1	1
5	1	1
6	1	1
7	1	1
8	1	1
9	1	0
10	0	1

A contingency table for the values of Table 1 is presented in Table 2.

TABLE 2. Proportions (Normal Group)

		Item 1	
		1	0
Item 2	1	0.8	0.1
	0	0.1	0.0

A phi coefficient based on the values of Table 2 would be -0.11.

Similarly, we can consider the typical responses of schizophrenics to the same two items as given in Table 3 and expressed as a fourfold table in Table 4.

TABLE 3. Responses of Schizophrenics

Person	Item 1	Item 2
11	1	0
12	0	1
13	0	0
14	0	0
15	0	0
16	0	0
17	0	0
18	0	0
19	0	0
20	0	0

TABLE 4. Proportions (Schizophrenics)

		Item 1	
		1	0
Item 2	1	0.0	0.1
	0	0.1	0.8

The value of the phi coefficient for the proportions of Table 4 is the same as that based on Table 2, namely, -0.11.

We are now in a position to demonstrate the consequences of varying proportions of schizophrenic and normal persons. The value of the phi coefficient for a group of persons consisting of 10% normals and 90% schizophrenics would be obtained by means of the matrix calculation:

$$\begin{matrix} 0.1 & 0.0 \\ 0.0 & 0.1 \end{matrix} \times \begin{matrix} 0.8 & 0.1 \\ 0.1 & 0.0 \end{matrix} + \begin{matrix} 0.9 & 0.0 \\ 0.0 & 0.9 \end{matrix} \times \begin{matrix} 0.0 & 0.1 \\ 0.1 & 0.8 \end{matrix} = \begin{matrix} 0.08 & 0.10 \\ 0.10 & 0.72 \end{matrix}$$

(Normals)   (Schizophrenics)   (Combined group)

The phi coefficient for the combined group would be 0.32.

If a phi coefficient were to be computed for every interval of 0.10 for the proportions of normal persons, the resulting curve would be that which is presented in Figure 3.

Fluctuations of such a type are not unique to the phi coefficient. Similar distortions, for example, can be demonstrated using tetrachoric correlation coefficients.

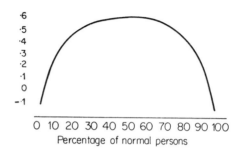

FIGURE 3. Effect of varying the proportions of normal and schizo-phrenic persons on the phi coefficient.

The effects of such fluctuations in correlational values on factor solutions have been shown in a previous paper (Holley 1966a). In a manner consistent with such a demonstration, let us consider the correlations, given in Table 5,

TABLE 5. Phi Coefficients

Test	Group A Test 1	2	3	4	5	Group B Test 1	2	3	4	5
1	—					—				
2	−0.12	—				−0.12	—			
3	−0.18	0.28				−0.18	0.28	—		
4	0.06	−0.03	0.08			0.06	−0.03	0.08	—	
5	−0.03	0.06	0.14	0.08	—	−0.03	0.06	0.14	0.08	—

Test	Group C Test 1	2	3	4	5
1	—				
2	−0.54	—			
3	−0.14	0.17	—		
4	−0.32	0.47	0.06	—	
5	0.47	−0.62	0.08	−0.44	—

of five tests for groups of persons A and B, and the two groups together, indicated by group C. The marginal values indicating performance levels for group A are 0.20, 0.10, 0.50, 0.20 and 0.90. The corresponding values for group B are 0.80, 0.90, 0.50, 0.80 and 0.10. When the two groups are combined to form group C, the marginal values will all be 0.50. The phi values for groups A and B, it may be observed, are identical, while the differences between the correlations of each and those of group C are extreme.

Factor analyses of the matrices of Table 5 can be shown to result in the loadings given in Table 6.

As might be expected, the factor loadings for groups A and B are identical, while each set is quite different from the factor loadings of group C.

TABLE 6. Factor Loadings

| Test | Group A | | Group B | | Group C | | |
	I	II	I	II	I	II	III
1	0.00	−0.30	0.00	−0.30	0.00	−0.24	0.60
2	0.10	0.40	0.10	0.40	0.06	0.24	−0.80
3	0.40	0.60	0.40	0.60	0.40	0.60	0.00
4	0.50	−0.20	0.50	−0.20	0.40	−0.16	−0.16
5	0.20	0.10	0.20	0.10	0.12	0.06	0.80

Such examples, it can be argued, represent instances which are unlikely to occur. Nevertheless, the illustrations serve their intended purpose of demonstrating the kind of serious difficulties that can arise when R factor analysis is applied in the clinical domain.

Now a point should be stressed! When there is no general, or reference, population, and when there are fluctuations such as those which have been described here, the findings of the various factor analyses cannot be combined so as to provide a factorial structure descriptive of the entire domain. Thus, the primary objective of the factorial method, as a basic research instrument, cannot be realized.

But it should be added that when Q factoring is used—which is based on the application of the G index of agreement (Holley and Guilford 1964)—the kinds of distortional fluctuations demonstrated here do not occur.

The G Index of Agreement

The G index is particularly suited for use in Q analysis, a method in which persons rather than tests are the variables of the matrix which is factored. The entries of the score matrix, then, used to compute correlations between persons, must meet three principal requirements. First of all, the mean score value for each person must be equal to zero. In addition, the standard deviation for the scores of each person must be equal to 1.00. Finally, reversals in scoring directions—a problem of special concern in clinical measurement—must not distort the correlational values between persons.

The problem of scoring directions has been discussed previously (Holley 1964b) in a manner consistent with the presentation of this paper, as illustrated by the hypothetical scores of Andrews and Wilson. The likes and dislikes of the two persons with respect to 10 different types of leisure-time activities are:

Andrews	*Wilson*
Likes football	Likes football
Dislikes radio	Dislikes radio
Likes concerts	Likes concerts
Dislikes films	Dislikes films
Likes TV	Likes TV
Dislikes reading	Dislikes reading
Likes hiking	Likes hiking
Likes fishing	Likes fishing
Dislikes golf	Likes golf
Likes bowling	Dislikes bowling

For purposes of illustration, let us consider the correlation between Wilson and Andrews with respect to the items which follow and which require responses of 'Yes' or 'No'.

1. You like football
2. You dislike radio
3. You dislike concerts
4. You dislike films
5. You dislike TV
6. You like reading
7. You like hiking
8. You dislike fishing
9. You like golf
10. You like bowling

The answers of the two persons, then, would be:

	Andrews	*Wilson*
1.	Yes	Yes
2.	Yes	Yes
3.	No	No
4.	Yes	Yes
5.	No	No
6.	No	No
7.	Yes	Yes
8.	No	No
9.	No	Yes
10.	Yes	No

The responses of the two individuals are summarized in Table 7.

TABLE 7

			Wilson	
		Yes	No	Both
Andrews	Yes	4	1	5
	No	1	4	5
	Both	5	5	10

A phi coefficient based on the entries of Table 7 would be $+0.60$.

Now let us rephrase items 1, 2, 4 and 7 so that their polarities are reversed. The items will then read:

1. You dislike football
2. You like radio
3. You dislike concerts
4. You like films
5. You dislike TV
6. You like reading
7. You dislike hiking
8. You dislike fishing
9. You like golf
10. You like bowling

The responses to the items with reversed polarities, then, would be:

	Andrews	*Wilson*
1.	No	No
2.	No	No
3.	No	No
4.	No	No
5.	No	No
6.	No	No
7.	No	No
8.	No	No
9.	No	Yes
10.	Yes	No

The responses to the items with reversed polarities are summarized in Table 8.

TABLE 8

			Wilson	
		Yes	No	Both
Andrews	Yes	0	1	1
	No	1	8	9
	Both	1	9	10

A phi coefficient based on the values of Table 8 would be -0.11.

Thus, correlations between individuals computed on the basis of tests of fixed attitudes or interests will vary according to the scoring directions of the items. It may be argued then that since the changes in the item polarities are in no way related to the psychological attributes of the two persons, the difference of 0.71 correlational points, as in the illustrative example here, must be regarded as error variance.

Now a point should be stressed! With very few exceptions, the polarities of clinical test items are reversible. The result is that no particular set of scoring directions is at all acceptable since any choice of item polarities can be expected to introduce spurious variance.

One system which might be used to avoid such distortional error would be to score each item twice—once positively, and again as a negatively poled item. The resulting scores, which can be written in the form of a 'double-extended matrix' (Holley and Guilford 1966), cannot be affected by changes in scoring directions.

When items are double-scored, the sums of the *columns*, indicating persons, will always be equal to zero. Such matrices, however, are not to be confused with 'double-centred' matrices in which the sums of both the *rows and the columns* are zero. To this it might be added that double-centred matrices, which are referred to later in this text, do not necessarily contain double-scored items.

As an illustration of the double-scoring of items, and of a double-extended matrix, let us assign two scores to each of the items which have been summarized in Table 8. Representing the 'yes' responses with ' + 1' and the 'no' responses with ' − 1' would result in a set of scores, standardized for columns, as given in Table 9.

Now it should be noted that the scores of Table 9 meet the requirements of Q analysis. The mean score value of each column, indicating a person, is zero. In addition, the standard deviation of each column is ± 1.00. Finally, the correlations between persons are invariant to reversals in scoring directions.

It may be shown that the values of the matrix $S'S/n$, when the S matrix contains scores which have been double-scored in the manner which has been illustrated here, will be exactly the same as a matrix containing G indices between persons—indices which are properly suited for Q factor analysis.

The G index has been previously cited under various names (Zubin 1938, Sandler 1948, Quenouille 1952, Sokal and Sneath 1963). Subsequent to its initial application, several generalizations of G have been offered (Sandler 1948, Sjöberg and Holley 1967, Cohen 1968, Holley and Lienert, In Press).

G indices are normally computed on the data found in an ordinary contingency table, as illustrated by the values of Table 10.

TABLE 9. Double-Extended Matrix*

Item	Person Andrews	Wilson
1	−1	−1
2	−1	−1
3	−1	−1
4	−1	−1
5	−1	−1
6	−1	−1
7	−1	−1
8	−1	−1
9	−1	+1
10	+1	−1
1′	+1	+1
2′	+1	+1
3′	+1	+1
4′	+1	+1
5′	+1	+1
6′	+1	+1
7′	+1	+1
8′	+1	+1
9′	+1	−1
10′	−1	+1

* The prime (′) indicates reversed polarity.

TABLE 10. Proportions.
Typical Contingency Table

		Variable 1 +	−
Variable 2	+	a	b
	−	c	d

The G index is based on the probability of agreement of responses, and requires no assumption about the data. The formula for G is

$$G = 2p_c - 1$$

where p_c is equal to the sum of $a + d$, as shown in Table 10.

Besides its suitability for Q factor analysis, G has additional attributes which recommend its use. The distortions illustrated in Figure 3, for example, do not occur when G is used. As a consequence, factors based on G do not appear or disappear, in a sudden and mysterious manner, as did the factor values of the demonstration presented in Table 6.

It should be pointed out, however, that when the G index is used in correlating tests rather than individuals, factors of means can be expected to result (Levy 1966, 1967, Holley 1966b, 1967)—a reason why its use has generally been restricted to the Q method of factoring.

The Burt Reciprocity Principle

The methodological basis for the task of structuring the clinical domain is found in the reciprocity principle of Burt (1941). Burt pointed out that when double-centred score matrices are used in factor analysis, equivalent sets of Q and R factors can be obtained, parameters which can be shown to be qualitatively identical. Thus, for any set of R factors, an equivalent set of Q factors can be obtained by means of a matrix transformation. Conversely, a set of Q factors can be converted to a qualitatively identical set of R factors. Such a bridge between Q and R factors, it should be emphasized, provides a mathematical rationale properly required for the empirical studies reported here, in which factorially structured tests are constructed on the basis of findings resulting from Q analyses.

An obstacle limiting the practical application of the Burt reciprocity principle has been the scarcity of double-centred matrices. Such score matrices are rarely encountered in real research problems. Subsequent to Burt's original work, therefore, a more generalized solution linking the two factor systems has been sought.

A breakthrough was first achieved by Sandler (1949), who provided a transformation between the Q and R systems of factoring which did not require that the score matrix be double-centred. Sandler's efforts resulted in a methodology which, without major modification in principle, remains currently applicable. It might be mentioned, too, that an earlier study on the Rorschach test by Sandler (1948), based on his transitional solution and using G indices, demonstrated levels of measurement accuracy far in excess of those customarily found in the literature. Subsequent to Sandler's initial work, three further generalizations of the Burt reciprocity principle were provided (Holley 1964a, 1970, Holley and Harris 1970), studies intended to extend the applicability of the original Sandler bridge.

An Empirical Application

The purpose of the first study on the Rorschach test (Holley, Fröbärj and Ekberg 1965) was to determine whether the method of Q analysis, based on the use of the G index, could discriminate with respect to three distinctly different types of clinical classes. Such an objective was intended to be only a first step towards the ultimate goal of providing a factorial description of the entire clinical domain—to be achieved as the result of a series of studies.

The first population sample of the study consisted of 20 women. The first six (persons 1–6) were normal, the next eight (persons 7–14) were depressive, while the last six (persons 15–20) had been diagnosed as schizophrenic. The 14 psychiatric cases had resided in a hospital near Gothenburg, Sweden, for a period of less than three weeks. Only three of the clinical cases had been treated previously.

The measures used were some 93 Rorschach items, in dichotomous form, examples of which are given later. The G indices which were computed between persons, as the first step in the analysis, are shown in Table 11.

TABLE 11. G Indices*

Person	1	2	3	4	5	6	7	8	9	10	11	12	13	14	15	16	17	18	19	20
1	—																			
2	29	—																		
3	25	10	—																	
4	23	−01	20	—																
5	14	03	12	14	—															
6	20	14	27	25	20	—														
7	−08	08	−31	−16	−12	−05	—													
8	−01	10	−12	−14	08	10	50	—												
9	16	18	14	16	12	18	25	36	—											
10	20	−05	−40	−29	−08	−18	57	38	20	—										
11	−14	−08	−29	−18	−05	−03	46	27	14	55	—									
12	−05	01	−25	−01	03	−03	50	36	36	59	48	—								
13	01	12	−14	−03	10	−01	48	46	42	53	55	55	—							
14	−16	03	−36	−38	−16	−18	61	29	12	57	50	42	40	—						
15	08	12	−01	−20	05	−01	05	12	16	23	25	33	48	36	—					
16	−12	12	−23	−12	01	−01	31	16	12	36	46	38	40	44	61	—				
17	05	03	−23	01	31	08	27	25	20	36	29	42	40	18	23	40	—			
18	12	10	−20	−05	03	05	46	48	27	42	44	44	55	46	38	59	38	—		
19	−03	−05	03	−29	01	03	18	12	25	18	29	20	14	31	36	27	14	16	—	
20	14	20	03	05	−03	29	23	25	42	18	16	29	23	14	18	14	14	38	27	—

* Decimal points omitted.

Since the use of an electronic computer was not convenient at the time, the centroid method was applied to obtain, by hand, some three factors. Unfortunately, the small number of items did not permit further extraction, as would be necessary for the isolation of clinical subclasses.

The graphic method of rotation (Zimmerman 1951) was then applied, resulting in the loadings presented in Table 12 and shown graphically in Figure 4.

It may be seen from the illustration of Figure 4 that the various psychiatric groupings emerged in a clearcut manner. Two persons, however, were not included in any of the three factors. Person 9 was not Swedish and had difficulty in understanding the Swedish language, while person 20 was a long-term patient who had been treated repeatedly over a period of many years.

TABLE 12. Rotated Factor Loadings. First Rorschach Analysis

Person	Factor I	Factor II	III	Person	Factor I	Factor II	III
1	0.16	−0.43	−0.38	11	0.59	0.26	0.28
2	0.24	−0.22	−0.16	12	0.54	0.44	0.30
3	−0.11	−0.54	−0.40	13	0.50	0.54	0.36
4	0.00	−0.47	−0.52	14	0.72	0.14	0.28
5	0.08	−0.36	−0.09	15	0.11	0.53	0.78
6	0.19	−0.46	−0.34	16	0.33	0.45	0.66
7	0.73	0.24	0.07	17	0.18	0.45	0.43
8	0.44	0.39	0.11	18	0.44	0.57	0.44
9	0.12	0.59	0.19	19	0.20	0.26	0.40
10	0.74	0.20	0.24	20	0.16	0.51	0.18

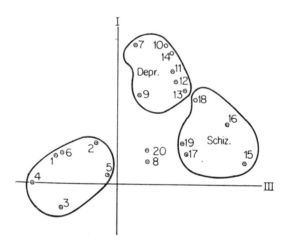

FIGURE 4. Rotated factor loadings. First Rorschach analysis.

Encouraged by the distinct patterns of the Q factors, the investigators decided that the study should be continued so that a validity coefficient for the Rorschach might be obtained—a value which, as previously mentioned, was not expected to exceed 0.30 correlational points.

In pursuit of such a goal, items were selected which were discriminatory with respect to the groupings obtained from the Q analysis, in a manner which has been described elsewhere (Holley and Fällström 1965). Thus, three sets of items were chosen, one set for each of the three groups of persons obtained as the result of the Q analysis. The mean scores of the three groups of persons with respect to the three sets of items were then computed, the terms M_N, M_D and M_S being used to indicate the average values for the groups of normals, depressives and schizophrenics, respectively.

A second sample of persons, similar in all relevant respects to the first, was then chosen. The population sample consisted of 42 persons—14 normals, 12 depressives and 16 schizophrenics. In order to provide for the placement of persons in the second group, on the basis of their scores with respect to the selected groups of items a 'factor index' was computed for each person, and for each clinical class, using the formulae:

Normal factor index (NFI) $\quad = \dfrac{100 \, X_N}{M_N}$

Depressive factor index (DFI) $\quad = \dfrac{100 \, X_D}{M_D}$

Schizophrenic factor index (SFI) $= \dfrac{100 \, X_S}{M_S}$

where X_N, X_D and X_S are the total scores of the individuals in the second population sample with respect to the groups of items allegedly differentiating groups of normal, depressive and schizophrenic persons, as subsequently illustrated, and the values of M_N, M_D and M_S have been previously defined.

The resulting factor indices, computed for each of the 42 persons in the second population, and with respect to each of the three categories, are presented in Table 13. The accuracy obtained by the placement procedures is given in Table 14.

TABLE 13. Factor Indices for Persons. Second Population Sample, First Rorschach Analysis

	Normal persons													
	1	2	3	4	5	6	7	8	9	10	11	12	13	14
NFI	62	95	85	81	100	76	71	85	109	66	118	95	71	81
DFI	63	24	32	16	16	24	32	39	24	39	24	24	24	24
SFI	16	00	47	16	00	16	31	31	31	31	31	47	16	00

	Depressive persons											
	15	16	17	18	19	20	21	22	23	24	25	26
NFI	14	52	09	00	28	33	19	14	24	47	24	00
DFI	55	102	71	95	63	102	55	87	102	47	102	71
SFI	31	00	31	63	00	16	16	00	47	31	16	16

TABLE 13. (continued)

	27	28	29	30	31	32	33	34	35	36	37	38	39	40	41	42
					Schizophrenic persons											
NFI	28	19	05	14	09	28	28	52	71	28	28	05	28	14	19	33
DFI	16	39	08	55	16	32	16	47	24	24	39	63	47	16	47	16
SFI	78	78	94	109	94	109	94	94	94	109	31	94	78	63	63	94

TABLE 14. Accuracy of Placement. First Rorschach Analysis

Actual	Predicted			
	Normal	Depressive	Schizophrenic	Total
Normal	13	1	0	14
Depressive	1	11	0	12
Schizophrenic	0	1	15	16
Total	14	13	15	42

It can be observed that, on the basis of their highest factor index, 39 out of 42 persons were correctly placed. The accuracy obtained, then, was about 93%, a respectably high magnitude for a beginning study!

In order to provide evidence of the credibility of the findings, the protocols of some 12 persons were selected from the books of Bohm (1957) and Rorschach (1957), as shown in the references of Table 15.

TABLE 15. Protocol References. Third Population Sample, First Rorschach Analysis

Person	Author	Page No.	Case No.
Normals			
N_1	Bohm	324	2
N_2	Bohm	330	5
N_3	Bohm	333	6
N_4	Bohm	337	7
Depressives			
D_1	Bohm	380	22
D_2	Rorschach	165	20
Schizophrenics			
S_1	Rorschach	154	14
S_2	Rorschach	156	15
S_3	Rorschach	157	16
S_4	Rorschach	158	17
S_5	Rorschach	161	18
S_6	Bohm	370	18

The individuals represented by the protocols of Table 15, and regarded as a third population, were assigned factor indices in the same manner as the persons in the second population, the items used in the analysis being presented in Table 16.

TABLE 16. Discriminatory Items.* First Rorschach Analysis

A. Responses characteristic of normal persons
    5. Whole responses (not popular) to card V
    7. Whole responses (not popular) to card VII
  21. Animal-movement response
  41. Colour–form response to card II
  60. Popular response (fur rug or bat) to card IV
  63. Popular response (fur rug) to card VI
  64. Popular response to card VII
  68. Popular response as first response to card X
  70. Light–dark response to card I
  87. Rejection of card I (scoring reversed)
  95. Rejection of card IX (scoring reversed)
  97. Number of responses 15 or more
112. Experience balance: extrasensive
115. Loose sequence
119. $F+ \%$ 80 to 90
127. % of original answers 6 or more
159. Colour symbolism
160. Colour descriptions
168. Impressions (or feeling responses)
169. Evaluative remarks (containing value judgments)
170. Emphasis on symmetry
181. Self-reference (projection of oneself into the perception)
212. Space response to card III
216. Space response to card VII
220. Mutilation response
222. Aggressive content
223. Oral complex determined responses
253. Percent of responses to the last 3 cards greater than 30

B. Responses characteristic of depressives
  96. Rejection of card X
103. Manner of approach: W
111. Experience balance: constrictive
137. The interpretation awareness: lowered
142. Colour shock to card IX
143. Colour shock to card X
145. Interference phenomenon VIII
151. Red shock to card II (scoring reversed)
167. Subject criticism
176. Perseveration: 'ruminating type'
187. Responses in question form
203. Kinesthetic shock (prevents M-response from developing)

* For further description of items see Bohm (1957).

TABLE 16. (continued)

C. Responses characteristic of schizophrenics
    2. Whole response (not popular) to card II
    3. Whole response (not popular) to card III
  101. Colour type: middle (scoring reversed)
  121. F% responses less than 65
  150. Dark shock to card VII
  162. Kinetic descriptions

The scores of the 12 persons with respect to the 46 items are given in Table 17, while the factor indices are given in Table 18.

TABLE 17. Score Matrix. Third Population Sample, First Rorschach Analysis

					Persons							
Item	N_1	N_2	N_3	N_4	D_1	D_2	S_1	S_2	S_3	S_4	S_5	S_6
Normals												
5	0	0	1	1	0	0	0	0	1	1	0	1
7	0	1	1	1	0	0	0	0	1	1	0	1
21	0	0	0	0	0	0	0	0	0	0	0	0
41	0	1	0	0	0	0	0	0	0	1	0	0
60	1	1	1	0	0	0	0	0	0	0	0	0
63	1	0	1	0	0	0	0	0	1	0	0	0
64	1	1	1	1	1	1	0	1	0	0	0	0
68	0	1	1	1	1	1	0	1	0	0	0	0
70	0	0	1	1	0	0	0	0	0	0	0	0
87	1	1	1	1	1	1	1	1	1	1	1	1
95	1	1	1	1	1	0	1	1	1	1	1	1
97	1	1	1	1	1	1	1	1	0	1	1	1
112	1	0	0	0	1	0	0	1	0	1	0	0
115	1	1	1	1	0	0	0	0	0	0	0	0
119	0	0	0	0	0	0	0	0	0	0	0	0
127	1	1	1	1	1	1	1	1	1	1	1	1
159	0	0	0	1	0	0	0	0	0	1	1	0
160	0	0	0	1	0	0	1	1	0	1	1	0
168	1	1	0	1	0	0	0	0	0	0	0	0
169	1	1	1	0	1	0	0	0	0	0	0	0
170	0	1	1	1	0	0	0	0	0	0	0	1
181	0	0	0	0	0	0	0	0	0	0	0	1
212	0	0	0	0	0	0	0	0	0	0	0	0
216	1	0	0	0	0	0	0	0	0	0	0	0
220	0	1	0	0	1	0	0	1	0	0	0	0
222	0	0	0	0	0	0	0	0	0	0	1	0
223	0	0	0	0	0	0	0	0	0	0	0	0
253	1	0	0	1	1	1	1	1	0	1	1	1
Totals	13	14	14	15	10	6	6	10	6	11	8	9

TABLE 17. (continued)

Depressives

96	0	0	0	0	0	0	0	0	0	0	0	0
103	1	1	0	0	0	0	0	0	1	1	1	1
111	0	0	0	0	1	1	1	0	1	0	0	0
137	0	0	0	0	1	0	0	0	0	0	1	0
142	1	1	1	0	0	0	0	0	0	1	1	0
143	1	0	1	0	0	0	0	0	0	0	0	0
145	0	1	0	1	0	0	0	0	0	0	0	0
151	0	0	0	1	1	1	1	1	0	1	1	0
167	0	0	0	0	1	0	0	0	0	0	0	1
176	0	0	1	0	1	1	1	0	0	0	0	1
187	0	0	0	0	0	0	0	0	0	0	0	0
203	0	0	0	0	0	1	0	0	0	0	0	0
Totals	3	3	3	2	5	4	3	1	2	3	4	3

Schizophrenics

2	0	0	1	0	0	0	0	0	1	0	1	0
3	0	1	0	0	0	0	0	0	1	0	1	1
101	0	0	0	1	0	0	1	0	1	1	1	0
121	0	0	0	0	0	0	1	1	1	0	1	1
150	0	1	0	0	1	0	0	0	0	1	1	1
162	0	0	0	0	0	0	1	0	0	1	0	0
Totals	0	2	1	1	1	0	3	1	4	3	5	3

It may be noted that sufficient data have been included to allow the reader to check the accuracy of the scoring and of the computations, if he wishes to do so.

Placement of persons on the basis of the factor indices of Table 18 would result in 11 accuracies out of 12 possibilities, indicating a validity of respectable magnitude. The results, then, in each of the three portions of the first study supported the hypothesis that validity might be demonstrated with the Rorschach test—providing the proper analytical procedures are used.

But, of course, such results must be verified, preferably on a large scale and by several independent investigators. In order to encourage further research of such a type, therefore, a second study demonstrating the validity of the Rorschach test was published (Holley and Fröbärj 1967). The report of the analysis included some 349 Rorschach items, in dichotomized form, which had been prepared by Fröbärj for application in subsequent analyses.

The demonstration study used 17 protocols from published references and one from the private collection of Dr Fröbärj. Nine persons comprised the analysis group, while the remaining nine individuals made up the validation group. The population consisted of nine normals, eight schizophrenics and one case of involutional paranoia—a variable which failed to emerge in either of the two isolated factors.

The perfect discrimination obtained from the factor analysis, and based on the use of 106 items, may be observed in the illustration of Figure 5.

On the basis of the items which had been selected as discriminatory, the total scores of the two groups of persons in the second sample were compared. A graphic presentation of the findings of the validity analysis is given in Figure 6.

TABLE 18. Scores on 'Factor Tests', and Factor Indices for Persons. Third Population Sample, First Rorschach Analysis

Person	Normal		Depressive		Schizophrenic	
	Score	NFI	Score	DFI	Score	SFI
Normals						
N_1	13	62	3	29	0	0
N_2	14	66	3	29	2	50
N_3	14	66	3	29	1	25
N_4	15	71	2	19	1	25
Totals	56		11		4	
Depressives						
D_1	10	47	5	49	1	25
D_2	6	28	4	39	0	0
Totals	16		9		1	
Schizophrenics						
S_1	6	28	3	29	3	75
S_2	10	47	1	10	1	25
S_3	6	28	2	19	4	100
S_4	11	52	3	29	3	75
S_5	8	38	4	39	5	125
S_6	9	43	3	29	3	75
Totals	50		16		19	

Factor indices have been based on the means of $M_N = 21.1$, $M_D = 10.3$, $M_S = 4.0$.

Thus, perfect placement of persons with respect to clinical categories was demonstrated. The probability of obtaining such accuracy by chance, it might be added, would be given by the value of $(\frac{1}{2})^9$, or 1 chance in 512, a probability which might properly be termed 'not very likely'.

Further analysis of the data from the study of schizophrenia just cited (omitting one case of involutional paranoia) was carried out in a demonstration of the factorial heterogeneity of clinical groupings (Holley and Fröbärj 1967).

As a result of the analysis, two factors of schizophrenia were isolated, as indicated by the illustration of Figure 7.

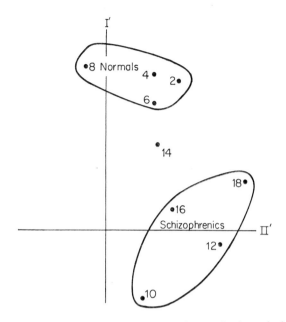

FIGURE 5. Rotated factors. Second Rorschach analysis.

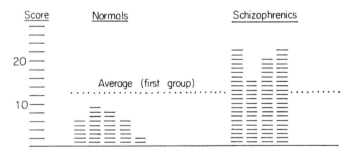

FIGURE 6. Total scores. Second population sample, second
Rorschach analysis.

It may be observed that three distinct clusters emerged as the result of the analysis. Two of the groups of persons represented different kinds of schizophrenic reactions. The normal control group, on the other hand, clustered around the origin.

The responses characteristic of the two types of schizophrenic reactions are presented in Table 19.

Thus, the factorial heterogeneity of the schizophrenic category has been demonstrated.

TABLE 19.* Discriminatory Items. Third Rorschach Analysis

Schizophrenic reaction A

28		Original responses (−)
51	reversed	Dilated experience balance
53	reversed	Introversive experience balance
80		Lack of subjective clearness in approach
116		'Or' responses
122		Absence of popular whole responses to card V
128		Great differences concerning sharpness of form
149		Only 0 or 1 movement+(M+, B+)
151		F+% less than 70
161	reversed	2 or more movement responses M+, B+
168	reversed	Human movement card I
177	reversed	Space response to card I
179	reversed	Card I regarded as neutral
180		Rejection of card II
207	reversed	Human movement to card III
243	reversed	Popular response (bat) as first to card V

Schizophrenic reaction B

6		F+% 65 to 79
11		Animal % 20 to 39
18		V responses 3 or 4
27		Original responses ±
31	reversed	Original responses 30 to 39%
37	reversed	% of responses to last 3 cards 40 and above
60		'Ruminating type' (same content but other answers between)
136		Flexor quality of movement response
141		Lowered interpretation awareness
146		S responses but not until cards VIII, IX or X
147		S responses but not until card VII
183	reversed	Whole response, not popular, to card II
190		Colour form CF, FbF to card II
296		Human movement to card VIII
301	reversed	Colour form CF, FbF to card VIII

* The items are from the Fröbärj item list (Holley and Fröbärj 1967).

A final study, using the Rorschach test, and concerned with the hypothesis of factorial heterogeneity, can be cited. In an investigation of epilepsy (Fröbärj and Holley 1968) four clearcut isolates, indicating subclasses of epilepsy, were obtained. Such findings provide strong evidence supporting the heterogeneity hypothesis. In addition, however, it should be emphasized that the groupings of persons in such sharply defined patterns could not possibly have been demonstrated had the Rorschach items comprising the basic score data not been discriminatory with respect to the clinical classes— and to a respectably high degree. The loadings of the isolates are given in Table 20, while their vector projections are shown in Figures 8, 9 and 10.

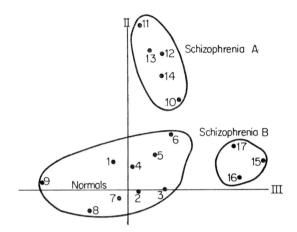

FIGURE 7. Rotated factors. Third Rorschach analysis.

TABLE 20. Rotated Factor Loadings. Fourth Rorschach Analysis

Persons	Factor				
	I	II	III	IV	V
Normals					
1	83	00	21	−03	−07
2	80	−11	02	−24	−10
3	63	−18	−26	17	−06
4	78	06	05	−13	21
5	80	04	04	08	22
6	72	22	02	00	22
7	70	−23	−12	07	08
8	81	−14	11	−05	−07
Epileptics					
9	15	−20	09	09	72
10	−05	19	78	−05	11
11	−22	64	10	28	−01
12	14	02	54	64	01
13	−09	12	02	77	29
14	24	−12	61	15	31
15	−21	39	00	58	03
16	16	52	−12	58	−12
17	−03	68	02	33	01
18	04	22	18	09	81
19	−09	66	27	01	−02
20	14	69	−44	−06	10

Decimal points are omitted.

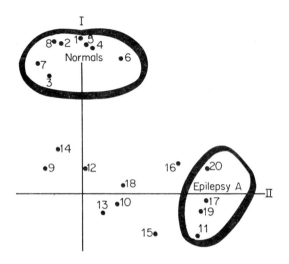

FIGURE 8. Factors I and II. Fourth Rorschach analysis.

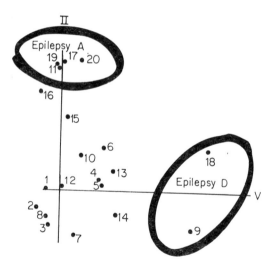

FIGURE 9. Factors II and V. Fourth Rorschach analysis.

Thus, the distinct groupings of persons into three subclasses of epilepsy and one normal cluster can be observed.

In summary, it can be stated that the findings of all four empirical studies reported in the present paper support the validity hypothesis—namely, that the Rorschach test, properly used, can yield data which, when properly analysed, can successfully demonstrate the validity of the Rorschach test.

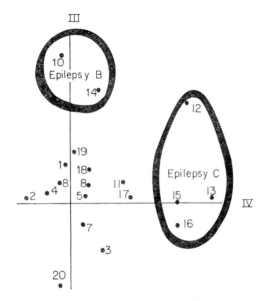

FIGURE 10. Factors III and IV. Fourth Rorschach analysis.

Critique

Several possible improvements with respect to the empirical studies which might be helpful in planning future research should be pointed out. One suggestion concerns the number of diagnostic categories (three) used in the first Rorschach investigation. The present writer would recommend that, in general, only two categories be included in a single analysis—as in the reported studies on schizophrenia and epilepsy.

A second comment concerns the relatively few persons used in the schizophrenic studies. An ideal number of individuals for a single factor analysis would be from 20 to 30, with a sample of comparative size comprising a second validation group. In addition, it must be admitted that not enough items were used in the empirical studies, the recommended minimum being about 200. While fewer items might be employed, in an analysis, such a practice would not be encouraged.

To such suggestions it should be added that the method of selecting items representative of each factor has improved since the earlier Rorschach studies. An objectively computed index, known as the D estimate (Holley and Risberg 1972), would now be recommended. The D estimate is a modified form of the G index, and expresses the probability that a given item response will indicate the correct placement of an individual with respect to a given clinical category.

Like the G index, a zero D value would be expected by chance, while a value of + 1.00 would indicate perfect discrimination. Unlike G, however, D is a coefficient which is not subject to distortions resulting from differences in the numbers of persons in the clinical groups. The D index, too, can be programmed for electronic computers and obtained directly from the original score matrix, once the category groupings have been determined.

As an illustration of the manner in which the D estimate is computed, we may consider the proportions of Table 21.

TABLE 21. Proportions

| Response | Clinical group | |
	'Epilepsy A'	Others
1	a	c
0	b	d

The D estimate may be computed on the basis of either frequencies or proportions by means of the formula

$$D = \frac{a}{a+b} - \frac{c}{c+d}.$$

It should be mentioned that D estimates will be illustrated later with empirical data.

Finally, in addition to the suggestions previously offered, criticism can be directed towards the procedures which were used to place persons into their appropriate clinical categories. In the studies reported here, representative items were selected for each factor. Persons were then assigned to the factorial groups on the basis of their relative performance with respect to the groups of selected items.

Two alternative methods of person placement, however, are suggested here. The first would require an electronic computer, and is documented here for possible application in the more distant future. Readers less interested in matrix notation, therefore, can bypass the derivation which follows. The formula for the matrix system presented later in equation (11) is derived in a manner which starts with the primary equation of Q factor theory, as presented previously (Holley and Risberg 1971), and consistent with the work of Dwyer (1937).

$$P_Q F_Q = S_G \tag{1}$$

where P_Q is the matrix containing factor loadings for persons, obtained by means of a Q analysis, F_Q is a set of reference scores for tests in which $F_Q F_Q'$ is equal to the diagonal matrix n and S_G is the $N \times n$ score matrix containing the scores of $+1$ and -1 for n tests and N persons.

Now let us multiply equation (1) from the left by the transpose of P_Q, indicated by P_Q', to obtain

$$P_Q' P_Q F_Q = P_Q' S_G. \tag{2}$$

Multiplying from the left by the inverse of $P_Q'P_Q$, indicated by $(P_Q'P_Q)^{-1}$, would result in

$$(P_Q'P_Q)^{-1}(P_Q'P_Q)F_Q = (P_Q'P_Q)^{-1}P_Q'S_G. \tag{3}$$

Since

$$(P_Q'P_Q)^{-1}(P_Q'P_Q) = I \tag{4}$$

where I is an identity matrix, equation (3) becomes

$$F_Q = (P_Q'P_Q)^{-1}P_Q'S_G \tag{5}$$

which in its transposed form is equal to

$$F_Q' = \{(P_Q'P_Q)^{-1}P_Q'S_G\}' \tag{6}$$

which, in turn, is the same as

$$F_Q' = S_G'P_Q(P_Q'P_Q)^{-1}. \tag{7}$$

It might be mentioned that since $(P_Q'P_Q)^{-1}$ is a symmetrical matrix, it is equal to its own transpose.

In order to continue our development, we return to equation (1) to multiply from the right by F_Q', in order to obtain the equation

$$P_QF_QF_Q' = S_GF_Q'. \tag{8}$$

Since F_QF_Q' is always a diagonal matrix equal to n, then

$$P_Q = S_GF_Q'/n. \tag{9}$$

Substituting equation (7) in (9) results in

$$P_Q = (S_GS_G'/n)P_Q(P_Q'P_Q)^{-1} \tag{10}$$

an equation which is basic to our analytical system.

Now it may be shown that if a P_Q factor solution is obtained for N persons in a given study, factor coordinates for additional persons, to be used for purposes of person placement, can be estimated on the basis of the G indices between the scores of the additional persons and the N persons in the original group.

In order to compute such estimates from G indices, an adaptation of equation (10) can be used to provide the relationship of

$$P_A = (_AS_GS_G'/n)P_Q(P_Q'P_Q)^{-1} \tag{11}$$

where P_A contains the factor coordinates for the additional persons in the study who are to be placed into appropriate factor groups, and $_AS_G$ contains the scores of the additional persons.

It should be mentioned that when the factor coordinates do not account for all of the variance between persons in the placement group, additional factors can be extracted from the residual matrix, such values being obtained by subtracting the cross products of the factor coordinates from the original G values.

The second alternative method to be used for person placement is an adaptation of the technique used in the Sandler (1958) system of 'delegate analysis', a scoring method which will be demonstrated later. With the Sandler model, total scores for the persons in the Q factor groupings are computed so that a total 'delegate score' is obtained for every item with respect to each factor. In its application by the present writer, persons who are to be 'placed' or 'evaluated' are then correlated, using a generalization of the G index, with the responses of the 'delegates' for each factor. Placement is determined on the basis of the highest G value.

The method is simple, and effective.

An Illustration of Some Suggested Procedures

In order to demonstrate some of the techniques which have been discussed, a description of the steps to be followed in the evaluation of the clinical tests and for the placement of persons into clinical groups is presented here. The data are from a study on epilepsy (Fröbärj and Holley 1968) which has been previously cited. The exercise first presents the scores of some eight persons in the 'analysis group' and three persons in the 'placement group' with respect to some 20 dichotomized Rorschach items. We are to carry out a factor analysis

TABLE 22. Score Matrix

Item	Persons in analysis group								Persons in placement group		
	1	2	3	4	5	6	7	8	9	10	11
3	0	0	0	1	0	0	0	0	1	0	0
4	1	0	0	1	0	0	0	0	1	1	0
11	1	0	1	1	0	0	0	0	1	0	0
18	0	1	1	0	0	1	0	1	0	0	0
26	1	0	0	1	0	0	1	0	1	0	0
35	0	1	0	1	1	0	1	0	0	1	0
40	0	1	0	0	1	0	1	1	0	1	0
46	1	0	0	1	0	0	0	0	1	1	0
53	1	0	0	1	0	0	0	0	1	1	0
59	0	0	1	0	0	1	0	0	0	0	1
71	0	1	0	0	1	0	0	0	0	1	0
125	0	1	0	0	1	0	0	0	0	1	1
143	0	0	1	0	0	0	0	1	0	0	1
148	0	1	0	0	1	0	1	1	0	1	0
150	0	1	1	0	0	1	0	1	0	0	0
157	0	1	0	0	1	0	1	1	0	1	0
168	1	0	0	1	0	0	0	0	1	0	0
224	0	0	0	0	0	1	0	1	0	1	1
301	1	1	0	1	0	0	1	0	1	0	0
336	1	0	0	1	0	0	0	0	1	0	0

of the responses of the first eight persons in the 'analysis group'. The next step will be to determine the qualities of the Q factors on the basis of an item analysis. Finally, the last three persons are to be assigned, or 'placed', into one of the isolated factor groupings. The placement is to be made, first, using the matrix method, and, secondly, using the Sandler scoring system.

G indices were computed between persons for the individuals in the analysis group as shown in Table 23.

TABLE 23. G Indices

Person	Person							
	1	2	3	4	5	6	7	8
1	—							
2	−0.50	—						
3	−0.10	0.00	—					
4	0.80	−0.50	−0.30	—				
5	−0.40	0.70	−0.10	−0.40	—			
6	−0.20	0.10	0.70	−0.40	0.00	—		
7	0.00	0.50	−0.10	0.00	0.60	0.00	—	
8	−0.50	0.40	0.40	−0.70	0.30	0.50	0.30	—

The application of the principal component method of factor analysis yielded three factors which, when rotated by means of the varimax system, resulted in the values of Table 24.

TABLE 24. Rotated Factor Loadings

Person	Factor		
	I	II	III
1	0.84	−0.13	−0.09
2	−0.47	0.65	0.02
3	−0.07	−0.10	0.76
4	0.86	−0.13	−0.34
5	−0.36	0.74	−0.08
6	−0.15	0.00	0.78
7	0.10	0.82	0.02
8	−0.48	0.32	0.57

The factor loadings of Table 24 can be observed in order to obtain the groupings of persons 1 and 4 for the first factor, persons 2, 5 and 7 for the second factor, and persons 3, 6 and 8 for the third factor. The persons of each factor can now be grouped together in a revision of the first eight columns of the matrix given in Table 22 to result in the matrix which is presented in Table 25.

TABLE 25. Revised Score Matrix

Item	1	4	2	5	7	3	6	8
3	0	1	0	0	0	0	0	0
4	1	1	0	0	0	0	0	0
11	1	1	0	0	0	1	0	0
18	0	0	1	0	0	1	1	1
26	1	1	0	0	1	0	0	0
35	0	1	1	1	1	0	0	0
40	0	0	1	1	1	0	0	1
46	1	1	0	0	0	0	0	0
53	1	1	0	0	0	0	0	0
59	0	0	0	0	0	1	1	0
71	0	0	1	1	0	0	0	0
125	0	0	1	1	0	0	0	0
143	0	0	0	0	0	1	0	1
148	0	0	1	1	1	0	0	1
150	0	0	1	0	0	1	1	1
157	0	0	1	1	1	0	0	1
168	1	1	0	0	0	0	0	0
224	0	0	0	0	0	0	1	1
301	1	1	1	0	1	0	0	0
336	1	1	0	0	0	0	0	0

Using the groupings of Table 25, D estimates can be computed in a manner which has been described in this paper. The D estimates which are presented in Table 26 indicate the relationships between the 20 items and each of the three Q factor isolates.

TABLE 26. D Estimates

Item	I	II	III	Item	I	II	III
3	0.50	−0.20	−0.20	71	−0.33	0.67	−0.40
4	1.00	−0.40	−0.40	125	−0.33	0.67	−0.40
11	0.84	−0.60	−0.07	143	−0.33	−0.40	0.67
18	−0.67	−0.27	0.80	148	−0.67	0.80	−0.27
26	0.84	−0.07	−0.60	150	−0.67	−0.27	0.80
35	0.00	0.80	−0.80	157	−0.67	0.80	−0.27
40	−0.67	0.80	−0.27	168	1.00	−0.40	−0.40
46	1.00	−0.40	−0.40	224	−0.33	−0.40	0.67
53	1.00	−0.40	−0.40	301	0.67	0.27	−0.80
59	−0.33	−0.40	0.67	336	1.00	−0.40	−0.20

With the D estimates of Table 26, representative items for each factor can be selected, as presented in Table 27.

TABLE 27. Items Descriptive of Isolates

Number	Content
First factor (normal)	
3	Number of responses 31 or above
4	F+ % 91 or above
11	Animal % 20 to 39
26	Original responses+
46	Whole responses
53	Experience balance introversive
168	Human movement (card 1)
336	Human movement for card 10
Second factor (epilepsy—type A)	
35	Responses % of last 3 cards 30 or less
40	W responses (more than average)
71	Illusion of similarity
125	Resignation formula: 'That is all, I don't know more'
148	Mean time more than one minute per response
157	Comment about the ease or difficulty of the test
Third factor (epilepsy—type C)	
18	V responses 3 or 4
59	'Sticking to a central theme', little variation in the same content category
143	Dark grey or black as colour
150	Colour naming—at least one
224	Dark shock, card 4
301 reversed	Colour form CF, FbF to card 8

The numbers used in Table 27 refer to the items developed by Fröbärj (Holley and Fröbärj 1967).

The items obtained by the application of the D estimate need only be used for the limited purpose of identifying the Q factors. It should be pointed out that it is not necessary to construct tests of the various Q factors, a procedure which had been followed in the empirical studies. Instead, placement of persons can be achieved directly from the factor matrix for persons, and from the score matrices, by means of the formula which has been described:

$$_A P_Q = (_A S_G S'_G / n) P_Q (P'_Q P_Q)^{-1}. \qquad (11)$$

Based on the data of Table 22, the values of $_A S_G S'_G / n$ can be shown to be those given in Table 28.

TABLE 28. Matrix $_AS_GS'_G/n$

Person	Person							
	1	2	3	4	5	6	7	8
9	0.9	−0.6	−0.2	0.9	−0.5	−0.3	−0.1	−0.6
10	−0.2	0.3	−0.5	−0.2	0.6	−0.2	0.2	0.1
11	−0.2	−0.1	0.5	−0.4	0.2	0.6	0.0	0.3

The values of the matrix $P_Q(P'_QP_Q)^{-1}$, computed from the entries of Table 24, are given in Table 29.

TABLE 29. Matrix $P_Q(P'_QP_Q)^{-1}$

Person	Factor		
	I	II	III
1	0.559	0.181	0.199
2	−0.125	0.308	−0.072
3	0.170	−0.016	0.545
4	0.491	0.161	0.014
5	−0.050	0.397	−0.106
6	0.149	0.031	0.545
7	0.356	0.616	0.137
8	−0.065	0.123	0.304

The final matrix, obtained from the multiplication of the values of Tables 28 and 29, is presented in Table 30.

TABLE 30. Factor Coordinates. Matrix $(_AS_GS_G/n)P_Q(P'_QP_Q)^{-1}$

Person	Factor		
	I	II	III
9	0.97	−0.22	−0.18
10	−0.33	0.40	−0.45
11	−0.15	0.00	0.63

The placements, indicated by the highest positive values, would be factors I, II and III for persons 9, 10 and 11, respectively. Such results are identical with those of the original analysis from which the data were obtained.

As an alternative technique for persons placement, an application of the Sandler scoring system will be illustrated. Using the data of Table 25, the totals for the persons in the three clinical groups are recorded—along with the scores of those individuals whose assignments are to be determined. The entries, given in Table 31, are to represent each item twice—once positively scored, and again with reversed polarity.

TABLE 31. Score Matrix C (Using Delegate Scores)

Item	Factor I	Factor II	Factor III	Person 9	Person 10	Person 11	Item	Factor I	Factor II	Factor III	Person 9	Person 10	Person 11
3	1	0	0	1	0	0	71	0	2	0	0	1	0
3'	1	3	3	0	1	1	71'	2	1	3	1	0	1
4	2	0	0	1	1	0	125	0	2	0	0	1	1
4'	0	3	3	0	0	1	125'	2	1	3	1	0	0
11	2	0	1	1	0	0	143	0	0	2	0	0	1
11'	0	3	2	0	1	1	143'	2	3	1	1	1	0
18	0	1	3	0	0	0	148	0	3	1	0	1	0
18'	2	2	0	1	1	1	148'	2	0	2	1	0	1
26	2	1	0	1	0	0	150	0	1	3	0	0	0
26'	0	2	3	0	1	1	150'	2	2	0	1	1	1
35	1	3	0	0	1	0	157	0	3	1	0	1	0
35'	1	0	3	1	0	1	157'	2	0	2	1	0	1
40	0	3	1	0	1	0	168	2	0	0	1	0	0
40'	2	0	2	1	0	1	168'	0	3	3	0	1	1
46	2	0	0	0	0	0	224	0	0	2	0	1	1
46'	0	3	3	1	1	1	224'	2	3	1	1	0	0
53	2	0	0	1	1	0	301	2	2	0	1	0	0
53'	0	3	3	0	0	1	301'	0	1	3	0	1	1
59	0	0	2	0	0	1	336	2	0	0	1	0	0
59'	2	3	1	1	1	0	336'	0	3	3	0	1	1

The correlations between the scores of the three persons and the delegate scores for the three factors, based on the use of the double-scoring technique, will yield correlational values which can be used in the placement of persons. Such values are presented in Table 32.

TABLE 32. Correlation Coefficients. Person and Delegate Scores

Person	Factor I	Factor II	Factor III
9	0.95	−0.47	−0.22
10	−0.21	0.43	−0.06
11	−0.32	0.04	0.32

On the basis of correlational values such as those of Table 32, individuals may be placed into their proper classificatory group. The assignment of

6

person 9 to the first factor group, person 10 to the second and person 11 to the third, in accordance with the system, is exactly the same placement as obtained by means of the matrix method.

Evidence of the greater accuracy of such placement techniques can be cited. In a recent validation of the Rorschach test by Karlsson (1971), 21 out of 24 persons were correctly placed, using the more crude assignment techniques originally described in the present paper. A reanalysis of the Karlsson data was carried out by the present writer, in a study as yet unpublished. Using a placement technique based on the Sandler scoring system, 23 out of 24 persons were correctly placed with respect to the clinical categories of normal, depressive and schizophrenic. One person, however, who had been incorrectly placed was schizophrenic, but with appreciably high depressive reactions, a finding consistent with psychiatric evaluation.

A rigorous comparison between the two techniques has not been made. The present writer would speculate, however, that the matrix method could be expected to give more accurate results. The system using delegate scores, on the other hand, is simpler to apply, is generally more convenient, and would appear to result in placement accuracy adequate for most practical problems of validation.

A General Demonstration

It should be emphasized that the use of the methodology given here need not be restricted to the Rorschach test, but can be applied to clinical measures in general.

Its use in such a manner has been recently demonstrated in a validity study using several clinical tests which included the Meta Contrast Technique and the Colour–Word Test developed by Professor Gudmund J. W. Smith of Lund University, Sweden (Kragh and Smith 1970). Two groups of persons, normals and schizophrenics, were used in the analysis group. The schizophrenics, from the psychiatric clinic of Saint Lars Hospital, Sweden, were newly admitted patients and had been tested early to avoid the effect of medication in the testing results. The normal control group was carefully matched with respect to age, sex and education.

A Q factor analysis (Nilsson 1971) resulted in perfect discrimination between the two groups. The general category of schizophrenia was found to be factorially heterogeneous, four factors being found to describe the subclasses. A follow-up study with 20 additional persons resulted in a placement validity of 100% accuracy.

Some Final Comments

The present paper has reported several validity studies on the Rorschach test in which encouraging results had been obtained. Such investigations were originally intended to provide empirical evidence to be used in the development of Q factor theory, as applied in the clinical domain. The validity studies, therefore, would be regarded by this writer as a by-product of the main efforts to achieve the theoretical objectives of the research.

In addition, evidence as to the effectiveness of the procedures which were used in the validation analyses was provided by the studies, recently completed, on the Smith tests.

Such studies, the present writer would submit, are in support of the view that the previous failures to demonstrate the validity of the Rorschach test (and perhaps many other clinical tests as well) can be attributed, not to the clinical measures themselves, but rather to the ineffectiveness of the validation procedures which were used.

References

Anderson, H. H., and Anderson, G. L. (1951), *An Introduction to Projective Techniques*, Englewood Cliffs, New Jersey, Prentice Hall.

Bohm, E. (1957), *Lehrbuch der Rorschach-psychodiagnostic*, Zeite Aufl., Bern, Hans Huber.

Brown, S. R. (1968), 'Bibliography of Q technique and its methodology', *Perceptual Motor Skills*, Monogr. Suppl., 4–126.

Burt, C. (1941), *The Factors of the Mind*, New York, Macmillan.

Cliff, Norman (1962), 'A note on the adjustment of fourfold tables for "curvilinearity" ', *Educational and Psychological Measurement*, **22**, 721–4.

Cohen, Jacob (1969), 'r_c: A profile similarity coefficient invariant over variable relection', *Proceedings, 76th Annual Convention*, American Psychological Association.

Dwyer, P. S. (1937), 'The determination of the factor loadings of a given test from the known factor loadings of other tests', *Psychometrika*, **2**, 173–8.

Eysenck, H. J. (1959), 'The Rorschach test', in *Vth Mental Measurement Year Book*, (Ed. O. K. Buros), New Jersey, Gryphon.

Fröbärj, G., and Holley, J. W. (1968), 'A Q factor analysis of some Rorschach protocols of epileptic and normal persons', Lund Univ. VIII: 6, *Psychological Research Bulletin*, **6**, 1–19.

Harris, C. W. (1953), 'Relations among factors of raw deviation, and double-centered score matrices', *Journal of Experimental Education*, **22**, 53–8.

Holley, J. W. (1964a), 'A note of the relationship between Q and R factors', *Scandinavian Journal of Psychology*, **5**, 143–8.

Holley, J. W. (1964b), 'A reply to some comments of Norman Cliff', *Educational and Psychological Measurement*, **24**, 313–17.

Holley, J. W. (1966a), 'A note of caution in the use of correlation coefficients in factorial studies in the clinical domain', *Scandinavian Journal of Psychology*, **7**, 93–6.

Holley, J. W. (1966b), 'A reply to Philip Levy—in defense of the G index', *Scandinavian Journal of Psychology*, **7**, 244–6.

Holley, J. W. (1967), 'Philip Levy and the G index—a final reply', *Scandinavian Journal of Psychology*, **8**, 250.

Holley, J. W. (1970), 'On the generalization of the Burt reciprocity principle', *Multivariate Behavioral Research*, **5**, 159–75.

Holley, J. W., and Fällström, K. (1965), 'A note on the construction of tests of Q factor isolates', *Scandinavian Journal of Psychology*, **6**, 237–40.

Holley, J. W., and Fröbärj, G. (1967), 'A demonstration study on the validity of the Rorschach test', *International Review of Applied Psychology*, **16**, 30–51.

Holley, J. W., Fröbärj, G., and Ekberg, K. (1965), 'On the validity of the Rorschach test', *Scandinavian Journal of Psychology*, **6**, 7–18.

Holley, J. W., and Guilford, J. P. (1964), 'A note on the G index of agreement', *Educational and Psychological Measurement*, **24**, 749–53.

Holley, J. W., and Guilford, J. P. (1966), 'A note on the double centering of dichotomized matrices', *Scandinavian Journal of Psychology*, **7**, 97–101.

Holley, J. W., and Harris, C. W. (1970), 'The application of the Harris bridge in the generalization of the Burt reciprocity principle—a demonstration study', *Scandinavian Journal of Psychology*, **11**, 255–60.

Holley, J. W., and Lienert, G. A., 'The G index of agreement in multiple ratings', *Educational and Psychological Measurement*, In Press.

Holley, J. W., and Risberg, J. (1971), 'An analytical technique for obtaining differential diagnoses on the basis of clinical data', *Psychological Research Bulletin* XI: 15, Lund University, Sweden, **15**, 1–13.

Holley, J. W., and Risberg, J. (1972), 'On the D estimate of discriminatory effectiveness', *Psychological Research Bulletin* XII: 12, Lund University, Sweden, **12**, 1–6.

Holley, J. W., and Sjöberg, L. (1968), 'Some characteristics of the G index of agreement', *Multivariate Behavioural Research*, **8**, 107–14.

Jonsson, H. (1973), 'The application of multivariate techniques in the study of differences between normal and schizophrenic persons', Academic Thesis, University of Lund, Sweden.

Karlsson, R. (1970), 'A study of the diagnostic power of the Rorschach', Report, Dept. of Psychology, University of Gothenburg, Sweden.

Kragh, U., and Smith, G. J. W. (1970), *Percept-Genetic Analysis*, Lund, Sweden, Gleeruds.

Levy, P. (1966), 'Properties of the Holley–Guilford "G index of agreement" in R and Q factor analysis', *Scandinavian Journal of Psychology*, **7**, 239–43.

Levy, P. (1967), 'A reply to Jasper Holley's defense of the G index', *Scandinavian Journal of Psychology*, **8**, 38.

Nilsson, I. K. (1971), 'A Q factor analysis of some experimentally derived measures of schizophrenia', Academic Thesis, Psychology Department, University of Lund, Sweden.

Quenouille, M. H. (1952), *Associated Measurements*, London, Butterworth.

Rorschach, H. (1957), *Psychodiagnostic Methodik und Ergebnisse eines wahrnehmungsdiagnostichen Experiments* (Deutenlassen von Zufallsformen), 7th Aufl., Bern, Hans Huber.

Sandler, J. (1948), 'A factor analysis of the Rorschach test with adult mental patients', *Proceedings, 12th International Congress of Psychology*.

Sandler, J. (1949), 'The reciprocity principle as an aid to factor analysis', *British Journal of Psychology*, Statistical Section, **2**, 180–7.

Sandler, J. (1952), 'A technique for facilitating the rotation of factor axes, based on the equivalence between persons and tests', *Psychometrika*, **17**, 223–9.

Sandler, J. (1958), 'Some notes on "delegate analysis" in Tacon, S. F. An investigation of some psychosomatic symptoms in adult neurotic patients', Ph.D. Thesis, University of London.

Sjöberg, L., and Holley, J. W. (1968), 'A measure of similarity between individuals, when scoring directions of variables are arbitrary', *Multivariate Behavioral Research*, **7**, 377–84

Sokal, R. R., and Sneath, P. H. (1963), *Principles of Numerical Taxonomy*, San Francisco, Freeman.

Stephenson, W. (1953), *The Study of Behavior: Q Technique and its Methodology*, Chicago, University of Chicago Press.

Thurstone, L. L. (1953), *Multiple Factor Analysis*, Chicago, University of Chicago Press.

Zimmerman, W. (1951), 'A simple method of orthogonal rotation of axes', *Psychometrika*, **16**, 51–5.

Zubin, J. A. (1938), 'A technique for measuring like-mindedness', *Journal of Abnormal and Social Psychology*, **33**, 508–16.

6

EVALUATING THE PERSON

D. Bannister

Bexley Hospital, Dartford

and

M. Bott

Hellingly Hospital, Hailsham

Psychological Measurement as a Political Act

MUCH OF the sterility of traditional measurement procedures in psychology derives from a concretistic attempt by psychologists to mimic what they imagine to be the process of measurement in the natural sciences. Yet physicists have long since recognized that measurement is an expression of the relationship between measurer and measured while psychologists seem to be struggling for some kind of absolute objectivity. They seek an ideal state in which people really will become 'organisms' and not know that they are being measured, not wonder why, not react to the general measurement situation and its implications and not, thereby, disturb the psychologist in his dream that he and they are unaffected by the act of measuring.

Consider the curious business of deception in psychological measurement, the endless search for the naive subject, the conviction that if a person knows what the test is driving at the whole business will collapse in ruins. Psychologists fear that their subjects are in search of social desirability (perhaps a projection of the fact that psychologists seem perpetually in search of social desirability) and therefore embed into their tests 'lie' scales. The essence of constructing and embedding a lie scale is that it should be done in such a way that the subject will not realize that it is being done—the psychologist must deceive the subject so that the subject does not deceive the psychologist. It is reminiscent of the old West—who is going to be quickest on the draw with the duel-winning lie? This tradition of bluff and double bluff is a long-established one. The numerous citations of the Hartshorne and May (1928) studies on honesty in schoolchildren attach little significance to the fact that in order to test whether children were honest, Hartshorne and May set out to trick the children into believing that they could cheat when the testing situation had been rigged by the deceiving Hartshorne and May. Whose honesty was thereby tested?

The psychologist's search for the Holy Grail of reliable measurement often seems to blind him to the fact that every occasion of measurement is accompanied by an implicit contract (honoured or broken) between psychologist and subject, covering such matters as secrecy, mutual understandings and misunderstandings about the purpose of making measurements of this kind on this person at this time, equally mutual agreements or disagreements as to what conclusions might fairly be drawn from the measurement. The titrating chemist or the stargazing astronomer has no contract to concern himself with, but it ought not to need the outbursts of outraged individuals or Governmental committees nor the acute embarrassment of such manifestations as Mensa to remind psychologists that their position in relation to 'objective' measurement is unique and uniquely dangerous.

Nor can psychologists continue to imagine that the dimensions which they construct for their measurement purposes are purely a matter of scientific or technical convenience. They cannot, much longer, ignore the moral, personal and political implications of measuring in terms of such value-saturated constructs as 'intelligence', 'psychopathy', 'creativity', 'authoritarianism', and so forth. The simple experience of saying to a child (Wechsler Intelligence Scale for Children) 'Why is it better to give money to an organized charity than to a street beggar?' ought to remind us that we are marketing attitudes while 'measuring intelligence'.

A cursory glance at the problems of measurement in psychology reveals a whole series of questions which would be inappropriate if asked of the measurement procedures of the natural sciences but which are of threatening relevance to psychologists. Is a reasonable degree of trust between psychologist and 'subject' necessary for effective psychological measurement, and if it is necessary how often does it exist? How many psychologists would be prepared to take the tests they habitually use on others and accept the kind of conclusions customarily drawn as valid for themselves? How far is testing not merely an abstract scientific procedure but an act of social judgment, carried out on behalf of authority? To what degree does the act of testing, followed by the claim that the subject has an unchangeable quantity of 'X', act as a self-fulfilling prophecy, engaging psychologist, subject and social agencies in the task of enforcing the test judgment?

Central amid this plethora of questions which face the measuring psychologist is the issue of who is to make use of the measurement, the psychologist, some social agency *or* the subject. The latter possibility is hardly likely to exist for the chemist or physicist, but it could reasonably be argued that it may be the key possibility, in many cases, for the psychologist. In psychotherapy it is often the client who, in collaboration with the psychologist, studies the results of testing in order to see what light may be cast upon his problems. Testing becomes, in effect, a format in terms of which the client may lay out his own ideas and reactions so that he can understand and develop them. The test is then not simply a measuring procedure but also a teaching device. If we extend this idea, that measurement is potentially part of the insight of the measured, into other areas of professional activity, we are bound to question many current procedures.

These, and many other problems of measurement, arise from the central situation in which the psychologist finds himself—a situation unique to psychology and not encountered in the natural sciences. The psychologist is a theorizing measurer who is attempting to assess other theorizing measurers, whom he has chosen to call 'subjects'. The challenge of this reflexive situation (Oliver and Landfield 1963) is evaded in a variety of postures. In some instances, measurement has been made so trivial (reaction time games, nonsense syllable learning, platitudinous questionnaires that question nothing) that the whole business is a matter of no concern to the subject, to his society or to anyone except psychologists who are professionally engaged in exchanging these trivia via the experimental literature. Alternatively, the person, *as a person*, is not measured at all, but some physiological function which is alleged to have psychological implications is taken as focus. Thereby, the act of measurement is removed from the psychological domain and has no *meaning* for the subject. This, for many psychologists, is highly desirable, since it is the ultimate in going behind the subject's back—rendering him truly an object. An equally prevalent practice is that of avoiding entanglement with the problem of measuring the person by submerging his individual performance in aggregate data and then letting him reappear only in comparison with the aggregate. Thus, Bakan (1954) and Beloff and Becker (1967) have shown how frequently aggregate scores fail entirely to represent, even approximately, *any* of the individuals whose data contributed to the aggregate, but the practice flourishes.

It is still possible, for example, to find solemn arguments in the literature about what 'percentage' of 'intelligence' or 'extraversion' or 'neuroticism' is to be attributed to heredity and environment, respectively. The reification of test concepts has here reached a point where it is difficult to imagine what on earth the term 'percentage' can possibly mean. If it is avowed that 75% of neuroticism is genotypical, this means what—75% of the person's 'neurotic' acts (as opposed to his 'normal' acts) are predictable from his ancestry? It is three to one that he will do what his parents did rather than what we tell him to? 25% of people are mavericks and the rest follow their ancestry? If we make all our predictions about 'neurotic' behaviour on the basis of a man's forebears, we should be right three times out of every four? Any single neurotic act would be only three-quarters as neurotic if it were not for environmental influences? The logical jump from test behaviour to statements about genetic or environmental 'percentages' is an intellectual suicide leap.

Psychological Measurement as a Process

An additional and central feature of psychological measurement which seems strangely ignored is the fact that it is essentially a process and not an instantaneous act; this at two levels. It is a process in that while measurement is taking place the measured person is evolving a view of the situation and the meaning of what he is doing, so that his end position is quite likely to be substantially different from his initial posture. Equally, the development of measurements is itself a cyclic process. No argument in psychology seems, on reflection, to be more foolish than the battle which raged about the relative merits of clinical *versus* statistical prediction. In this argument, initiated by Meehl (1954), one group contended that 'objective measurement' of the kind where the counting system is basically mechanical, interjudge agreement is absolute and testing procedures are formal and rigid is superior to clinical measurement, where the nous, guesswork, experience and imagination of the clinician are primary tools. Apart from the fact that the experimental evidence was largely bound to favour the actuarial school, because the experimental criteria were themselves actuarial (Holt 1970), the whole argument revolves on treating as two separate and distinct approaches what should be merely stages in a single endeavour. Today's standardized tests (good, bad or indifferent) are formal versions of yesterday's clinical insights. If we stop trying to perceive our fellow men in broad clinical and imaginative terms, then we are committing ourselves eternally to our present level of actuarial achievement. This whole sad dichotomy is an example of the habit of making permanent intellectual residences out of what should be parts of an endless cyclic process. Other samples of this kind of sterile polarizing (the hard *versus* soft science argument and its kissing cousin the arts *versus* science argument) are discussed in Bannister (1970).

Psychological Measurement as a Paradox

The central paradox of psychological measurement hinges on the fact that not only does the measurer affect the measured, but the measurer and the measured are one and the same, being both men. Specifically, they are the same in relation to what is being measured. Psychological measurement is a business of mind understanding mind, and even if we try to evade the issue by saying that we are measuring a man's 'behaviour' we are still inevitably faced by the question of how do we find a common language in which to discuss our behaviour of measuring his behaviour. The limitations imposed by too simple-minded a view of objectivity are well specified in Mair (1970), who commented as follows.

'Psychologists, in recognising their personal limits and predilections as people, have generally sought to overcome these by *excluding* themselves as thoroughly as possible from the contexts within which they act as scientists. Thus we have often tried to use, or acknowledge, as little of ourselves as possible in our professional roles. But, as noted already, our subjects still persist in viewing psychologists, even when they act as experimenters, as human beings like themselves. If we are inevitably to be seen as this, why not make the best rather than the worst of it? Why not intentionally begin to use *all* our capacities of feeling, thought and action to aid us in creating more sensitive means to extend our understanding of ourselves and others (who are the subject matter of psychology)? It was William James who said somewhere: "It takes the whole of us to spell the meaning out completely". This being so we can convert our personal preferences in thought and action into our greatest scientific assets rather than our shameful secrets. What we discover about ourselves can contribute to our own growth and to the possible development of others, just as our discoveries about others may aid them and extend the range of possibilities we personally can employ. In all this remembering that when we study others the conclusions we reach are about *persons in relation* (Macmurray 1961) and not specifically about us or them.'

The kind of objections raised here to standard practices in the field of psychological measurement are sometimes dismissed as 'philosophical', 'political' or even 'literary'. That the practices condemned have *empirical* effects of the most disturbing kind is made manifest by the work of Rosenthal (1967 *et seq.*) on experimenter bias, by the work of Milgram (1965) on the dangerously 'liberating' quality of experimenter status, by the work of Orne (1962) on the 'demand characteristics' of the experimental situation, and many others. However, the sheer weight of psychologists' investment in testing is such that no clear professional response to such work is yet evident.

Reliability and Validity

While the twin concepts of 'reliability' and 'validity' were useful guidelines for pioneer test constructors, they seem of later years to have rigidified—it is as if we were suffering from what Kelly called the dread disease of hardening of the categories. The repeated stress on the need for reliability in psychological measures is a sign of the only half-realized but persistent dominance of trait psychology and the belief that what we must seek and find are fixed characteristics of an object rather than an understanding of process. Had psychologists been in charge of developing the anemometer, it is difficult to believe that we should yet have had an instrument for measuring changes in wind force. The most obvious feature of persons is that they change, and grievous though this may be to the champions of reliable psychological measurement, it must be recognized that we must seek to understand change and to measure our degree of understanding by the degree to which we can predict it. We do not need to regard change in test scores as indicating 'error variance'. If we can anticipate such change and relate it to process, then we might rejoice at finding tests which reflect such change rather than pursue such *chimera* as the constant IQ.

Equally, if we substitute for validity the notion of usefulness, or at least make usefulness the central feature of validity, we shall be less concerned with the correlation between a test and some relatively arbitrary criterion and more concerned with the values which users of a test find in it. This might bring to an end such curious practices as declaring a test valid because it has some degree of correlation, small but significant, with, say, diagnostic judgments by psychiatrists, when we know such psychiatric diagnostic judgments to be themselves of little use (see Bannister, Salmon and Leiberman 1964).

Individually Oriented Measures

An early formal attempt to measure aspects of the individual person treated as someone who imposes his own peculiar meanings on his life and his world was the development of the projective test. Yet, though it was inspired by a recognition of the meaningfulness of personal viewpoints, the broad technique can be argued to be deficient in three respects. Firstly, it was assumed that projective test material would have to be standard, and thus was born the fixed set of ink-blots for the Rorschach and the standard pictures of the Thematic Apperception Test. Undoubtedly, any fixed material of this kind must be, to a greater or lesser degree, inappropriate as from one person to another, but the traditional value placed on the identical fixed stimulus saddled the projective tester with materials which must, for many subjects, come near to being wellnigh meaningless. It will be noted later in relation to the development of grid method that this assumption is both unnecessary and burdensome. Kelly (1955) specifically comments: 'It might be easier to predict what a subject would do on a Rorschach test, for example, from a knowledge of how he deals with people in his world, than it would be to predict what he would do with the people in his world from a knowledge of how he deals with ink blots'. Secondly, the designers of projective tests followed the hallowed psychological tradition of maintaining a decent trade union differential in the form of a substantial psychological distance between themselves and their subjects. Tests are to be interpreted in a manner and language which is meaningful only to the psychologist and not to the 'subject'. Indeed, it could be that the tremendous fascination of the Rorschach resides in its 'mystery', which underlines both the expertise of the psychologist and the simple-mindedness of the subject. He (poor subject) cannot possibly see what he is revealing by undertaking the alien task of interpreting ink-blots. Thirdly, projective tests are only partially articulated into general psychological theories. They do not effectively escape the limitation common to most tests of being operational definitions inadequately linked to any comprehensive theoretical framework.

An interesting example of the difficulties that psychologists experience in trying to recognize the extent and significance of change is illustrated in the personal questionnaire designed by Shapiro (1961). Here, standard questionnaire procedure is promisingly redesigned for use with a single individual. An individual patient is asked to supply the dimensions in terms of which he sees his complaints, for example, 'I feel nervous', 'I worry about what people think of me', and so forth. Each form of complaint is then scaled so that at set time intervals the patient can record the intensity of his feelings about that area in a form which quantifies fluctuation along a time line without any need for reference to group norms. On the one hand, we have a genuine attempt to work within terms elicited from the patient, and the comparisons made over time are essentially intra-individual. On the other hand, the patient is forced to render a possibly complex problem into the form of simple 'complaints', and the possibility that the patient might wish to change the very terms in which he construes his complaint is not catered for by the test. Wright (1970), using grid technique, well illustrates the complexity of the apparently simple complaint.

On this question of the terms in which subjects are to express themselves within the frame of psychological measurement, the usual assumption is that such terms will have to be standard and generalized, nomothetic rather than idiographic. Nowhere is this assumption more massively elaborated than in the semantic differential developed by Osgood, Suci and Tannenbaum (1957). The relationship between the semantic differential and grid method in both theoretical and operational terms is discussed at length in Bannister and Mair (1968), but the central difference that concerns us here is the question of whether dimensions have to be public and standard in order for measurement to take place. In developing the semantic differential, Osgood used factor analytic techniques to establish what he came to view as three major orthogonal dimensions of meaning designated by the terms 'evaluation', 'potency' and 'activity'. Thus, though individuals can vary in the meaning they attach to different words within this framework, it is assumed in the test that, for all subjects, these broad dimensions are meaningful, it is assumed that they cover a major part of the variance in the subject's personal meaning, and it is assumed that the three dimensions are orthogonal to each other for each individual. All these assumptions are, of course, questionable and experiments using grid method (Fransella 1968) raise grave doubts about them.

Grid Method

Grid method *is* a method and not a test. This statement has been repeated time and again since the original presentation of the technique (Kelly 1955), yet the tradition of 'the test' in psychology seems so strong that the implications of calling the grid 'a method' are by no means accepted. If they had been accepted, then repertory grid technique would have been welcomed as, say, the equivalent of a new series of statistical forms of analysis, or as the equivalent of a new interviewing technique, or as the equivalent of a method of exploring postures and interrelationships such as sociodrama. Instead, it was greeted as yet another test. It seems worthwhile, therefore, to specify the primary implications of referring to it as *a method*. Grids are sorting procedures wherein we focus on the relationship *between sorts*. Consider the range of possibilities which attend a simple exemplary form of grid. Suppose we elicit from a person the names of twenty people known personally to him and then repeatedly group these people in threes and ask him to tell us some important way in which two of them are alike and thereby different from the third. Thereby we might obtain from him a series of constructs ('*worrier–relaxed, likes me–doesn't like me, old–young*) in the traditional way. We might then ask him to categorize each individual as belonging to one pole or the other of these constructs and enter his judgments in the form of a matrix as shown in Table 1.

TABLE 1

Constructs	Elements 1 2 3 4 5 6 7 8 9 10 11 12 13 14 15 16 17 18 19 20
1. Worrier–relaxed	X X X X X X X X X X X
2. Likes me–doesn't like me	X X X X X X X X X X X
3. Old–young	X X X X X X X X X X

We might then derive a simple measure of relationship between sorts (commonly called a matching score) by looking at the degree of correspondence of cross and blank for each pair of rows (in each row the subject has presented us with an operational definition in terms of his acquaintances of that construct, just as in each column he has given us a personality profile of the acquaintance). Thus, the relationship between construct 1 and 2 is expressed as a matching of 6 out of 20 and, if we assume that chance expectancy

TABLE 2

Matching scores	
1–2	6 out of 20 $= -4$
1–3	16 out of 20 $= +6$
2–3	7 out of 20 $= -3$

would be a matching of 10 out of 20, we can represent this by a value of -4, whereas the matching between constructs 1 and 3 on the same basis would be $+6$, and so forth. In this way we can build up a complete matrix of the inter-relationships between all pairs of constructs used in the grid (Table 2).

Now consider the number of variations possible within the terms of this relatively simple operation.

(1) The elements (objects sorted) have here been elicited from the subject but could have been supplied to him. For that matter, they could have been anything at all (films, chess openings, religious beliefs, types of rose, proverbs, poems, coital positions, psychological theories, members of family only, computer programs, and so forth), depending upon the area of construing that we wish to explore.

(2) Consider the constructs: these have been elicited from the subject by asking him to make distinctions within triads of people–elements. They could have been elicited from him on a general interview basis by getting him to talk about people and noting the kind of constructions he used. They could have been elicited from him by giving him a projective test such as the TAT and noticing the kind of constructions which were utilized in the stories he told. The verbal labels of the constructs could have been supplied to him. (*Note. It is only the verbal labels of the constructs that can be supplied, and a construct is not a verbal label. A construct is the discrimination made by a person among his elements.*) These verbal labels could have been supplied on all sorts of bases—that they are commonly used, that we have a particular interest in certain of them because they have to do with, say, particular kinds of interpersonal relationships, or with 'self', and so forth. They could have been supplied on the basis of selecting a particular group of verbal labels be-cause it is alleged that they constitute a usable language and we wish to see if the matching scores are stable enough over time, similar enough across individuals and separate enough from other terms to function as a workable specialist language as in Agnew and Bannister (1973).

(3) In the example given, the format was such that the person was asked to dichotomize his elements on to the poles of the constructs in a yea/nay fashion. He could have been asked to rank order his elements, in which case the equiva-lents of the matching score between constructs would have been Spearman rhos between rankings. He could have been asked to rate the elements on some sort of scale, in which case a Pearson product-moment correlation could have been run between the lines of pairs of ratings so as to yield, once again, a matrix of interrelationships between constructs.

(4) Ways of analysing the matrix of construct interrelationships or other grid data are numerous, and doubtless many are as yet uninvented. The initial matrix of relationships between constructs can be factor analysed to give a picture of the 'clusters' of the constructs in an attempt to give some sort of summary view of the 'personality theory' behind the judgments (Slater

1964). Structural analyses can be devised to show how far a person's world is compartmentalized (Makhlouf-Norris, Jones and Norris 1970) or which issues dominate the construct system (Thomas 1972). The analysis may be limited to looking at the content of the grid in terms of relationships between specific constructs which are themselves a focus of interest (Fransella and Adams 1966). The person's degree of insight into his own constructional system could be measured by asking him to predict his own grid (Bannister 1962). On the same basis, the degree of agreement between an individual's grid and some public norms for the set of construct relationships might be analysed (Bannister, Fransella and Agnew 1971). Some features such as 'lopsidedness' (the degree to which elements are allotted to one pole of the construct more than the other) might be under investigation (Radley 1973). The degree to which one person can recognize and understand the construct of another might be a focus of interest (Adams-Webber 1969, Smail 1972). Direct judgment of John by Jane may not be the focus; it could be Jane's view of John in his relation to Jack (Ryle and Lunghi 1970).

(5) Grids need not take the form of simple element on construct allotment. The Implication Grid (Hinkle 1965) allows the subject directly to index the relationship between constructs, and the same writer's Resistance to Change Grid is a method of analysing a person's differential willingness to change along the construct dimensions which have been elicited from him. Equally, in his development of 'laddering' technique, Hinkle has devised what is still essentially a grid, but here the subject is repeatedly asked, 'Why do you prefer to be at one end of this construct rather than at the other?' (e.g. *work for a firm* rather than *be your own boss*). The person's answer supplies a more superordinate construct (e.g. *secure* rather than *always taking risks*), which in turn can be queried to elicit a yet more superordinate theme.

Kelly (1955) outlined a dependency grid in which the constructs are situations in which a person might want help (at times of emotional crisis, at times of financial crisis, and so forth) and where the elements along the top of the grid are people. The intersects are marked to show whether the subject would turn to that person in such a crisis or not. From such an array an analysis of the distribution of a person's dependencies (are all eggs in one person's basket?) can be worked out. The dependency grid could clearly be inverted to formalize information about how the person sees others as depending on him.

Since grids are a broad methodological approach, attempts to pre-empt them into specific categories are inappropriate. Grids are not intrinsically 'cognitive tests' nor 'measures of attitudes' nor 'measures of meaning'. Equally, we could abandon the curious notion that tests are intrinsically nomothetic or idiographic and accept that it is we who construe test data in either an idiographic or a nomothetic manner. It is quite possible to analyse the grid of one person in idiographic terms, particularly since grid format permits measures of statistical significance to be made on data from a single case. Equally a grid format can be standardized and normative data collected and that particular form can be used thenceforth in a highly nomothetic manner (e.g. the Grid Test of Thought Disorder, Bannister and Fransella 1966).

Personal Construct Theory and Grid Method

A second oft-reiterated statement about grid method is that it is derived from personal construct theory and perhaps best makes sense when viewed in terms of its parent framework. Again, the purely empirical lusts of psychologists have proliferated uses of the grid as some kind of general measure of 'attitudes' or 'concepts' entirely divorced from personal construct theory.

A brief look at the formal corollaries of construct theory in relation to grid method indicates the ways in which each defines the other.

Construction corollary: A person anticipates events by construing their replications. The placing of elements in terms of constructs in a grid is a formalization of this construing of replicative features of the person's world—the constructs are the *replicated features*.

Individuality corollary: Persons differ from each other in their construction of events. Grids illustrate this notion of individual differences at two levels. Firstly, individuals differ in how they construe the same elements and secondly, the implications of their *constructs* (relationships between constructs) differ.

Organization corollary: Each person characteristically evolves, for his convenience in anticipating events, a construction system embracing ordinal relationships between constructs. Techniques such as laddering and the derivation of clusters by factor analytic procedures are operational definitions of the ordinal relationships between constructs to which this corollary refers.

Range corollary: A construct is convenient for the anticipation of a finite range of events only. This generates a basic rule of grid constructions, which is that there is little point in asking a subject to construe an element in terms of a construct which does not include the element in its range of convenience. For a subject for whom only young people may be thought of as *keen on sex* or *afraid of sex* there is little point in asking him to decide whether his grandfather is *keen on sex* or *afraid of sex*. It can be argued that the relationships between any groups of constructs for a single person can only be stated for a particular context. If the context is changed (consider *honesty* in politics, *honesty* in sex, *honesty* in science), then the ramifications of constructs change even though the themes are related enough to merit a single name. Grids may well need to be developed as 'contextual interviewing methods', with the psychologist seeking to understand the reservations, emphases and ambiguities that subjects experience in completing the grid if he is to understand the meaning of grid-analysed data.

Sociality corollary: To the extent that one person construes the construction processes of another, he may play a role in a social process involving the other person. This is grid method's *raison d'être* and specifies that the psychologist's task is to see how the subject (the non-professional psychologist) makes sense of his life and world in his own terms rather than imagine an object/person who moves predictably in the psychologist's terms.

The technical possibilities and problems of grids have been dealt with extensively in Bannister and Mair (1968) and the discussion has been extended in later writings (Landfield 1971, Fransella 1972). However, professional use of grids to date seems not fully to have explored the implications of the idea that the grid is a method, a strategy, a language system, a variable format for data, a set of principles for formalizing information and judgments—it is anything but a test. Equally, professional discussion of grid method has failed, as yet, adequately to explore the relationship between grid and construct theory and the problems of using grid formats within studies utilizing other theoretical frameworks.

Until these wider problems are confronted, grid methods may well contribute too generously to the testing ironmongery with which the psychological scene is cluttered.

Grid Design and Use

To illustrate the design problems and uses of grid method, examples will be drawn entirely from psychotherapy cases undertaken by the writers. This is done, in part, to stress that measurement must have a meaningful context. The therapist who 'measures' his client has an immediate use for, and test of the value of, his assessment procedures. Psychologists whose assessments have been limited to a research context or to providing information for third parties (psychiatrists, courts, and so forth) may not appreciate how vivid and relevant assessment becomes when it is linked to work directly undertaken with another person.

An unsuccessful joint therapeutic venture by the two authors with a married couple illustrates a number of possibilities and difficulties in grid method. The couple had been married for some years but had never had sexual intercourse and, apart from a brief and unhappy encounter at the beginning of the marriage, had no kind of sexual relationship. The wife was a virgin but had experienced mild and acceptable love play with two boy friends before marriage—her husband had no kind of sexual experience other than masturbation. For some years after marriage the non-existent sexual aspect of the partnership was never discussed, but eventually the wife explained her unhappy situation to her doctor and she and her husband agreed to try to work through their problem with the authors of this paper.

As part of the general interviewing exploration of the situation, both husband and wife were given identical grids with supplied construct labels (particularly labels dealing with constructs to do with sex, i.e. *keen on sex, sexually attractive, afraid of sex*) and elicited constructs which were a mixture of those derived from the two partners. Thus the grid included the constructs already mentioned, plus *selfish, good, moody, intelligent, artistic, like I am, sensitive, moral, like I would like to be* and either *like my wife* or *like my husband*. The elements for all the grids used with this couple were 10 photographs of people unknown to the subjects, which they were asked to rank order on the constructs.

The couple were also asked to complete a 'duo' grid utilizing the constructs from the individual grid. In this duo grid the couple completed one grid together. It must be stressed here that this was not a group test in the conventional sense, i.e. separate tests completed at the same time. The husband and wife were faced with the same photographs and the same constructs, and were asked to argue out each decision between them so that the final rank ordering consisted of their agreed placings. The specific purpose of the duo grid was to try to see whose construct system was, in this rather mechanical sense, 'dominant', and to see how the issue of dominance related to the level of sexual activity between the couple. The relationship between the duo grid and the individual grids of the married couple was measured by rank ordering the matrices of intercorrelation between constructs (from highest positive through zero to highest negative) and calculating the rho between the matrices. On this latter point, it is interesting to note that the correlation between the duo grid and the individual grids of each partner and the relationship of this in turn to level of sexual activity was (for the four grids given over the period of therapy) as follows: the initial grid (given when sexual activity was non-existent), husband +0.59, wife +0.09; second grid (given when sexual activity had reached a fairly high level), husband +0.19, wife +0.64; third grid (given when sexual activity seemed to be declining again), husband +0.33, wife +0.48, and the final grid (given when sexual activity had almost entirely ceased again), husband +0.83, wife +0.56.

Construct relationships on the two initial grids of husband and wife were examined to check their respective views of 'sex'. Two marked features of the husband's grid were, firstly, that *keen on sex* had a high negative correlation with *artistic*, and the latter construct had a high positive relationship with *like I'd like to be*. Speculatively, this might indicate that sexual relationships were aesthetically unacceptable to this essentially 'aesthetic' man. Secondly, *sexually attractive* was significantly and negatively correlated with *keen on sex*. One possible explanation here would be that any woman who indicated to him that she was keen on sex would represent a threat to him and thereby immediately lose her sexual attraction—he was in practice a mild flirt with essentially non-responding women. In general, the construing system seemed broadly 'anti-sex', except that *being afraid of sex* was seen as *selfish* (though this may have been more how he saw it in the context of his relationship with his wife than his general view) and there was some indication of a desire to be *sexually attractive*.

The initial approach based on this grid picture was to try to utilize the husband's interest in literature and history to get him to explore the idea that sex was 'aesthetic' in the sense that it was a major inspiration in art and literature, and also to underline the notion of being *afraid of sex* as *selfish*.

The wife's grid was pro sex except for a tendency to see *moral* as negatively related to *sexually attractive* and, more importantly, sexual constructs were only weakly related to each other and to other constructions. This (unsurprisingly) indicated relatively undeveloped construing in this area.

Our initial approach was to try to articulate and extend her construing of sex, while exploring with her the possibility that *sexually attractive* was at least a neutral, if not a morally laudable, characteristic.

By the time the second grid was completed some eight months after the beginning of therapy, progress seemed to have been made. The couple were indulging in a substantial amount of sexual play, and although this stopped short of intercourse, their mood could fairly be described as one of optimistic interest. In grid terms, the husband was certainly no longer seeing *keen on sex* as *anti-artistic*. He was seeing it as both an ideal to be aimed at and as a mildly laudable characteristic. More ominously (though the therapist did not clearly note this at the time), he had ceased to see being *afraid of sex* as at all *selfish* and, in general, correlations between sex constructs were tending to diminish, making the whole area perhaps more acceptable but also somewhat less important.

The wife's second grid showed a change of view of her husband, since she apparently saw him as much more *keen on sex*, and additionally *sexually attractive* now correlated positively with *moral* and with *sensitive* and had become much more part of her *ideal self* picture. She also saw herself as much more *sexually attractive* and *keen on sex*.

In this general mood of optimism, the therapists moved on to a much more behaviour therapy style of approach on the assumption that the construing problems were largely solved and that, given more frequent and energetic 'practice', the couple would achieve intercourse. Programmes of sexual exercises were drawn up and faithfully followed by the couple and the emphasis was put much more on adventurous behaviour and much less on discussion of basic outlook. However, at the end of another eight months, it seemed clear that the level of sexual involvement was declining and consummation, though devoutly to be wished, was somewhat farther away. A third set of grids was administered and these revealed that, for the husband, *sexual attractiveness* was now negatively related to *good* and *intelligent* and was again significantly and negatively related to *moral*. *Afraid of sex* was again positively related to *artistic* and he no longer saw himself as *keen on sex*. Perhaps most significant, the relationship between *like I'd like to be* and *like my wife* had changed over the three grids from 0.02 to 0.86 to 0.41. The wife's grid continued, in a milder form, the generally favourable picture of sex manifested in the second grid, but ominously she now saw herself and her husband as less *sexually attractive.*

Therapy was continued for a further four months (wavering uncertainly between attempts to desensitize sexual anxieties by behavioural methods and trying to alter viewpoints) and further grids were administered. The husband's grid was very similar to his previous one, with *like I am* and *keen on sex* being negatively related and with no relationship existing between *like I'd like to be* and *keen on sex.*

In the wife's grid a generally favourable view of sex was still indicated but the level of correlation had now sunk to a new low, and this may be taken as indicating a spreading vagueness and apathy around the whole area of sex. Eventually, with the agreement of the couple, therapy was discontinued with the problem unsolved.

With the wisdom of hindsight it is possible to see a number of inadequacies in the therapeutic attack here briefly described. For example, no attempt was made (in spite of the interesting development of the duo grid) to get each partner to predict the other's grids, so as to investigate their picture of each other and to see how this related to their situation. If we see sex as a role relationship and note Kelly's dictum that to the extent that one person construes the construction processes of another he can play a role in a social process involving the other person, then this seems a glaring oversight in the therapists' grid exploration of the partnership.

Equally, the grids seem in retrospect to have been overfocused, so that other constructions to do with sex stemming from more remote areas of construing were missed initially and no attempt was made to extend the grids on retesting. For example, it became fairly obvious towards the end of therapy that one of the husband's major problems hinged on the issue of 'control'. In his working life, on holiday and in his domestic life he seemed to require an obsessional degree of control, planning and logical clarity, if he was to feel secure. Thus, any display of emotion (the couple had never quarrelled) was strenuously avoided, and it seems likely that sexual intercourse represented for him a prime risk of losing control and was thereby immensely threatening. This aspect of his construing system was never properly explored in the grids, since the constructs which would have brought it to light had not been elicited initially and the grids were unextended.

It seems clear on re-examination that the changeover from more generally exploratory kinds of therapy to a behaviour therapy focus was premature. It may have arrested the process of change rather than facilitated it. The obvious moral seems to be that, of themselves, grids will not ensure good therapy unless they are adequately designed and sensitively interpreted *in relation to* an understanding generated by the ongoing experience of therapy.

'The Problem'

If a test is designed to measure, say, 'neuroticism', then its use in a particular instance presupposes not only that the test is a valid measure of 'neuroticism' but that 'neuroticism' is relevant to the problem which inspired the act of testing. Often this is a questionable supposition. Granted, a strategy such as the personal questionnaire (Shapiro 1961) does not beg the question of relevance to the subject—it is focused directly on to the problem ('illness', 'symptom') in the subject's own terms. However, such a procedure does not include any method of discovering if there are alternative terms in which both subject and measurer might prefer to reframe the problem. The case now to be discussed illustrates the capacity of grid method to act as a way of posing the question 'What is the problem?' as well as a measure of its 'severity'.

P was a railway worker who had, in psychiatric terms, 'led a normal life' until he was involved in a catastrophic shunting accident in which he saw two of his mates killed and was himself injured and as a result had his left foot amputated. This was followed by months in hospital, a period of work, a reamputation below the knee and a long compensation dispute. For some three years he worked very irregularly, suffered from nightmares and pervasive anxieties, disturbed sleep, feelings of depression, violent outbursts of aggression and very severe persistent headaches. Eventually he was admitted for psychiatric treatment and failed to respond to drug therapy. When he was taken on for psychotherapy he centred his complaint on the fact that he was a cripple—under abreaction he described himself as a cripple and was very angry about the loss of his limb, feeling that he was no longer able to do manual work and earn his living. In the initial stages of psychotherapy both patient and therapist were focusing their attention upon the accident and the consequent physical disablement. The patient's general malaise was attributed to this and a solution to his problem was seen largely in terms of how the patient was to adapt to life and work as a partially disabled man. At this point, he completed a grid in which the elements were 10 significant figures in his life and the constructs were a mixture of supplied verbal labels and elicited constructs. Elements and constructs are listed in Table 3.

It was decided to use the grid, in part, as a measure of the therapist's understanding of the patient's construct system. The therapist was asked to predict the matrix of interrelationships between the constructs shown in Table 3, and for each pair of constructs he predicted either that they would be unrelated (correlation between $+0.3$ and -0.3) or positively related (correlation above $+0.3$) or negatively related (correlation below -0.3). His predictions were compared with the grid matrix of intercorrelations between constructs, and the number of matrix entries he had correctly predicted was very much above chance level. However, the therapist was wrong in a number of his predictions, and these wrong guesses were not scattered randomly across the matrix but tended to hinge on a particular interpretation of the patient's construct system—an interpretation which seemed to be shared by the patient. The therapist had assumed that the patient viewed his life prior to the accident as being more or less satisfactory, and saw his problems as having derived from the accident. Therefore, the therapist predicted positive relationships between such constructs as *achieved something, have confidence in themselves, understanding people* and the construct *like I used to be*. He predicted a negative relationship between these constructs and *like I am*. In line with this view, he predicted a positive relationship between *like I'd like to be* and *like I used to be*, since the patient was presenting his problem in terms of trying to achieve some former state of grace. From this derived most of the errors of prediction, since the grid indicated that the patient's earlier life had contained many problems about confidence and relationship with people and extreme feelings of aggression which in therapy he was presenting as the consequences of the accident.

TABLE 3. P's Grid

Elements	Constructs designated as either elicited (E) or supplied (S)
A—best friend	Admired v. not admired (E)
B—father	Most like me (S)
C—liked boss	Hot-tempered v. cool, calm and collected (E)
D—mother	Good worker v. bad worker (S)
E—disliked boss	Like I would like to be (S)
F—wife	Understanding people—aggressive (E)
G—sorry for	Good mixer socially v. good loser (S)
H—brother	Handicapped v. healthy outlook (E)
I —ex-friend	Like I used to be (S)
J —sister	Likes a laugh v. takes offence (E)
	Clever v. stupid (S)
	Achieve something v. not achieving anything (E)
	Secure v. uncertainty of having cash (E)
	Attractive to the opposite sex v. not (S)
	Have confidence in themselves (S)
	Have confidence in other people (S)
	Manual v. clerical worker (E)

The implications of the grid were conveyed to the patient, and on reflection P was prepared to admit that he had always felt poorly educated and therefore shy, had often used alcohol in quantity in an attempt to give himself confidence. He acknowledged that he always had great difficulty in understanding people and that this contributed to his lack of confidence in meeting them. When meeting people his mind was constantly occupied with the question of what the other person was thinking about him.

Over the succeeding months the therapy discussions and the patient's exploratory behaviour outside therapy sessions were focused on this issue of relating to other people. When he undertook an unpaid job in a friend's shoeshop, this was not simply 'work practice' in the normal rehabilitation sense. The situation was seen as one in which he might improve his social skills and his ability to relate to other people initially in a formal situation. A second grid confirmed that he was, in interpersonal terms, moving towards *like I'd like to be*, and not only did his relationships with other people and his feelings of confidence about them improve but his aggressive outbursts, disturbed sleep, nightmares and persistent headache disappeared. At the point at which therapy was concluded, he was not simply 'coping' with his life in spite of his disablement, but was reshaping his relationships with his family and with other people in terms of ideals which were clearly more elaborate than his pre-accident demands on life.

Self-Characterization

Although very different in format from grid method, the technique of self-characterization (Kelly 1955) is very much akin to it in enabling a person to show how he sees his situation *in his own terms*. The procedure is simple, being a derivative of Kelly's 'first principle'—if you don't know what is wrong with the patient ask him, he *may* tell you. In order to allow the person to stand back a little from himself in writing the characterization, he is invited to write it in the third person. Thus, Harry Brown is told, 'I want you to write a character sketch of Harry Brown, just as if he were the principal character in the play. Write it as it might be written by a friend who knew him *very intimately* and *very sympathetically*, perhaps better than anyone ever really could know him. Be sure to write it in the third person. For example, start off by saying "Harry Brown is".'

Methods of analysing self-characterizations are discussed in some detail in Kelly (1955, p. 315) and briefly illustrated in Bannister and Fransella (1971). The aim is not to quantify but rather to consider what the message means *as a message* and to identify the alternatives and issues it raises.

For example, below is a self-characterization supplied by a person being given psychotherapy on an outpatient basis.

'G.M. is a person of noble character. He has the quality of understanding which motivates all his actions regarding people. He is completely honest but he would bend this honesty if it meant saving the feelings of almost anyone (perhaps everyone). His latent courage will stem from the pity that is invoked through other people's suffering. Whilst he knows no person can help being born "good or bad" he still derives his pleasure from the thought that he is greater than anyone else. He hasn't got any weak characteristics, but whilst he would die for principle it is unlikely he could seek to do so for quite some time yet, until, in fact, he has strengthened his nerve considerably.'

Direct examination of this self-characterization reveals four features which are unusual and which suggest some of the qualities of the person and his life situation. Firstly, the whole characterization is written in a very 'abstract way', without reference to examples, specific situations or explanatory details —it is curiously without content. Secondly, the characterization makes no references to the views of anyone else, nothing is said of how other people regard G.M. It is an internal portrait. Thirdly, the claims it makes are so extensive and extreme as to seem more characteristic of private fantasy than of the kind of evaluation which one writes of oneself to communicate to someone else. Fourthly, there is a major obvious contradiction in the assertions in that G.M. 'hasn't got any weak characteristics' but within the same sentence he will not do something 'until, in fact, he has strengthened his nerve considerably'.

This self-characterization was written by a man in his middle 20's who had lived, and was living, a life of extreme isolation, almost entirely without involvement with other people. He did not work and had only superficial contacts even within his own family. Along with the view set out in the self-characterization, he saw himself as psychologically 'frozen' at the age of eight.

The characteristics of his life are well reflected in the characteristics of his self-description. There is no evidence or event or other person's view in his description because his life is largely uncommitted and eventless. Because his life is lived as a prolonged fantasy, with no committal to action, his self-description is idealized and uninformed by experience. The contradiction at the end of the self-description is reflected in the conflict which brought him to psychotherapy—the alternating and irreconcilable (because equally untested) views of himself as a man uniquely saint and martyr (the purity of inaction) and uniquely failing and undeveloped. Perhaps, in using the construct of *latency* in his self-description ('latent courage'), he is offering a construction on the basis of which some part of the conflict might eventually be resolved.

Measurement to What End?

A wander through the ever-growing volumes of the *Mental Measurements Yearbook* suggests that psychologists have a great desire to measure, or possibly a great fear of being discovered not measuring. It is as if we suffered from a kind of counting fever, and often measuring procedures are justified by the assumption that operational definition is, of itself, a good thing almost regardless of what we are operationally defining. Kelly (1955, p. 203) commented on the purposes of testing in a clinical setting but the point he makes is of wider import. He argues that the psychologist 'can seek to fix the position of the subject with respect to certain dimensions as coordinates—such as intelligence, extraversion and so on—or to classify him as a clinical type—

such as schizoid, neurotic, and the like. On the other hand, he can concern himself with the subject's freedom of movement, his potentialities, the resources which can be mobilized, and what is to become of him. From the point of view of the psychology of personal constructs, in which the emphasis is upon process rather than upon fixed position, the latter represents the more enlightened approach. Let us say, then, that the primary purpose of psychological measurement in a clinical setting is to survey the pathways along which the subject is free to move . . .'.

References

Adams-Webber, J. R. (1969), 'Cognitive complexity and sociality', *British Journal of Social and Clinical Psychology*, **8**, 211.

Agnew, Joyce, and Bannister, D. (1973), 'Psychiatric diagnosis as a pseudo-specialist language', *British Journal of Medical Psychology*, **46**, 69.

Bakan, D. (1954), 'A generalisation of Sidman's results on group and individual functions and a criterion', *Psychological Bulletin*, **51**, 63.

Beloff, N., and Becker, S. W. (1967), 'On the futility of aggregating individual learning curves', *Psychological Reports*, **20**, 183.

Bannister, D. (1962), 'The nature and measurement of schizophrenic thought disorder', *Journal of Mental Science*, **108**, 825.

Bannister, D., (1970), 'Science through the looking glass', in *Perspectives in Personal Construct Theory* (Ed. D. Bannister), London, Academic Press.

Bannister, D. and Fransella, Fay (1966), 'A grid test of schizophrenic thought disorder', *British Journal of Social and Clinical Psychology*, **5**, 95.

Bannister, D. and Fransella, Fay (1971), *Inquiring Man—the Theory of Personal Constructs*, Harmondsworth, Penguin.

Bannister, D., Fransella, Fay, and Agnew, Joyce (1971), 'Characteristics and validity of the grid test of thought disorder', *British Journal of Social and Clinical Psychology*, **10**, 144.

Bannister, D., and Mair, J. M. M. (1968), *The Evaluation of Personal Constructs*, London, Academic Press.

Bannister, D., Salmon, Phillida, and Leiberman, D. M. (1964), 'Diagnosis–treatment relationships in psychiatry: a statistical analysis', *British Journal of Psychiatry*, **468**, 726.

Fransella, Fay (1968), 'Self-concepts and the stutterer', *British Journal of Psychiatry*, **114**, 1531.

Fransella, Fay (1972), *Personal Change and Reconstruction*, London, Academic Press.

Fransella, Fay, and Adams, B. (1966), 'An illustration of the use of repertory grid technique in a clinical setting', *British Journal of Social and Clinical Psychology*, **5**, 51.

Hartshorne, H., and May, M. (1928), *Studies in the Nature of Character*, Vol. 1, London, Macmillan.

Hinkle, D. N. (1965), 'The change of personal constructs from the viewpoint of a theory of implications', Unpublished Ph.D. Thesis, Ohio State University.

Holt, R. R. (1970), 'Yet another look at clinical and statistical prediction', *American Psychologist*, **25**, 337.

Kelly, G. A. (1955), *The Psychology of Personal Constructs*, Vols. I and II, New York, Norton.

Landfield, A. W. (1971), *Personal Construct Systems in Psychotherapy*, New York, Rand McNally.

Macmurray, J. (1961), *Persons in Relation*, Faber and Faber.

Mair, J. M. M. (1970), 'Psychologists are human too', in *Perspectives in Personal Construct Theory* (Ed. D. Bannister), London, Academic Press.

Makhlouf-Norris, Fawzeya, Jones, H. G., and Norris, H. (1970), 'Articulation of the conceptual structure in obsessional neurosis', *British Journal of Social and Clinical Psychology*, **9**, 264.

Meehl, P. E. (1954), *Clinical versus Statistical Predictions: A Theoretical Analysis and a Review of the Evidence*, University of Minnesota Press.

Milgram, S. (1965), 'Some conditions of obedience and disobedience to authority', *Human Relations*, **18**, 57.

Oliver, W. D., and Landfield, A. W. (1963), 'Reflexivity: an unfaced issue of psychology', *Journal of Individual Psychology*, **29**, 187.

Orne, M. T. (1962), 'On the social psychology of the psychological experiments: with particular reference to demand characteristics and their implications', *American Psychologist*, **18**, 776.

Osgood, C. E., Suci, G. J., and Tannenbaum, P. M. (1957), *The Measurement of Meaning*, University of Illinois Press.

Radley, A. R. (1973), 'A study of self-elaboration through role change', Unpublished Ph.D. Thesis, London University.

Rosenthal, R. (1967), 'Covert communication in the psychological experiment', *Psychological Bulletin*, **67**, 356.

Ryle, A., and Lunghi, M. E. (1970), 'The dyad grid: a modification of repertory grid technique', *British Journal of Psychiatry*, **117**, 323.

Shapiro, M. B. (1961), *The Personal Questionnaire. A Method of Measuring Changes in the Symptoms of an Individual Psychiatric Patient*, London, Institute of Psychiatry.

Slater, P. (1964), *The Principle Components of a Repertory Grid*, Vincent Andrews.

Smail, D. J. (1972), 'A grid measure of empathy in a therapeutic group', *British Journal of Medical Psychology*, **45**, 165.

Thomas, L. F. (1972), 'A McQuitty hierarchical programme for analysing grids', Personal Communication.

Wright, K. J. T. (1970), 'Exploring the uniqueness of common complaints', *British Journal of Medical Psychology*, **43**, 221.

7

ASSESSMENT IN PSYCHODYNAMIC PSYCHOLOGY

Paul Kline

University of Exeter

PSYCHODYNAMIC psychology we shall define as referring to the theories of Freud, Jung and the Neo-Freudians. Consequently, this chapter is concerned with the problems of measurement and some recent solutions in this highly complex area.

Academic psychologists typified by Eysenck (1953) in Great Britain and Skinner (1954) in the US have strongly attacked psychoanalysis, especially, and its related theories on the grounds that they are non-scientific. They are held to be so because they are not stated in a testable refutable form, thus breaking one of the hallowed canons of scientific method (Popper 1959), because by invoking novel and specific concepts they are unparsimonious, breaking another canon (Bacon's), and because they involve apparently insuperable problems of quantification. It is, of course, this last point which is the concern of this chapter.

Now it is not our intention in this chapter to demonstrate the truth or falsity of any of these theories although this may be one incidental result. Rather, it is our aim to elucidate the problems of quantification in psychodynamic theories. Thus if precise measures could be constructed relevant to these theories, we could go a long way in dismissing the objections to them. For theories can usually be restated in a testable form despite the claim of Martin (1964) that such a procedure changes the theory, at least in the case of psychoanalysis, and with precise measuring instruments the restated theories could be put to the normal scientific test. This seems to us a useful not to say essential procedure for psychology, because these psychodynamic theories have impressive explanatory power embracing such diverse fields as the arts, anthropology, psychiatry and, indeed, the whole basis of civilization. Perhaps more relevantly for psychology, they purport to lay bare the secrets of human motivation.

Since, as we have seen, the development of precise quantification would enable us to establish these theories on a scientific basis, it is clearly important in any discussion of assessment in this area to establish that the measures are in fact adequate for this. Thus, for example, it would not be convincing to a sceptical scientist, despite the impressive results discussed by Holley in a previous chapter of this book, to invoke the Rorschach test as scientific evidence to support these theories. Similarly, as is also clear from Chapter 4 by Semeonoff, projective test results may be invoked only when the particular scores have been cross-validated empirically.

In brief, as in the other areas of psychology, reliable and well-validated measures are essential. Consequently, in this chapter we shall limit our discussion to measures of this sort which offer some evidence of their validity. In practice, this means that it will be confined to studies using personality questionnaires usually designed (often using factor analytic techniques) specifically to test psychodynamic hypotheses, objective test techniques as discussed by Hundleby in Chapter 3, and finally projective test scores where evidence for their validity is offered other than clinical intuition or *a priori* assumptions.

The approach here followed means that the chapter is a curious blend of theoretical and applied psychology. Thus it draws on some of the work discussed in earlier chapters of this book, for example the findings from objective tests in Chapter 3. In this sense it may be described as applied psychology. On the other hand, its field of application being psychodynamic theories, it is clearly theoretical.

Now we must briefly discuss what aspects of psychodynamic psychology we shall be concerned with in this chapter. Obviously, in one chapter it would be impossible to outline even the problems of quantification in *one* of the major psychodynamic theories. This limitation of space, however, is not as disadvantageous as might first appear. For, as has been pointed out by Farrell (e.g. 1964) on many occasions, psychoanalytic theory is not one unified theory but a vast collection of theories each of which needs proof or disproof, and disproof of one of these theories does not necessarily disprove all (or even any) of the others. This same point applies to the other psychodynamic theories to be discussed here, and it is our contention that quantification is far more relevant to some parts of these theories than others. In a previous publication Kline (1972) surveyed all the objective evidence relevant to Freudian theory and pointed out that certain aspects of it were not testable in that they could not be restated in a form possible to refute. An obvious example is the death instinct, *thanatos*. A similar example from Jungian theory is the racial unconscious. Although the problems of measurement of the death instinct are doubtless interesting, with our present techniques we cannot approach obtaining a valid or reliable test of it. Consequently, these are considered to be aspects of psychodynamic psychology meriting but the briefest discussion. Defence mechanisms, however, have proved to be, to many investigators, amenable to measurement, thus opening out new and important areas of research, so that discussion of problems in this area would seem most valuable. Therefore discussion of quantification will be restricted to those aspects of the theories which appear most suited to measurement by tests.

We shall not discuss, therefore, all the testable parts of the theories since Freudian dream theory, for example, may be subjected to the scientific test without the use of psychometric or projective tests, and the castration complex may be similarly subject to experimental verification again without recourse to testing. All these studies have been fully reviewed by Kline (1972). In summary, then, we shall discuss below those aspects of psychodynamic psychology in which testing seems most scientifically valuable.

In fact, quantification in the areas set out below will be discussed.

(1) Personality syndromes of Freudian psychosexual theory

(1A) Fixation at psychosexual stages

(2) Defence mechanisms

(3) Motivation (as it is pertinent to psychodynamic theories) and the basic parameters of personality and mental activity

(4) Jungian personality types

Examination of these topics shows clearly that they provide a reasonable coverage of psychodynamic psychology and are not unduly restricted to trivial parts of the theory. Thus, topic 1 is concerned with the personality theory of Freud and also of Neo-Freudians such as Fromm with his biophilous character (Fromm 1965) and Horney with her typology (Horney 1945). Topic 1A is closely related and differentiates orthodox classical psychoanalytic theory from the later adaptations. Similarly, defence mechanisms are fundamental to Freudian theory and implicated in the Neo-Freudian concepts. The topic of motivation obviously is relevant to all psychodynamic theories, and if the objective results can stand scrutiny they should help us to choose among the different theories. Similar remarks apply to the area of the basic parameters of mental activity and personality. Finally, topic 4 refers to specific parts of Jungian theory. There seems little doubt that should it be demonstrated that all these concepts can be subjected to rigorous quantification then one of the myths of academic psychology, that psychodynamic variables are not amenable to measurement, will have been quashed. At the same time, we must reiterate that this scheme does not attempt to embrace all psychodynamic theory. Certain parts of this, the metapsychology, to use Rapaport and Gill's (1959) term, are indeed impossible to quantify. After this preamble we now turn to a consideration of the central thesis of the chapter.

Personality Syndromes of Freudian Psychosexual Theory

Freudian psychosexual theory (Freud 1905, 1908) claims that as a result of fixation at the oral, anal or phallic phase of development (usually due to overindulgent or oversevere training procedures) certain characteristic personality patterns develop in adulthood. These patterns are defence mechanisms against (as in the case of anal erotism) or direct expressions of (as in the case of oral erotism) pregenital erotism. Even from this simple outline of the theory it should be obvious that objective measurement techniques have a good target—the different personality syndromes. Do they exist or not? If they do, what are the factors influencing their development?

In fact, there have been considerable efforts to verify the existence of these personality syndromes since the early forties. To put these into a brief historical perspective, Table 1 summarizes the main investigations.

TABLE 1

Investigator and date	Subject of study	Method and sample
Goldman-Eisler (1948, 1950, 1951)	Oral pessimists and optimists	Rating scales for 115 adults of oral traits
Barnes (1952)	All syndromes	Personality test items factor analysed
Krout and Krout (1954)	All syndromes	Krout personal preference scale used in a number of investigations by various researchers
Beloff (1957)	Anal character	Personality test items factor analysed: student sample
Grygier (1961)	All syndromes	Dynamic Personality Inventory developed and used in various investigations
Gottheil (1965a,b) Gottheil and Stone (1968)	Anal and oral characters	Scales developed and finally subjected to a 'P' factor analysis
Lazare, Klerman and Armor (1966)	Anal and oral characters	Scales given to a sample of female neurotics and factor analysed
Kline (1971)	Anal character	Ai3Q factor analytic scale developed and validated

We do not intend to discuss in any detail the early researches in Table 1 because the advent of powerful computers has enabled later investigators to improve considerably on their methodology. However, they merit mention because in some cases recent investigations have made use of their tests, for example Lazare, Klerman and Armor (1966). Elsewhere the present author has examined all these studies in some detail (Kline 1972).

The value of looking at these early investigations in assessing the later ones may be seen most clearly when we attempt to clarify the developments over two decades of research. The basic approach to the measurement of psychosexual personality syndromes has remained the same—the construction of personality tests to measure the relevant personality traits. However, in early investigations it was usually considered sufficient to construct face-valid, homogeneous scales and assume validity. Recent studies have used factorial analyses to demonstrate the construct validity of the tests and in one case to isolate types.

Thus, for example, Barnes (1952) constructed a large number of items which appeared to be relevant to psychosexual personality syndromes. The resulting tetrachoric correlations between these items were factor analysed and the factors were compared with psychosexual personality syndromes. No account was taken of response sets, which Cronbach (1950) rightly points out can destroy the validity of this type of personality test, and there was no evidence that the scales formed by the items were valid.

Kline (1971) in his study of the anal character began the investigation just as did Barnes. Items were written which appeared to tap the anal triad—obstinacy, orderliness and parsimony. These were then item analysed by the top and bottom $27\frac{1}{2}$ per cent method. However, social desirability was checked by examining the response split for each item. An item with a fifty-fifty response split may hardly be described as biased by social desirability. Acquiescence was examined by comparing responses to items keyed 'No' to items keyed 'Yes'. Furthermore, after the scale had been shown to be homogeneous with several different samples its construct validity was demonstrated by factor analysis with the 16 PF test, the MMPI and the Beloff (1957) anal scale, and finally with the DPI (Grygier 1961). Thus, if the scale is measuring the anal or obsessional personality syndrome factor, loadings and correlations with these various tests can be hypothesized. Thus, for example, there should be no high correlations with the scales of the 16 PF test and the MMPI, for these contain no measure of the anal or obsessional personality. On the other hand, there should be correlations with the DPI and Beloff anal scales. As for factor loadings, Ai3Q, the anal test, should be independent of Cattell's extraversion and neuroticism factors and the MMPI general factor, but should load on factor G superego. It should also form a common factor with other obsessional or anal scales. In fact, in the studies reported in Kline (1971) all these predictions were confirmed. With such a scale as Ai3Q, an apparently valid measure of the anal or obsessional personality, it is possible to investigate quantitatively the Freudian theory of the anal character. Thus, then, this present study illustrates how the modern approach to the measurement of psychosexual syndromes using factor analytic techniques to validate psychometric measures has enabled one part of Freudian theory to be opened up to quantitative investigation. As a final illustration of work in this area, the studies carried out by Gottheil and his associates (1965a, 1965b, 1968) deserve scrutiny. These began their research in the usual fashion. Items apparently relevant to oral and anal characters were written and subjected to item analysis to produce two independent and homogeneous scales. An attempt to demonstrate their validity was made by having psychiatrists and psychologists classify the items as oral and anal. Although there was an impressive degree of agreement in the classification of these items, it must be stressed that this validity is no more than a kind of super face validity. Had the studies stopped here they would be of little interest and little different from those that had gone before. However, Gottheil and Stone (1968) administered these items together with items pertaining to mouth and bowel habits to another large sample. The resulting inter-item correlations were factored—the usual procedure—and although anal and oral personality factors emerged, they were not related to mouth and bowel habits as predicted from Freudian theory. The novel part of this study was to apply inverse factor analysis (Q technique) and cluster analyses to the data. If there were indeed anal or oral characters, both these last techniques should pick them out. Neither method revealed an anal or oral type.

This study has been discussed because it illustrates the possibilities of inverse factor analysis in the elucidation of Freudian theory. Too much must not be made of the results. In the first place, there were no checks on social desirability or acquiescence and the scales were, as mentioned above, of unknown validity. Furthermore, the number of variables and subjects was almost the same (186 items, 179 subjects), a ratio undesirable for factor analysis. As Harman (1964) points out, there should be at least twice as many variables as subjects for a factor analysis, and conversely for the P technique used here. In addition, the sample was probably too small and too homogeneous, in that there were no extreme psychiatric cases, for there to be much hope of picking out characteristic types by either cluster analysis or inverse factor analysis. Indeed, a recent study of the Gottheil oral trait scale by the present author (Kline, In Press) on a sample of 241 students revealed that, in Great Britain at least, the scale could not be valid. Only 16 of the 40 items formed an adequate scale (revealed by item analysis) and these in content seemed to be extraversion items. This finding could account for the failures with this test to confirm Freudian theory.

Thus, then, we would argue that in the case of psychosexual personality syndromes psychometry has developed an approach well able to deal with the problems. Given sufficiently large samples, there is no reason why valid psychometric techniques should not be constructed. This of itself supports Freudian theory. If certain scales prove impossible to develop, for example there is as yet no phallic scale, this in itself tends to refute the theory. The very fact of such studies indicates that this part, at least, of Freudian theory is not untestable.

Fixation at Psychosexual Stages

In the preceding section we discussed the measurement of the personality syndromes claimed in Freudian theory to arise from fixation during the first five years at pregenital stages. Obviously, as regards the validation of Freudian theory, and the resolution of the conflicting views of Neo-Freudians such as Fromm and Horney who accept the existence of these personality syndromes but deny their aetiology, the question of psychosexual fixation to be discussed in this section is vital.

The requirement of any quantification is that the object of measurement be accurately described. In this respect pregenital fixation is hard to measure. Nevertheless, it can be inferred from Freudian psychosexual theory that over-concern with pregenital zones and an exaggeration of their importance are to be expected—direct expressions of pregenital erotism rather than defence mechanisms against it. This vagueness of definition has led to a variety of techniques being developed. These techniques are of two kinds—specifically designed projective tests and preference inventories.

Preference Inventories

The most widely used preference inventory relevant to psychosexual fixation is that of Wolowitz (1964), who has used it to study the psycho-analytic theory of peptic ulcer (Wolowitz 1967, Wolowitz and Wagonfeld 1968) and also in the investigation of alcoholism (Wolowitz and Barker 1968, Story 1963). From this it should be obvious that it is a measure of oral fixa-tion. It consists of forced-choice items where the subject has to state a prefer-ence for either a sweet milky food or a sharp pungent one—semolina versus curry. A liking for soft pallid food is claimed to measure fixation at the oral passive level, for highly flavoured pungent foods fixation at the later oral sadistic level.

Evidence for the validity of the Wolowitz food preference inventory since there is no clear criterion measure of oral fixation must be of the kind relevant to construct validity—a notoriously devious concept in the case of psycho-analytic theory. All that can be done is to see to what extent results from using the inventory accord with Freudian theory. Wolowitz and Wagonfeld (1968) did find that peptic ulcer patients were significantly higher on the oral passive scale than controls (surgical patients with other gastrointestinal complaints). Now, this finding certainly fits in with the psychoanalytic theory of psycho-somatic symptoms as developed by Alexander (1950) and may therefore be held to support the validity of the measure. However, a more parsimonious explanation of this finding would be that peptic ulcer patients prefer soft milky diets because these cause them less discomfort. Wolowitz and Barker (1968) also found that alcoholics, as predicted by Freudian theory, were more oral passive on the food preference scale than other comparable groups. Story (1963) in his doctoral thesis demonstrated that scores on this food inventory were related to the scales of putative oral personality traits used by Goldman-Eisler (1948, 1950, 1951) in her study of the oral character (see p. 182). All this evidence confirms to some extent the validity of the food preference inventory as a measure of oral erotism. It certainly suggests that this test deserves further and more extensive use as a possible method of assessing psychosexual fixation.

The Wolowitz food preference inventory is, naturally, not an entirely new and novel test. Rather, as most tests, it is a development of previous attempts to measure oral fixation. Thus, for example, the Krout Personal Preference scale (Krout and Krout 1954) contains oral passive and oral sadistic scales. As well as personality trait items, it has items pertaining directly to fixation, for example, sucking candy or eating soft-boiled eggs, and for the sadistic scale items such as chewing on celery and the taste of rare meat. Similarly, the Dynamic Personality Inventory (Grygier 1961) contains a mixture of personality trait and fixation items. However, considerable doubt regarding the validity of these scales was raised by a study by Kline (1968b), who showed that the so-called oral scales did not load on a common factor.

If it were to emerge that food inventories were an adequate measure of oral fixation, the problem remains with them that responses to them are likely to be strongly influenced by variables that in all likelihood are sources of error to the investigator of psychodynamic theory. Thus, for example, cross-cultural studies, potentially of great interest and importance in the elucidation of psychodynamic psychology, can hardly be undertaken with a food inventory. Suffice it to say that spaghetti and roast beef are quite different items in Italy and Great Britain. National differences would also be expected to affect cultures as similar as those of America and Great Britain. Indeed, even within each society, social class and educational status differences affect food inventories. This means that even within the culture for which the test was constructed sampling must be carefully done if, as in the Wolowitz and Wagonfeld (1968) study, special groups are to be compared. This means in practice that food inventories specific to each country must be adopted. Ongoing work at Exeter by the present author (Kline 1973) suggests that the construction of a British food inventory suitable for the measurement of oral fixation is no simple matter. Thus, in a study of orality and smoking no relationship was found between two independent food scales (liking for sweet milky foods, and liking for hot spicy ones) and other oral measures—the Blacky Pictures (Blum 1949) and the Gottheil oral scale. Even if we admit that the Gottheil scale may be invalid (see p. 184), this finding is contrary to theory. Furthermore, smokers were not differentiated from non-smokers on the scales, although there were differences on the Blacky Pictures.

It should be noted, at this point, that Cattell and Warburton (1967), in their survey of objective test measures of personality and motivation, have a form of food and drink preference test. However, for them the interest of the test lies in the commonness of the foods liked and in the daring shown of actual foods claimed to be eaten. Thus, despite the problems outlined, it is probably fair to say that a carefully developed food inventory would prove a useful measure in this area of psychodynamic psychology although its use must be necessarily limited.

Useful or not, food inventories at best can apply only to oral erotism. The question remains as to whether there are or can be any similar tests for other forms of pregenital erotism. In a previous section we mentioned the work of Gottheil and Stone (1968), who factor analysed a questionnaire consisting of items relevant to oral and anal personality traits and mouth and bowel habits. This latter might be, if sufficiently developed, the anal equivalent of a food inventory. However, in our opinion no high hopes of such a measure should be entertained on account of the problems of response sets, especially social desirability. Furthermore, in Western culture excretory references are usually regarded as humorous, so that the chances of such a questionnaire being taken seriously are remote. For this reason the objective approach to the measurement of pregenital erotism cannot be extended beyond oral erotism.

Projective Tests

A quite different method of measuring pregenital erotism has been through projective tests. This is not the place to argue the merits of these tests, and readers should peruse the chapters of Semeonoff and Holley, before either rejecting them out of hand (as Eysenck would have us do) or accepting them without reserve. Our position as regards the use of projective tests in the evaluation of psychodynamic psychology must, however, be made clear. The whole point of attempting the precise assessment of psychodynamic psychology is to put it on a scientific basis. From this point of view, *the general use* of projective tests for this purpose would be unsatisfactory. A major weakness of many of them is in their lack of evidence for validity. On the other hand, if there is empirical support for the validity of scores derived from projective tests, we have no *a priori* objection to them. Of course, scores derived in this way do not necessarily involve any of the assumptions behind projective testing. Rather, the test cards may be regarded as stimuli peculiarly relevant to the pregenital stage under assessment.

Two tests have been developed which to some extent, at least, meet the criteria for using projective tests—the Blacky Pictures (Blum 1949) and its Gallic offspring, le Patte-Noire (Corman 1969).

The Blacky Pictures are, of course, in no sense new, having been first shown in 1949. They merit discussion because they represent exactly the type of projective test which can be used in psychodynamic quantification. Blacky, it will be remembered, is the eponymous hero of a family of dogs who thanks to their author find themselves in a number of situations which in psycho-analytic theory are held to be critical for development. As each situation is presented to the subject, he has to describe what is going on in Blacky's mind. Thus the cards relevant to oral erotism show Blacky tearing his mother's collar (oral sadism) and Blacky sucking at his mother's teats (passive oral erotism). Now, even without accepting the whole of Freudian psychosexual theory, it is still an undeniable fact that these two cards are oral stimuli and therefore responses of subjects fixated at the oral level would be expected to be different from subjects not so fixated. Similar arguments apply to the anal and phallic cards. Thus, if evidence were produced which demonstrated that, for example, peptic ulcer patients (in Freudian theory oral) were more oral than controls on the oral dimension, or that colitis patients were more anal than controls, these results could be accepted as supporting the validity of these dimensions and, *ipso facto*, psychoanalytic theory.

Originally (Blum 1949), these Blacky Pictures were based closely on psycho-analytic theory. For example, denial was regarded as a disturbed response: if when presented with a picture of Blacky tearing his mother's collar a subject says, 'You might think that shows Blacky tearing his mother's collar but really it's a piece of old bone . . .', then this subject is scored high on oral sadism. However, more recently (Blum 1962) a factor analysis of Blacky responses has led to a revised scoring system the validity of which remains to be proven. Taulbee and Stenmark (1968) produced a useful annotated biblio-graphy of research done with the Blacky Pictures which showed that there is as yet from about 150 researches little firm evidence that oral or anal erotism are important variables in personality dynamics. This failure to demonstrate Freudian theory can, of course, be due to defects either in the test, the theory or both.

Certainly the test may be criticized. For a projective technique it is satis-factorily reliable with most populations (Berger and Everstine 1962) mainly because some of the responses are of the multiple-choice type—thus one major source of error, marker variance, is eliminated. However, the present author has found in a number of studies with this test (Kline 1968a, 1970, Kline and Gale 1969, Kline and Trejdosiewicz 1971), using university students (with and without a formal knowledge of psychology) and student teachers, that the situations are so obvious that some subjects spot the purpose of the test (despite the claim in the manual that psychologists find it difficult to fake results) and, to put the least damaging interpretation of this fact, these sub-jects produce stories that are hard to score. If the purpose of each card is understood, it must be easy to distort results if desired. This problem was overcome by establishing good rapport in testing and thus, it was hoped, gaining cooperation. Nevertheless, it is undermining of confidence to be told on presenting the Oedipal card that 'Blacky has got a real problem here—the old Oedipus complex . . .' or on seeing the anal card that 'Blacky has received too severe toilet training and we all know what that does to you . . .'. It is also our impression that the crudity of the drawings together with the obviousness of the situations creates unfavourable attitudes to the test, especially among highly educated subjects.

Nevertheless, as a method of presenting stimuli critical for psychosexual developmental theory, apart from the details of its execution and realization, and for the quantification of results, it is argued that the Blacky Pictures Test is essentially a useful technique.

These objections do not apply to its use with children, and there is some evidence (e.g. the work of Blum and Miller 1952 with oral children, and the case study of an Oedipal child by Michal-Smith *et al.* 1951) that it is an effective measure with young subjects.

Corman (1969) has developed a form of the Blacky Pictures for use in France especially with children: le Patte-Noire (PN). It may be regarded as a form of the Blacky Pictures in that, as in those, an animal (a black-legged pig) is presented in certain critical situations. However, unlike the Blacky Pictures it contains also measures of defence mechanisms and is far less structured. A brief discussion of this test is merited because it may well turn out as more results are collected that it has succeeded in eliminating the defects of the Blacky Pictures and retaining the qualities. The points stressed will be the differences from the Blacky Pictures.

The PN test has 17 cards plus a frontispiece covering the following dimensions: urethral sadism, Oedipal conflicts, oral sadism and sibling rivalry, intrapunitiveness, fantasy of being a changeling, leaving home, castration fears, anal sadism, birth, self ideals, orality, fear of being excluded, and finally three wishes. From this it is clear that the PN test is well equipped to measure psychosexual pregenital fixation if, in fact, it is valid. The pictures relevant to psychosexual fixation are:

(1) *Urethral sadism.* This shows PN urinating into a trough. Curiously, although a piglet, PN is lifting its leg like a dog. Ongoing research with this test at Exeter by the present author will *inter alia* determine whether this is anomalous for farming children.

(2) *Oral sadism.* PN biting another piglet.

(3) *Anal sadism.* Young pigs are rolling and splashing in thick mud and liquid dung and have heavily splashed an adult pig.

(4) *Oral erotism.* PN being suckled.

These are the psychosexual fixation variables of the PN. However, it differs from Blacky, most importantly, not in its cards, although these are more pleasant, in our estimation, to look at, but in the method of administration which allows more variables than the developmental ones outlined above to be measured. Freedom is the keyword in the administration of the PN. When the frontispiece is shown to the child, the pig family is entirely uncharacterized. The child can perceive any of the figures as any age or sex. Furthermore, the order in which the cards are administered is chosen by the child, and if he doesn't wish to say anything about a card he does not have to. As in most projective tests, there are no constraints in telling the stories about each picture or in any responses concerned with the test.

This freedom, according to Corman (1969), is most important. Thus, whereas in the Blacky Pictures the family is fixed—mother, father and two siblings—in the PN test this is not the case. Sometimes the piglets are not regarded as siblings, sometimes the 'parents' are conceived as outsiders, and so on. Very curiously, the clearly female sow may be regarded as a father! Corman warns the tester to appear unsurprised. Again, when the relationships of the family have been discovered from the frontispiece, the procedure is free. The child is presented with the cards and asked to tell a story about those that interest him. Then attention is turned to the cards the child has rejected. Sometimes the child changes and is unwilling to talk, however there is no insistence. This is because after the stories have been told there is another procedure—*preference identification*, which Corman believes truly distinguishes the PN from the Blacky, and indeed from all other projective tests.

Preference Identification. For this the tester gathers up all the cards, whether stories to them have been produced or not, and says to the child that he is going to play a game—the game of the preferred picture. The child then makes two piles of liked and disliked pictures, and selects the picture he likes best of all. The child indicates why he likes this picture and which of the characters in it he would like to be. This process is then repeated for all the pictures in the liked pile. At any stage the child can deny identification with the pigs in the picture. A similar procedure is then adopted for the pile of disliked pictures, only this time the child selects the least liked of the pictures.

After the preference identification the tester can ask any questions he thinks might be worthwhile. For example, in Card 1 which shows PN urinating, many children fail to perceive this salient fact and questions can often reveal whether it was a deliberate suppression or a failure to comprehend the drawing. When they realize their mistake, some of the subjects will make a new identification.

The last part of the test consists of questions aimed to elucidate the general impression of the child about the test. Subjects are asked to name, with reasons, the happiest and unhappiest character, the most and least gentle, and the pig they most like. At this stage the wishes card can be shown so that the child's three wishes may become known. In all, this complex procedure of administering the PN takes around 1½ hours, although it may, of course, be split into two sessions. Most educational and clinical psychologists would agree that a test of this length, to justify itself, must produce results that not only could not be produced in any other way but were also of high value. We have described the PN test in some detail for a number of reasons. The main one is that it appears to us to offer enormous possibilities for quantification in psychodynamic psychology, and yet it is but little used outside France. Buros (1971) in his almost complete review of personality tests makes no mention of it and there are no papers in which it has been used in recent British journals. Its promise resides in the fact that, like the Blacky Pictures, it presents stimuli critical for the study of psychodynamic psychology but it lacks the crudity of the earlier technique. In addition, the preference identification procedure enables it to measure more variables than the Blacky Pictures—especially defence mechanisms. However, a test of this sort, if it is to be used for precise quantification, needs a good manual. Reliabilities, evidence of validity and normative data all need to be known.

Vol. 1 (Corman 1969) of the manual has appeared. In this some normative data, based on 100 girls and 100 boys, are given. Although the size of this sample is very small, it is larger than that used in the manuals of many projective tests and is certainly superior to the clinical impressions on which the scoring and interpretations of such tests are based. Furthermore, there are many examples in the manual of responses representative of all the scoring categories of the test such that the reader is left in little doubt as to how a response should be scored and interpreted. One disappointing aspect of the manual lies in the fact that there is no firm evidence offered of either reliability or validity. For example, it would have been informative to know the degree of agreement of each PN score between occasions and between different markers. Similarly, we should like to know which cards if any discriminate difficult or malajusted children from normal, and how it relates to other tests, such as Blum's Blacky Pictures, which we know from the manual were administered to some of the normative sample. Thus it may be admitted that the manual is clinically rich but psychometrically quite unsatisfactory. There is no evidence for the validity of PN presented, and a rational researcher or tester could not be persuaded to use the test.

Thus in summarizing the PN test as a measure of psychosexual fixation we regard it as a test of rich promise. Needed are careful psychometric parametric studies so that its full efficacy may be judged. Mention of the possibilities inherent in this test will be made in the sections dealing with defence mechanisms and the dynamic structure of the mind.

The projective approach typified by the Blacky Pictures and the PN test, both specifically designed to measure psychosexual fixation, can be applied to any projective technique. For example, we would arbitrarily, perhaps, decide that oral themes to Rorschach cards were evidence of oral fixation and use the number and intensity of such themes as a measure of oral erotism. Such a measure would not carry much weight unless it were shown to be a reliable and valid discriminator of groups hypothesized as oral from controls. In fact, Masling, Rabie and Blondheim (1967, 1968) have used just such oral measures derived from both the TAT and the Rorschach with alcoholics and obese patients. The reason that it is preferable to design tests for specific purposes is that any projective card has a particular specific 'pulling' power, i.e. it is likely to produce some themes rather than others. The art of constructing a good projective test is, of course, to design cards that tend to produce the kind of themes one wants (but not with all subjects!).

What may be fairly concluded from our study of measurement techniques relative to pregenital fixation? First, it is clear that there is no test which most psychologists would agree is a valid measure, contrary to, for example, intelligence. On the other hand, it is equally clear that it is wrong to say that the concept is not susceptible to quantification, since there are two methods, one projective, the other psychometric, which have been used tentatively in attempts to measure psychosexual fixation. To what extent these tests are valid, indeed to what extent the concept can be said to be confirmed by these studies, is unclear. For this reason, little emphasis has been placed on any results so far achieved with these measures. Nevertheless, we contend that we have shown pregenital erotism to be a quantifiable concept.

Since we have shown the Freudian psychosexual personality theory to be capable of refutation, it is appropriate at this point to consider the Jungian personality typology (Jung 1949). Here Jung makes a fourfold classification: introvert or extravert (attitudes), sensation or intuition (perceptions) and thinking or feeling and judgment and perception (judgments). It should be noted that Jung's scheme is a typology and thus his concept of extraversion cannot be equated with the factor analytically derived dimensions of that name to be found in the work of Eysenck, Cattell and Guilford.

In point of fact, two questionnaires have been developed which purport to measure these variables—the Gray–Wheelwright Questionnaire (Gray and Wheelwright 1946) and the Myers–Briggs Type Indicator (Myers 1962). Since the construction of this last test was begun in 1943, neither test can be really described as new except that there have been relatively few researches using them. Indeed, the Gray–Wheelwright test has not yet been published.

Since both tests claim to identify types rather than place subjects on a continuum, a brief description of each is necessary. For whether or not these tests can thus categorize subjects is crucial for assessing their validity and for interpreting certain aspects of the psychometric data reported about the Myers–Briggs Type Indicator.

The Gray–Wheelwright Test. This consists of 85 forced-choice items. Subjects have to indicate which of two things they prefer. Each response places a subject into a category. The instructions to this test are curious in the extreme in that subjects are asked to choose the answer which best reflects 'your original inborn tendency rather than what you wish to do or what you have made of yourself'. Experience in testing educated subjects in Great Britain suggests strongly that these instructions would be insuperable obstacles to satisfactory test completion.

The Myers–Briggs Test (form F). The first part consists of 71 forced-choice items as above. Part 2 contains 52 pairs of words. For each pair subjects have to choose the more appealing, whereas the third part is identical with part 1 in form (43 items).

Scoring. These inventories categorize subjects into types. If a subject has more

E responses than I responses he is classified extravert. His score is the difference between extraversion and introversion. Similarly for the other scales. A continuous scale score (like a dimension) is also available for parametric statistical analysis.

From this description it is clear that two independent tests have been constructed such that subjects, depending on their choices, can be placed into Jungian categories. Thus Jungian theory has shown itself amenable to test. A number of difficulties with these tests must be mentioned.

Although the manual to the Myers–Briggs test (Myers 1962) quotes satisfactory reliabilities in the order of 0.7 to 0.8, these are for the continuous scores (which are not apposite to Jungian theory), not the category scores. For the category scores, Myers reports a similar figure but she used tetrachoric correlations (notoriously unreliable) corrected for length. Even if we accept the test as reliable, evidence for validity is far more difficult to come by. Is, then, the Myers–Briggs Indicator a valid test of Jungian categories?

Mendelsohn (1965) and Sundberg (1965), surveying the evidence, both agree that there is not good support for the validity of this test. The classic study is that of Stricker and Ross (1964), who correlated the continuous scores with a large number of other tests—notably the MMPI, the Strong Interest Blank, the Edwards Social Desirability scale, the Californian Psychological inventory and the Gray–Wheelwright test. Although this kind of construct validity study is difficult to interpret, these authors are forced to conclude that there was no strong evidence for its validity. However, there were good correlations with the Gray–Wheelwright test. Indeed, Myers (1962), correcting these correlations for the unreliability of both scales, arrives at correlations greater than +1—i.e. the two tests' true variances are identical. Thus from this study of the correlations with the continuous scores of the Myers–Briggs Indicator, three conclusions appear warranted: (1) that the Myers–Briggs test and the Gray–Wheelwright are measuring very similar variables; (2) that the Myers–Briggs test is of unproven validity; (3) that the Myers–Briggs test used empirically may be highly useful (as claimed by Myers 1962 in the manual).

However, Stricker and Ross (1964) also investigated the typological side of the test. Here, by a study of the distributions, they were forced to conclude that there was little evidence for the Jungian types. Evidence in the manual from regression lines of scales on IQ which appear to change slope at the 0 or cutting point does not seem convincing. Indeed, the conclusion from all this would appear to be negative were it not for a study by Bradway (1964) reprinted in Vetter and Smith (1971).

Bradway (1964) overcame the problem of validity by getting Jungian analysts to put themselves into their personality groups. This is a true criterion. For the meaning of a category is only that given it by a Jungian analyst. In fact, compared with the 28 analysts' self-typing both the Gray–Wheelwright and the Myers–Briggs showed full agreement for introverts and extraverts. Both tests were better than chance as regards the sensation/intuition. For thinking, feeling and perception judgment the Gray–Wheelwright also showed better than chance matching. These are sound impressive findings in support of the validity of the tests; clearly, they measure what these Jungian analysts regard as Jungian types. What we do not know, of course, is to what extent these analysts are a random sample of Jungian analysts or whether their theoretical knowledge was sound.

In conclusion, we should like to propose that both these tests merit further study and development, especially perhaps the Gray–Wheelwright. If they do measure variables similar to those implicit in Jungian theory it might be possible using them to elucidate the Jungian theory and relate it to other theories of personality. Certainly it seems to us that both these tests offer forms of measurement applicable to Jungian theory.

Defence Mechanisms

The mechanisms of defence are a highly important part of Freudian theory. Indeed, were it ever demonstrated that these processes do not occur, one of the cornerstones of psychoanalysis would be removed. The empirical investigation, therefore, of psychodynamic psychology should certainly be aimed at defence mechanisms. Freud (1923) has argued that the neurotic conflict is between the ego and the id. To bar the instinctual impulses of the id, the ego uses mechanisms of defence which can vary in their effectiveness. A list of Freudian defences is set out below:

(1) *Sublimation*. Strictly not a defence mechanism, it refers rather to any successful defence—i.e. one in which the impulse is expressed without endangering the ego. Its commonest form is deflection of aims, for example maternal instinct expressed in schoolteaching.

(2) *Repression*. (a) Primal repression—denial of entry into consciousness. (b) Repression proper—this relates to the material associated with the primal repression. (Freud 1915)

(3) *Denial*. Clearly seen in the child who, on being suddenly leapt upon says, 'It didn't frighten me'.

(4) *Projection*. In this defence, the person imputes to others his unacceptable impulses. The most celebrated example of this is to be seen in the Freudian theory of paranoia (Freud 1911), where the paranoid's delusions are attributed to homosexuality—'I love him' turns by reaction formation into 'I hate him', which by projection becomes 'He hates me'.

(5) *Reaction formation*. The creation of an attitude opposite to the instinctual impulse. Love becomes hatred, hatred love.

(6) *Undoing*. Freud (1909) says this is typical of the obsessional neurotic. It is the imaginal undoing of a real or imaginal action.

(7) *Isolation.* In this defence, experiences are separated from associations and emotions.

(8) *Regression.* A retreat to earlier modes of mental activity and behaviour. All these defence mechanisms are, of course, unconscious. Finally, it should be noted that there are similar defences against affects. One of these, *displacement* (kicking the dog rather than the wife), is most commonly seen in this sphere. Such is the list of the classical Freudian mechanisms of defence. Anna Freud (1946), however, lists one further mechanism—*identification with the aggressor.* An example of this would be the anti-semitism of some Jews.

Some of the Neo-Freudians (Anna Freud is truly in direct descent), especially Fromm (1942) and Horney (1942), have also described mechanisms of defence. Fromm has three main defences:

(1) *Masacho-sadistic striving.* The desperate effort to dominate or be dominated—caused by the terror of being alone.

(2) *Destructiveness.* This is caused by feelings of individual powerlessness in the face of a constricting society.

(3) *Automaton conformity.* This is the usual defence. The individual abandons his real self and hides beneath the shield of a national or social stereotype. National differences, therefore, are real differences.

Horney (1942), as indicated above, postulates a number of defence mechanisms—in her terminology neurotic trends—developed to overcome what for her is the basis of neurosis—basic anxiety. Of her 10 trends, four are regarded as most important:

(1) Neurotic need for affection

(2) Neurotic need for power

(3) Neurotic withdrawal

(4) Neurotic submissiveness

Horney (1945) groups these trends into three categories, moving towards, moving away from and moving against people. Normals balance these three trends rationally, neurotics do not.

In fact, the basic anxiety and the neurotic need for power of Horney and the masacho-sadistic striving of Fromm closely resemble the inferiority feelings of Adler—for him the driving force of man. However, both Fromm and Horney argue that their defences are unconscious, whereas for Adler the feelings of inferiority were not (Adler 1930).

From this necessarily brief outline of the theories of Freud, Fromm and Horney concerning mechanisms of defence it will be seen that all postulate unconscious mental processes which profoundly affect behaviour. We can now turn to the tests which have been developed in the attempt to verify and quantify these theories.

At this point we must stress the fact that in this chapter we are not primarily concerned with demonstrating, even were it possible, the truth or falsity of any of these theories. The aim is to indicate the variety of assessment techniques which enable such verification to be made. This is especially important here in the case of defence mechanisms since some of them (notably repression) are open to verification using experimental procedures rather than tests. This means, therefore, that even if no tests of these defences have been developed, no readers should assume that the concepts are unverifiable. A full discussion of experimental methodology for the verification of Freudian theory may be found in Sarnoff (1971) and, together with a survey of all research findings relevant to Freudian theory, in Kline (1972).

In the previous section on the measurement of pregenital fixation we discussed both the Blacky Pictures (Blum 1949) and the Patte-Noire (Corman 1969). The Patte-Noire was notable because it was so designed that defence mechanisms, it was claimed, could be measured by it. Blum (e.g. 1956) has developed from the Blacky Pictures a measure known as the Defence Preference Inquiry. This is not a separate test (in that it is not listed in Buros 1971) but consists rather of special questions about the Blacky Pictures, the answers to which, it is claimed, reveal the preferred mode of defence. Thus, for each picture subjects have to rank a series of descriptions of Blacky's thoughts and feelings in terms of their applicability and accuracy. Since each description is a definition of one of the Freudian defence mechanisms, the mean ranking for a defence over the 11 pictures gives a quick measure of the preferred mode of defence. Furthermore, it indicates how particular developmental problems are dealt with. For example, anality may be repressed, orality sublimated. Unfortunately there is, as yet, little evidence that this measure of the mechanisms of defence is valid. Perhaps the best argument comes from the studies of perceptual defence conducted by Blum's group (e.g. Blum 1955), where subjects classified as repressors by the Defence Preference Inquiry showed greater perceptual defence to emotional stimuli than did other subjects.

Corman (1969), while freely acknowledging his debt to Blum, argues that there is one essential (and novel) difference between the PN and the Blacky test—the procedure of preference identification. This we have already described in the previous section. Suffice it to say here that from the preference identifications and the responses to any further questions which the tester may ask about them Corman claims that the habitual mechanisms of defence may be observed. However, it must be noted that the PN test of defence mechanisms differs considerably from the Defence Preference Inquiry on one essential point. The Blum test is objective in that it is independent of the marker's skill. It has, therefore, complete intermarker reliability. Corman's test, as is obvious from the manual, is highly interpretative and therefore is highly dependent on the tester's interpretative ability—a procedure usually fatal for reliability and hence, inevitably, for validity. No figures are quoted in the manual regarding the reliability of the measures of defence mechanisms. On the other hand, there is little doubt that the cards of the PN are well suited for eliciting Freudian defence mechanisms. Again, as with the Defence Preference Inquiry, there is no evidence of validity in the manual other than case studies and examples from protocols. These, it is fair to say, are convincing to those who believe in defence mechanisms but cannot constitute scientific proof. About both these tests of defence mechanisms we are at present forced to conclude, as so often in psychology, that more research is needed before they may be accepted. At best, they look promising.

There are some other measures of the mechanisms of defence which deserve mention. Gleser and Ihilevich (1969) have devised an objective measure of defences which departs from orthodox psychoanalytic theory in that it is aimed at five basic defences which, the authors claim, embrace all the Freudian defences outlined at the beginning of the section. Their five categories are: turning against object, projection, principalization, turning against self, and reversal. To some extent, therefore, this test is relevant to the theories of Horney rather than Freud. The test itself consists of 10 stories, two per conflict area. Questions about these stories are claimed to tap the five defence categories and to indicate which kind of defence is used in various areas of conflict. The areas are: authority, independence, competition, situations, and masculinity and feminity. Although this is an interesting attempt to measure the mechanisms of defence, it is at present entirely vitiated by the unreliability of the scoring system. Thus, 60 per cent agreement is the best figure for a defence category and some fall below this figure. Until a more reliable and objective form of scoring can be devised this test cannot be recommended.

Kragh (1960) has developed the Defence Mechanism Test in Sweden which is based on a combination of conventional projective testing theory, percept-genetic theory and psychoanalysis (Sjoback 1967). Sjoback, indeed, in the paper cited described the test in some detail and our description here is, in effect, a brief summary of this. The Kragh test is interesting if only because in it the stimulus is presented tachistoscopically.

Basic Theory. The defence organization is studied as it appears in the perception of pictures with aggressive themes. Indeed, the way a perception develops can be observed—'percept-genesis'.

Method. For group testing a stimulus card is repeatedly shown through a tachistoscope at gradually increasing speeds—10 msec, 13 msec, 17 msec, in geometrical progression up to 2 sec. For individual administration a viewer and electronic timer may be used. Subjects after each exposure record what they have seen either orally or in writing. 'Distortions', 'additions' and 'eliminations' at each viewing speed form the data of the test, which are interpreted as reflecting the workings of various defence mechanisms.

The Cards. Two pictures differing in detail. Each picture has three elements, a central figure the hero (boy/girl, young man/woman), hero's attribute (gun, car, etc.) and a threat figure—man or woman with a horrid face. In addition, there is a demonstration picture and a 'distractor picture' which is shown before, between and after the two series of test pictures. This distractor shows a couple in their nightclothes on a bed. The pictures are repeatedly shown until three successive complete recognitions have been made.

Since percept-genesis theory lies so much behind this test, it is perhaps apposite to explicate the rationale of the testing procedure. Briefly, as Sjoback (1967) points out, the early phases of perception (when the tachistoscope is fast) are primary processes, individual rather than stimulus directed. However, as the perceptual process continues (and the tachistoscope becomes slow) the perceptual process becomes more directed, 'more stripped of irrelevant contents in favour of stimulus . . .' (Sjoback 1967, p. 5). Thus, by means of the defence mechanism test it is possible to study directly a percept-genesis and thus observe primary process influences (defence mechanisms) at first hand.

In this percept-genesis theory there is one crucial assumption—the parallelistic assumption. This assumes a correspondence between 'an individual's ontogenesis and his percept-genesis. This implies that in his percepts . . . the whole of the individual's previous experience is released in chronological order' (Sjoback 1967). However, Kragh (1960), clearly aware that these assumptions would be acceptable only to those who already accept percept-genesis theory, argues that the DMT does not necessarily presuppose acceptance of this model.

Our position on this must be made clear. Without a large body of evidence we could not accept this assumption. There seems to be little or no support for it. Without this assumption the rationale of the test becomes much weaker —why should defence mechanisms (formed early in life) otherwise show themselves early in the sequence? On the other hand, we should be prepared to accept that defence mechanisms could determine the perception of stimuli presented below the perceptual threshold if evidence were adduced for the theory. Indeed, this DMT would appear to be a highly promising method.

At present, there is no definitive evidence supporting the validity of the DMT. However, some examples of the scoring procedure are not without interest and suggest again that it may be a valid technique. The examples are taken from Sjoback (1967).

(a) *Repression*—if the hero or the secondary figure have a stiff or lifeless quality, or are seen as animals or objects.

(b) *Isolation*—if the hero and the secondary figure are separated by a line or object; if the secondary figure is seen but not experienced as threatening.

(c) *Denial*—the existence of a threat in the picture is explicitly denied.

(d) *Reaction formation*—the secondary figure is kind or happy or the atmosphere is said to be pleasant.

These examples are sufficient to indicate that this test seems capable of providing evidence of defence mechanisms. Of course, this means little other than that it has face validity. Other defences tapped are turning against the self, identification with the aggressor, identification with the role of the other sex, introjection, projection and regression.

Although this test has been used in a number of investigations (e.g. Kragh 1959), there is still no definitive evidence concerning the validity of the scores. Certainly, the assumptions behind the percept-genesis theory, as has been stated before, would need very considerable support if they were to be accepted, and without these assumptions much of the rationale of the test disappears, certainly much of what makes it distinctive compared with other projective techniques. Nevertheless, the fact that it is shown through a tachistoscope at below threshold speeds and that the emotional characteristics of the stimuli are so clearcut does allow, in psychoanalytic theory at least, the defence mechanisms to show themselves in perception (see the work of Wenig 1952).

Our view of this test is that it might prove, on further examination, an effective measure for quantifying defences. However, it needs research to establish its validity. Finally, before passing on to other measures of the defensive processes, two further points need to be made about the DMT. First, there is no reason why the test should only be used to investigate Freudian defences. Unlike the Blacky Pictures and the PN test, the stimulus cards are not critical only for psychoanalytic theory; rather, as heroes hideously threatened by others, they would appear to be of a more general significance. Thus, researchers could use the test to investigate both Horney's and Fromm's defences and, indeed, evidence of the inferiority feelings of Adler. Again, what is needed is evidence. The second point concerns the stimulus cards. There is no reason for investigators to stick to the DMT cards (although, obviously, the use of different cards would create another test). In fact, the procedure would seem suitable for any well-structured stimuli, such as, for example, certain of the TAT cards. Empirical studies of other stimuli presented as in the DMT might produce tests of remarkable quality.

At this point a brief mention must be made of Byrne's (Byrne 1964) Repression–Sensitisation scale. Byrne (1964) has an excellent summary of the history and development of this scale together with all the studies up to this date, including many not then published. This Repression–Sensitisation scale is made up from items in the MMPI and is based on the work of Altrocchi, Parsons and Pickoff (1960). It also clearly resembles, to the extent of sharing half the items, Ullman's (1962) Facilitation–Inhibition scale, with which it correlates (not unnaturally) extremely highly. Byrne (1964) quotes figures ranging from 0.76 to 0.94. Since its internal consistency reliability is 0.94 and its test–retest reliability 0.82, the repression scale may be regarded, as Byrne (1964) points out, as an alternative form of the facilitation scale.

However, despite the large number of studies carried out with the test certain findings quoted by Byrne (1964), notably those of Joy (1963) and Endler (1963), throw such doubts on its validity as to make the use of the test hazardous (at least). Thus Joy found very substantial correlations with many of the MMPI clinical scales, findings which do not support its clinical validity. For example, the R–S scale correlates 0.72 with the repression scale, 0.84 with the social introversion and 0.91 with the K scale. The same writer found a negative correlation of 0.91 with the Edwards Social Desirability scale (Edwards 1957). In view of the reliabilities of these tests, these correlations are astonishingly high. Endler in general supported these findings and he found a correlation of 0.92 with the Psychasthenia scale. The final nail in the coffin of this test lies in the finding that repressors come from permissive backgrounds (Byrne 1964). This is not in accord with the Freudian notion of repression and renders the scale invalid. For this reason, then, the results with the R–S scale will not be examined.

Freudian Motivational Theory

We shall now consider the problems and techniques of assessment of the motivational hypothesis of Freudian theory. At this point we enter what Rapaport and Gill (1959) refer to as the metapsychology of psychoanalysis, an area generally considered alien and antithetical to quantification. To some extent we are in agreement with this position. Thus Freud (1923) in *Ego and the Id* argued that man is governed by two instinctual forces—*eros* and *thanatos*, the life and death instincts. These forces in their opposition create the essence of life. The death instinct shows itself as the tendency to return to the original inorganic state. *Eros* is the life force. There appears to be no way to refute these statements and it is certain that these forces cannot be measured. Hence we accept, in full, the objection that this part of the theory is unscientific.

However, as we pointed out at the beginning of this chapter, it is an error to regard Freudian theory as unitary. Rather, it is best considered as a collection of theories, and some of these do have bearing on motivation. Basic to Freudian motivational theory is his structural theory of mind (Freud 1933) that there are three mental provinces, id, ego and superego. According to this the id obeys the pleasure principle and seeks to discharge the instinctual drives. In civilized society this is impossible and the ego and superego strive to control it, the ego being in contact with reality, the superego representing the parental morals—conscience. On how this balance of the trinity is achieved depends, according to the theory, the mental health and behaviour of the individual. The obsessional is ruled by his superego, the psychopath by his id. The aim of psychoanalysis is to redress the balance, 'where id was there shall ego be'. The motivation of behaviour, therefore, lies in the id. Scientific curiosity is sublimation of infantile sexual curiosity.

If we leave, for the moment, the concepts of *eros* and *thanatos*, which many psychoanalysts have ignored (see Fenichel 1945), it is possible to argue from the tripartite division of the mental apparatus that the main motivational drives should be sex and aggression—the normally hidden unconscious contents of the id. We have, therefore, two sets of complementary hypotheses which, logically at least, are open to measurement. What are required if we are to quantify Freudian motivational theory are tests of sex and aggression as drives and measures of ego, id and superego.

Work of Cattell

In a previous chapter by Hundleby, we saw how the objective measures of personality described in Cattell and Warburton (1967) have been used to elucidate the underlying structure of personality especially, and also motivation. These studies, as is typical of the work of Cattell, were to as large an extent as possible atheoretical. Thus Cattell attempts to sample the whole universe of variables and he interprets the factor analysis in the most psychologically meaningful way. If the resultant factor analysis resembles any already existing theory, it is fair to argue that it may be regarded as strong support for that theory. If, as frequently happens, the factor analysis is quite different from any theory, we can consider it as putting these theories into considerable doubt. Of course, this argument assumes (a) that Cattell has truly sampled the whole universe of relevant variables, (b) that the sample of subjects to whom the tests were administered was representative of some known population, and (c) that the tests were reliable and valid. Thus, then, we have to answer two questions about Cattell's studies of drives. To what extent do they fulfil the technical criteria mentioned above, and to what extent do the results support the Freudian hypothesis? Obviously, if the answer to the first question is negative and it is agreed that there are serious technical shortcomings, the second question is not worthy of consideration.

About the first point we intend to say little, other than make the modest and cautious assertion that despite doubts about the validity of some of the measures and the nature of the samples, the results are probably sufficiently robust to merit consideration. We shall not attempt here to justify fully the claim, although it has already been done, in part, in an earlier chapter of this book. Thus, as was mentioned above, Hundleby's chapter on objective tests in the measurement of personality indicates that over the last 10 years sufficient evidence has now built up that they are valid.

Motivational factors

Cattell (1957) has argued that motivation is probably best assessed through studying attitudes and interests. This approach is well suited to the empirical examination of Freudian motivational theory in that, as Toman (1960) has shown, in psychoanalysis interests are regarded as reflecting motivation, for example, the surgeon sublimates his aggression, the fireman his phallic erotism, in his work. In a sample of 374 adult males whose interests and attitudes were sampled in five areas—job, disreputable and respectable hobbies, and attitudes with moral and unconscious roots—five factors of motivation emerged.

(1) *Alpha*—the id component of interest. It appears to be the 'I desire' component, of which the individual is partly conscious but which has not been tested against reality.

(2) *Beta*—the realized ego. This component was loaded on good knowledge of the interest, and a capacity to learn relevant material. It could not be intelligence because all these scores had been ipsatized.

(3) *Gamma*—the superego or ideal-self component, only identified by Cattell with great caution.

(4) *Delta*—loading on physiological variables—perhaps the entirely unconscious id.

(5) *Epsilon*—component from repressed complexes—loading on memory and PGR, as often found in word association studies.

These five factors were oblique and their intercorrelations were themselves subjected to factor analysis. Two second-order factors emerged—integrated interests (beta and gamma) and unintegrated interests, mainly unconscious (delta, epsilon and alpha).

It is not relevant here to discuss the neatness of this fit to psychoanalytic Freudian theory although there is clearly a more than passing resemblance, especially at the second-order stage. However, what the study does demonstrate is that by using objective motivation tests the Freudian dynamic theory of motivation does become testable and hence refutable and scientific. We are forced to agree with Cattell (1957) that these motivational investigations need further research. So far little has been reported. Pawlik and Cattell (1964) subjected objective measures of personality (rather than motivation) to third-order factor analysis. Here three factors emerged—immature self-centred temperament, restrained acceptance of external norms and high self-assertion. Pawlik and Cattell (1964) point out that these personality factors are a remarkably close fit to the id, superego and ego of Freudian theory. This, of course, is the more remarkable in that these objective personality tests have been empirically devised to measure the whole personality sphere (Cattell 1957) without any theoretical preconceptions.

Finally, as regards the Cattell personality tests, Warburton (1968) subjected questionnaire personality factors to fourth-order factor analysis. Two factors finally emerged, integration and morality. This finding does not so well support the Freudian theory, although these factors resemble the ego and superego to some extent.

Thus, to conclude our discussion of Cattell's factor analytic approach to studying motivational factors as they impinge on the first of the hypotheses implicit in Freudian theory—that there will be three factors accounting for behaviour of every kind, id, ego and superego—it is obvious from the results discussed above that this part of the theory is amenable to test and, indeed, that many of the results so far obtained go some way to supporting it. Clearly, then, id, ego and superego are not incapable of measurement even though with these techniques they are measured indirectly at some remove.

Another approach to the study of motivation, which Cattell has also explored, is to attempt to investigate drives. It is common to assume, with animals at least, that there exist certain fundamental drives which motivate appetitive behaviours—thirst and hunger are obvious examples. In the past it was also assumed that man's behaviour was motivated by similar drives, the number and nature of which being constantly a matter for speculation and argument. The work of McDougall (1932), Murray (1938) and Burt (1940) bears eloquent witness to this particular dialectic. Cattell, however, using motivational objective test devices (each loading on the three motivational factors found above), has managed to isolate 10 drives which he calls ergs. These are, in order of variance accounted for—the sex erg, gregariousness, parental protectiveness, exploration, escape, self-assertion and narcissism. These seven are the best validated. In addition, there emerged from these studies a number of sentiments, for example, sentiments to profession, to sports and to religion. These sentiments are, however, of less interest to this chapter since they are clearly culturally moulded.

Although as yet there is little firm evidence for the validity of the MAT ergs and sentiments (Comrey 1972), a recent study by the present author strongly supports the validity of this measure (Kline and Grindley, In Press). In this research the MAT was completed every day for a 28-day period by one subject. The peaks and troughs of the fluctuations of each variable were examined in relation to a detailed diary record of this period. To avoid obvious contamination of scores and diary, none of the tests was scored until the 28-day period was completed. A brief summary of the findings of this case study is hardly useful in that the interest of the study lies in the particular details. However, most of the fluctuations clearly fitted the diary record and very few notable diary events failed to show a corresponding change in ergic tension. One of the most amazing (except to a convinced Freudian) data was the fact that on the day the sex drive was at its highest point, the subject went out and bought smoked eels as a gift to her father!

The fact that it has been possible to measure drives with some degree of validity points strongly to the fact that the Freudian theory of drives (sex and aggression) is not untestable. The existence of so many ergs must be regarded as evidence against the psychoanalytic theory, although the deeper factor structure has not yet been worked out. The importance of sexuality too is noteworthy. One point must be stressed. The population used by Cattell was homogeneous—airmen. For this reason, hunger did not appear as an erg. In the West hunger is a trivial drive, quite otherwise in Bangladesh.

All this work by Cattell on ergs and motivational factors demonstrates that with objective test devices and factor analysis it is possible to test the motivational theories of Freud. In addition, it must be noted, they have received some support.

Since, in Freudian theory, id, ego and superego are fundamental components of behaviour, it is to be expected that they would emerge as higher-order factors rather remote from the original test scores. This expectation was confirmed in the factorial studies of Cattell discussed above. However, Dombrose and Slobin (1958) have described a projective test, the IES test, which purports to measure directly id, ego and superego. There are four subtests. (a) *Picture title test*. In this subjects give a title to 12 pictures. Scoring depends on the title given. For example, if a subject integrates all the components of the picture in his title, he is given an ego score. (b) *Picture story completion test*. Subjects have to complete, with one of three cartoons, sets of cartoon pictures. Their choice reflects, again, ego, superego or id components. (c) *Photoanalysis test*. Subjects here have to answer multiple-choice questions about photographs. Responses are claimed to indicate id, superego or ego since subjects project their own desires on to the pictures. (d) *Arrow–dot test*. For this subjects have to trace the shortest path from start to goal avoiding barriers of barred lines. Other 'barriers' not mentioned in the instructions are present. If these are crossed, for example, as they can be, this is an ego score. Disobeying the rules to reach the target is an id score, avoiding the unmentioned barriers is a superego score.

The test–retest reliability of the test is 0.62 (Dombrose and Slobin 1958) overall, for a small sample of men under outpatient therapy. This suggests that it may be used with caution for research purposes, certainly with groups. However, there are few norms for the test and the user has to make do with the results from a few published studies (e.g. Rankin and Johnston 1962) which use rather homogeneous groups of students. In addition to this, most published reports have concerned American or Canadian samples. A further disadvantage of the test is that there is really no evidence of its validity. Herron (1966), surveying all the reports in which the test was used up to that date, was unable to present a powerful argument for its construct validity. Certainly the IES has discriminated latents, adolescents, seniles and psychotics (see Dombrose and Slobin 1958) yet, as Crowne (1965) points out, this cannot be used to demonstrate its validity without also showing what it does not measure. After all, an intelligence test would make such discriminations. The IES test has been mentioned here because it is one of the few attempts to measure with any degree of quantification these particular variables and because none of the reported studies actually contraindicates the validity of the test. The IES demands, therefore, further research. However, as Crowne (1965) points out, the lack of evidence for validity, the moderate reliability and, above all, the crude nature of the test materials so that the purpose of the test is transparent all tend to discourage rigorous researchers from using this test.

Kline and Trejdosiewicz (1971a, b) carried out a pilot study of the construct validity of the test by administering it individually to a small sample of male students together with the Blacky Pictures. There was little to support the validity of the IES in this sample in that there were no significant correlations with the Blacky Pictures. Furthermore, the scores of the British sample were significantly different from those of comparable American samples but not in any consistent way. Thus, IES scores were both larger and smaller than the American norms depending upon from which test they were derived. We were compelled to conclude that in this British university sample the sources of variance for the IES test scores were complex and related in part to the interaction of the educational background of the sample with the particular stimulus properties of the test rather than the putative test variables.

What may we conclude, therefore, from this study of Freudian theories of motivation? First, it demonstrates beyond reasonable doubt that the concepts of id, ego and superego are amenable to test, both indirectly (higher-order factors) and, albeit less convincingly, directly (the IES test). This puts this part of Freudian theory on to a scientific basis. It shows also that the objective test devices of Cattell are unquestionably the most potentially useful measures in this field. Another clear finding to emerge from this section is that the objective devices are capable of measuring the dynamics of motivation drives. This means that this aspect of Freudian theory may be considered as refutable and hence scientific. Here the evidence suggests at this early stage of research that psychoanalytic theory seriously underestimates the number of drives underlying human behaviour. However, until ergic factor structure is convincingly explicated we cannot be sure of this. We await with interest higher-order ergs.

One further point needs discussing. At the beginning of this section it was perhaps baldly stated that *eros* and *thanatos* were considered to be unmeasurable. The observant and sceptical reader may perhaps wonder why it was not argued that these two concepts imply a bipolar theory of motivation. The difficulty with this is conceiving what variables might load on the *thanatos* pole. Suppose interests in dangerous occupations and hobbies loaded at one pole of an unknown factor, it follows that interests in the opposite would load at the other. It means only that dangerous sports fall into a different group from safe ones. It remains impossible to define operationally a *thanatos* or an *eros* factor.

Conclusions

What final conclusions can we draw, then, from this study of assessment procedures in psychodynamic psychology? One fact seems to be clear. To reject such psychology as unquantifiable and unscientific is false. In the chapter we have cited tests of psychosexual personality traits, psychosexual fixation, Jungian personality types, defence mechanisms, drives, and even the dynamic equilibrium. Furthermore, these tests have not been restricted to projective measures. Some indeed, notably those of Cattell, have relied on multivariate statistical methods in their validation and construction. From this we therefore conclude that psychometrists can, given imagination and insight, provide sound quantification into psychodynamic psychology and thus help to elucidate these theories and to establish whatever truths they may contain as part of the science of psychology.

References

Adler, A. (1930), *Individual Psychology*, See C. Murchison (Ed.) (1930), *Psychologies of 1930*, Worcester, Mass., Clarke University Press.

Alexander, F. (1950), *Psychosomatic Medicine*, New York, Norton.

Altrocchi, J., Parsons, O. A., and Pickoff, H. (1960), 'Changes in self-ideal discrepancy in repressors and sensitizers', *Journal of Abnormal and Social Psychology*, **61**, 1, 67–72.

Barnes, C. A. (1952), 'A statistical study of the Freudian theory of levels of psychosexual development', *Genetic Psychological Monographs*, **45**, 109–74.

Beloff, H. (1957), 'The structure and origin of the anal character', *Genetic Psychological Monographs*, **55**, 141–72.

Berger, L., and Everstine, L. (1962), 'Test–retest reliability of the Blacky Pictures Test', *Journal of Projective Techniques*, **26**, 225–6.

Blum, G. S. (1949), 'A study of the psychoanalytic theory of psychosexual development', *Genetic Psychological Monographs*, **39**, 3–99.

Blum, G. S. (1955), 'Perceptual defence revisited', *Journal of Abnormal and Social Psychology*, **51**, 24–9.

Blum, G. S. (1957), 'An investigation of perceptual defence in Italy', *Psychological Reports*, **3**, 169–75.

Blum, G. S. (1962), 'A guide for the research use of the Blacky Pictures', *Journal of Projective Techniques*, **26**, 3–29.

Blum, G. S., and Miller, D. R. (1952), 'Exploring the psychoanalytic theory of the "oral character"', *Journal of Personality*, **20**, 287–304.

Bradway, K. (1964), 'Jung's psychological types', *Journal of Analytical Psychology*, **9**, 129–34.

Buros, O. K. (Ed.) (1965), *The VIth Mental Measurement Year Book*, New Jersey, Gryphon.

Buros, O. K. (Ed.) (1971), *Personality Tests and Reviews*, New Jersey, Gryphon.

Buros, O. K. (Ed.) (1972), *The VIIth Mental Measurement Year Book*, New Jersey, Gryphon.

Burt, C. A. (1940), *The Factors of the Mind*, London, University of London Press.

Byrne, D. (1964), 'Repression-sensitisation as a dimension of personality', in B. A. Maher (Ed.) (1964), *Progress in Experimental Personality Research*, Vol. 1, New York, Academic Press, pp. 169–220.

Cattell, R. B. (1957), *Personality and Motivation Structure and Measurement*, Yonkers, New World.

Cattell, R. B., and Warburton, F. W. (1967), *Objective Personality and Motivation Tests*, Urbana, University of Illinois Press.

Comrey, A. L. (1972), 'The Motivation Analysis Test', in Buros, O. K. (Ed.) (1972), *The VIIth Mental Measurement Year Book*, New Jersey, Gryphon.

Corman, L. (1969), *Le Test P.N. Manuel*, Paris, Presses Universitaires de France.

Cronbach, L. J. (1950), 'Further evidence on response sets and test design', *Educational and Psychological Measurement*, **10**, 3–31.

Crowne, D. P. (1965), 'Review of the I.E.S. Test', in Buros, O. K. (Ed.) (1965), *The VIth Mental Measurement Year Book*, New Jersey, Gryphon.

Dombrose, L. A., and Slobin, M. S. (1958), 'The I.E.S. Test', *Perceptual and Motor Skills*, **8**, 347–89.

Edwards, A. L. (1957), *The Social Desirability Variable in Personality Research*, New York, Dryden.

Edwards, A. L. (1959), *The Edwards Personal Preference Schedule*, New York, Psychological Corporation.

Endler, N. S. (1963), Paper quoted by Byrne (1964) q.v.

Eysenck, H. J. (1953), *Uses and Abuses of Psychology*, Harmondsworth, Penguin.

Farrell, B. A. (1964), 'The status of psychoanalytic theory', *Inquiry*, **7**, 104–22.

Fenichel, O. (1945), *The Psychoanalytic Theory of Neurosis*, New York, Norton.

Freud, A. (1946), *The Ego and the Mechanisms of Defence*, London, Hogarth Press and the Institute of Psychoanalysis.

Freud, S. (1905), 'Three essays on sexuality', Vol. 7, 135–243.

Freud, S. (1908), 'Character and anal erotism', Vol. 9, 169–75.

Freud, S. (1909), 'Notes upon a case of obsessional neurosis', Vol. 10, 153–318.

Freud, S. (1910), 'Leonardo Da Vinci and a memory of his childhood', Vol. XI, 63–137.

Freud, S. (1911), 'Psychoanalytic notes on an autobiographical account of a case of paranoia (dementia Paranoides)', Vol. 12, 3–82.

Freud, S. (1915), 'Repression', Vol. 14, 143–58.

Freud, S. (1923), 'The ego and the id', Vol. 19, 3.

Freud, S. (1933), 'New introductory lectures on psychoanalysis', Vol. 22.

Fromm, E. (1942), *The Fear of Freedom*, London, Routledge & Kegan Paul.

Fromm, E. (1965), *The Heart of Man, its Genius for Good and Evil*, London, Routledge & Kegan Paul.

Gleser, G. C., and Ihilevich, D. (1969), 'An objective instrument for measuring defence mechanisms', *Journal of Consulting and Clinical Psychology*, **33**, 51–60.

Goldman, F. (1948), 'Breast-feeding and character formation I', *Journal of Personality*, **17**, 83–103.

Goldman, F. (1950), 'Breast-feeding and character formation II. The etiology of the oral character in psychoanalytic theory', *Journal of Personality*, **19**, 189–96.

Goldman-Eisler, F. (1951), 'The problem of "orality" and its origin in early childhood', *Journal of Mental Science*, **97**, 765–82.

Gottheil, E. (1965a), 'Conceptions of orality and anality', *Journal of Nervous and Mental Diseases*, **141**(2), 155–60.

Gottheil, E. (1965b), 'An empirical analysis of orality and anality', *Journal of Nervous and Mental Diseases*, **141**, 308–17.

Gottheil, E., and Stone, G. C. (1968), 'Factor analytic study of orality and anality', *Journal of Nervous and Mental Diseases*, **146**, 1–17.

Gray, H., and Wheelwright, J. B. (1946), 'Jung's psychological types: their frequency of occurrence', *Journal of Genetic Psychology*, **34**, 3–17.

Grygier, T. G. (1961), *The Dynamic Personality Inventory*, London, N.F.E.R.

Harman, H. H. (1964), *Modern Factor Analysis*, Chicago, University of Chicago Press.

Herron, W. (1966), 'The I.E.S. Experiment', *Perceptual and Motor Skills*, **23**, 279–90.

Horney, K. (1942), *Self Analysis*, New York, Norton.

Horney, K. (1945), *Our Inner Conflicts*, New York, Norton.

Joy, V. L. (1963), 'Repression-sensitisation personality and interpersonal behaviour', Unpublished Ph.D. Thesis, University of Texas.

Jung, C. G. (1949), *Psychological Types*, London, Routledge & Kegan Paul.

Kline, P. (1968a), 'Obsessional traits, obsessional symptoms and anal erotism', *British Journal of Medical Psychology*, **41**, 299–305.

Kline, P. (1968b), 'The validity of the Dynamic Personality Inventory', *British Journal of Medical Psychology*, **41**, 307–11.

Kline, P. (1970), 'A projective and psychometric study of the oral character', *Proc. VII Internat. Conf. Soc. Rorsch. & Proj. Tech.*, Vienna, Hans Huber.

Kline, P. (1971), *Ai3Q Test*, Windsor, N.F.E.R.

Kline, P. (1972), *Fact and Fantasy in Freudian Theory*, London, Methuen.

Kline, P., 'The concept and measurement of orality', *British Journal of Projective Psychology*, In Press.

Kline, P., 'The validity of the Gottheil personality scale', *Journal of Projective Techniques and Personality Assessment*, In Press.

Kline, P., and Gale, A. (1969), 'An objective method of administering a projective technique—The Blacky Pictures', *British Journal of Projective Psychology*, **15**, 12–16.

Kline, P., and Grindley, J., 'The validity of the M.A.T.: a 28 day case study', *J. of Multivar. Clin. Psychol.*, In Press.

Kline, P., and Trejdosiewicz, L. (1971a), 'I.E.S. Test Scores of students in Great Britain', *Perceptual and Motor Skills*, **33**, 1209–10.

Kline, P., and Trejdosiewicz, L. (1971b), 'The I.E.S. Test and the Blacky Pictures', *British Journal of Projective Psychology*, **16**, 19–21.

Kragh, U. (1959), 'Types of pre-cognitive defence organisation in a tachistoscopic experiment', *Journal of Projective Techniques*, **23**, 315–22.

Kragh, U. (1960), 'The Defence Mechanism test: a new method for diagnosis and personnel selection', *Journal of Applied Psychology*, **44**, 303–9.

Krout, M. H., and Krout, T. J. (1954), 'Measuring personality in developmental terms', *Genetic Psychological Monographs*, **50**, 289–335.

Lazare, A., Klerman, G. L., and Armor, D. J. (1966), 'Oral, obsessive and hysterical personality patterns: an investigation of psychoanalytic concepts by means of factor analysis', *Archives of General Psychiatry*, **14**, 624–30.

McDougall, W. (1932), *The Energies of Man*, London, Methuen.

Maher, B. A. (Ed.) (1964), *Progress in Experimental Personality Research*, Vol. 1, New York, Academic Press.

Martin, M. (1964), 'Mr. Farrell and the refutability of psychoanalysis', *Inquiry*, **7**, 80–98.

Masling, J., Rabie, L., and Blondheim, S. H. (1967), 'Obesity, level of aspiration, Rorschach and T.A.T. measures of oral dependence', *Journal of Consulting Psychology*, **31**, 233–9.

Masling, J., Weiss, L., and Rothschild, B. (1968), 'Relationships of oral imagery to yielding behaviour and birth order', *Journal of Consulting and Clinical Psychology*, **32**, 89–91.

Mendelsohn, G. A. (1965), 'The Myers–Briggs Type Indicator', in Buros, O. K. (Ed.) (1965), *The VIth Mental Measurement Year Book*, New Jersey, Gryphon.

Michal-Smith, H., Hammer, E., and Spitz, H. (1951), 'Use of the Blacky Pictures with a child whose Oedipal desires are close to consciousness', *Journal of Clinical Psychology*, **7**, 280–2.

Murchison, C. (Ed.) (1930), *Psychologies of 1930*, Worcester, Mass., Clarke University Press.

Murray, H. A. (1938), *Explorations in Personality*, New York, Oxford University Press.

Myers, I. B. (1962), *Manual to the Myers–Briggs Type Indicator*, Princeton, E.T.S.

Pawlick, K., and Cattell, R. B. (1964), 'Third-order factors in objective personality tests', *British Journal of Psychology*, **55**, 1–18.

Popper, K. (1959), *The Logic of Scientific Discovery*, New York, Basic Books.

Rankin, R. J., and Johnston, J. D. (1962), 'Influences of age and sex on the I.E.S. Test', *Perceptual and Motor Skills*, **15**, 775–8.

Rapaport, D., and Gill, M. M. (1959), 'The points of view and assumptions of metapsychology', *International Journal of Psychoanalysis*, **40**, 153–62.

Sarnoff, I. (1971), *Testing Freudian Concepts*, New York, Springer.

Sjoback, H. (1967), *Defence Mechanism Test*, Lund, The Colytographic Research Foundation.

Skinner, B. F. (1954), 'Critique of psychoanalytic concepts and theories', *Science Monitor*, **79**, 300–5.

Story, I. A. (1963), 'The relationship between the effects of conflict arousal and oral fixation on thinking', Unpublished Ph.D. Thesis, University of Michigan.

Story, I. A. (1968), 'Effects on thinking of relationships between conflict arousal and oral fixation', *Journal of Abnormal Psychology*, **73**, 440–8.

Stricker, L. J., and Ross, J. (1964), 'Some correlates of a Jungian Personality Inventory', *Psychological Reports*, **14**, 623–43.

Sundberg, N. D. (1965), 'The Myers–Briggs Type Indicator', in Buros, O. K. (Ed.) (1965), *The VIth Mental Measurement Year Book*, New Jersey, Gryphon.

Taulbee, E. S., and Stenmark, P. E. (1968), 'The Blacky Pictures Test. A comprehensive annotated and indexed bibliography (1949–67)', *Journal of Projective Techniques*, **32**, 105–37.

Toman, W. (1960), *An Introduction to the Psychoanalytic Theory of Motivation*, Oxford, Pergamon.

Ullman, L. P. (1962), 'An empirically derived M.M.P.I. scale which measures facilitation–inhibition of recognition of threatening stimuli', *Journal of Clinical Psychology*, **18**, 127–32.

Vetter, H. J., and Smith, B. D. (Eds.) (1971), *Personality Theory: A Source Book*, New York, Appleton Century Crofts.

Warburton, F. W. (1968), 'The structure of personality factors', Unpublished Ms., University of Manchester.

Wenig, P. W. (1952), 'The relative roles of naïve, autistic, cognitive and press compatability misperception and ego defence operations in tests of misperception', Unpublished M.Sc. Thesis, University of Illinois.

Wolowitz, H. M. (1964), 'Food preference as an index of orality', *Journal of Abnormal and Social Psychology*, **69**, 6, 650–4.

Wolowitz, H. M. (1967), 'Oral involvement in peptic ulcer', *Journal of Consulting Psychology*, **31**, 418–9.

Wolowitz, H. M., and Barker, M. J. (1968), 'Alcoholism and oral passivity', *Quarterly Journal of Studies on Alcohol*, **29**, 592–7.

Wolowitz, H. M., and Wagonfeld, S. (1968), 'Oral derivatives in the food preferences of peptic ulcer patients. An experimental test of Alexander's psychoanalytic hypothesis', *Journal of Nervous and Mental Diseases*, **146**, 18–23.

8

THE PSYCHOPHYSIOLOGY OF INDIVIDUAL DIFFERENCES: STUDIES OF EXTRAVERSION AND THE EEG

Anthony Gale

University of Wales Institute of Science and Technology

THIS CHAPTER has four sections. The first is concerned with the aims of psychophysiological research in general. The second section describes in detail experiments concerned with extraversion–introversion and the EEG. This is followed by a critical discussion of the defects in those studies and recommendations for future research. Finally, there is a brief description of some recent psychophysiological studies which might provide a basis for future work on the psychophysiology of individual differences.

Introduction

It is a reflection of the youthful state of psychophysiology that there exists no integrated review of research upon the psychophysiology of individual differences. Research in this area is considerable but fragmented, and although it is ripe for synthesis, no suitable framework for integrating all the experimental data has yet been formulated. We now know a great deal about the patterning of psychophysiological response over a variety of normal and abnormal states, providing sufficient material for a volume with individual chapters devoted to psychophysiological studies of anxiety, psychopathy, schizophrenia, psychosomatic disorders, extraversion–introversion and intelligence. It is impossible within the short scope of this chapter to give an adequate account of what has been achieved so far. I propose instead to focus upon research into the relationship between extraversion and the electroencephalogram or EEG. This is a topic which exhibits many of the problems, pitfalls and errors which may be observed in studies of the psychophysiology of individual differences as a whole, and I shall therefore pick out some of the good and poor features of these studies to see what general lessons may be learned. My approach will be rather simple-minded, in contrast with many of the foregoing chapters, for I am no master of the arts of psychometric wizardry which they exemplify. It is proper, however, that this chapter should appear in a volume which is largely psychometric in character, for psychophysiology has much to learn from the simple and straightforward practices of psychometrics in matters concerning sampling, reliability of the instruments of measurement and the standardization of procedures. Psychophysiology does have its own brand of sophisticated alchemy, of course; there are now several manuals of a very technical nature, which discuss (in what may appear to the outsider as obsessional and excruciating detail) problems of electronic circuitry, electrode preparation and placement, waveform analysis, computer storage of data, and so on. My view is that this sophistication has been misplaced, since technical aspects have often been overemphasized at the expense of the art of experimentation. Too many psychophysiologists have been so enchanted by hardware and gadgetry that they have forgotten to carry out experiments.

There is a disease to which many scientists are prone. To purloin a copyright and coin a phrase, we may call it Meccanophilia. The symptoms are recognized without difficulty. The Meccanophiliac suffers from a love of experimental apparatus, rather than a love of experimentation. He tinkers, plays and fidgets with apparatus, but rarely uses it. Computeritis is a related disorder with an equally poor prognosis which hits young scientists in their prime, quite often in the first year of study for a doctorate. The key symptoms are continuous absence from the laboratory and the acquisition of a neologistic but apparently systematic quasi-language. When more than one are affected, it can take upon it the appearance of *folie à deux*. Supervisors who observe these symptoms in their research students are advised to act quickly. If their own training has been of the paper-and-pencil variety, they should be particularly cautious. Only those who have suffered from disorders of this nature and have pulled through intact are really capable of effecting a cure. Rational appeals to the patient, on the grounds that computers are tools and not masters, are likely to fail.

What is required is more meta-discussion concerning the basic assumptions of the discipline together with a disinterested consideration of the sort of question which the psychophysiologist wishes to put to nature. It is reasonable to ask whether individual differences as measured by tests or clinical diagnosis are reflected in individual differences in the patterning of physiological response, but unfortunately questions of this nature are rarely put properly. Thus the psychophysiology of individual differences is replete with first-rate questions and second-rate answers. I hope to illustrate these problems in discussing studies of extraversion and the EEG.

On the Distinction between Psychophysiology and Physiological Psychology

Why does one need yet another new label like 'psychophysiology'? Many psychophysiologists convey the impression that they are poor relatives of physiological psychology, condemned to the mere study of man, rather than predictable rat. There are in fact real and important distinctions to be drawn, which have several implications, and the study of man has many advantages which, of late, some psychologists have come to recognize.

Physiological Psychology

The physiological psychologist is primarily concerned with tampering with the nervous system and then drawing inferences about its normal modes of operation on the basis of the behavioural disruption which ensues. He cuts, burns, ablates, sucks out and even rewires parts of the brain and may also induce reversible chemical lesions. He then observes how behaviour is changed and attempts to describe or determine the normal role of the part which has been damaged. There are great logical difficulties with an approach of this nature and many researchers appear to be oblivious to them. A key problem is that control operations are required in *other* brain areas to ensure that damage in areas other than the one under inspection does not bring about identical effects. Secondly, the part damaged may be only necessary rather than sufficient to the function it is said to subserve. Its removal or damage may have an adverse effect on a psychological 'function', but that does not imply that it 'subserves' that 'function'. It may merely be part of a larger system which is dependent upon its integrity for the proper functioning of the whole. Again, the sort of block diagram which physiological psychologists are wont to produce is *not* like those produced by engineers, since engineers know *before* they draw the diagram what the system it describes actually does and what are the functions and *modus operandi* of its individual parts and units. The illusion the physiological psychologist wishes to create concerning his engineering skills is a false illusion which derives from a failure to understand the logical rationale of engineering models themselves. This localization of function approach is essentially both causal and reductionist. It attempts to identify those parts of the brain which subserve certain psychological 'functions'. Quasi-anatomy is often dressed up as *bona fide* neurophysiology. The psychological terms employed in such models are often barely removed from the vernacular. For example, the subtle distinctions employed by those who work with the psychology of memory are forgotten by those who claim to work with the physiology of memory. Some of the models devised for describing or explaining the functioning of the brain, the most complex machine we know of, are barely adequate to the description of the functioning of the pedal bicycle. Psychophysiology is not open to such criticism, since it rarely engages in discussion of causal mechanisms or in attempts to 'explain'. It focuses much more upon observation, measurement and correlation.

The general rule in physiological psychology is to employ physiological variables as independent variables and behavioural variables as dependent variables. Until quite recently, however, the dependent variable has been poorly quantified and has leaned heavily upon simple observational techniques. Quite often, the extensive study of behavioural variables is limited because of the critical effects of surgery upon the experimental animals. Indeed, it sometimes appears that experiments are carried out in indecent haste, to ensure their completion before the death of the subjects. Needless to say, such experiments are performed at present upon lower vertebrates rather than upon man. There are studies of the behavioural effects of lesions in the human brain, but the experimental subjects are usually the unfortunate victims of illness, accident and/or of the eager surgeon's knife. Such 'natural' experiments are not a reliable source of information, since either there are no pretest data or the pretest data are themselves contaminated by the very disorder which necessitates surgery. Even where controlled and reversible lesions are employed, as in the sodium amytal technique for the detection of speech 'localization', the dangers involved in the procedure preclude extensive periods of experimentation and the behaviour which is sampled is in consequence limited. Possibly the best studies upon humans are those reporting the effects of discrete gunshot wounds, since the gradual accumulation of cases provides a pattern of lesions in different brain areas. The behavioural effects of such wounds may be quite subtle and discrete and may have little effect upon the general functioning of the individual, which for most intents and purposes may remain intact. The key difficulty which these studies overcome is that within a group of subjects they provide damage controls in different brain areas. The lack of such controls in earlier work explains the phenomenally broad range of functions and characteristics ascribed to the same part of the human brain by different authorities. For example, the frontal lobes have at one time or another been said to subsume or contain: reasoning, the highest intellectual centre, higher levels of emotion and personality, foresight, volition, skin and motor analysers, immediate memory, inhibition, attention, and so on. . . .

We see then that physiological psychology is more physiological than psychological. The logical basis of the reasoning employed is suspect and the interpretation of experimental data is often overgenerous. It is essentially a causal or reductionist approach. Thus psychological variables are inadequately treated. Because surgical techniques are an essential feature of the discipline, human subjects are rarely employed. Thus the proportion of space allocated to human psychology in standard textbooks of physiological psychology is remarkably small. It is much easier to talk about rats and cats than it is to talk about man.

Psychophysiology

Psychophysiology presents a considerable contrast. Experiments are performed almost exclusively upon intact human subjects. The activity of the nervous system is studied from the outside. No particular advantage is thought to be gained from the capacity to probe about inside the system. Models or theories about the functioning of the system are at present rare. The emphasis is upon adequate quantification of the physiological variables which in this case are employed as dependent variables. Psychological state is manipulated and physiological and psychological outcomes are measured. Because human subjects are employed, the experimenter is able to take account of the subjective report of the person upon whom the experiment is being carried out. This provides an additional source of information which the student of the animal brain denies himself. Three different aspects of the person may be studied concurrently, along a common time scale: performance or behaviour, verbal report of subjective experience, and physiological state. The capacity to study events in three universes of discourse at once is the hallmark of the psychophysiologist. His job is to construct units and scales of measurement which enable him to make sense of what is occurring concomitantly in all three universes: (i) physiology, or what is going on in the nervous system (e.g. as measured by variation in heart rate, electrodermal activity, respiration, muscle activity and the EEG), (ii) what the subject is observed to be doing (reaction time, learning, social behaviour, activity level, and so on) and (iii) subjective report of experience (what is thought, felt or imagined). This is essentially a correlational approach. It does not necessarily involve discussion of cause nor is it a commitment to reductionism. One rarely hears the psychophysiologist make the arrogant claim that behaviour is 'really only the activity of the nervous system' or that all psychology is ultimately reducible to the activity of neurons. This approach to psychophysiology is merely a recognition that man may be looked at in different ways, but at the same time, and that none of the three ways of looking is necessarily superior or primary. This view may not be philosophically palatable to some, for it involves the psychophysiologist in a sort of 'naive parallelism' since events in the three universes of discourse are considered to be sharing a common time scale. Certainly, this view enables the psychophysiologist to sidestep the Cartesian *cul-de-sac*. A commitment to correlation rather than cause can provide a therapeutic escape from the worries of the mind–body problem.

The ideal psychophysiological experiment asks questions of the form: 'When S performs classes of action X_b, Y_b and Z_b, may we also differentiate parallel changes in classes of physiological state X_p, Y_p and Z_p and also classes of experiential event X_e, Y_e and Z_e (where the subscripts b, p and e stand for behaviour, physiology and experience)?'. For X, Y and Z we might substitute, for example, anger, fear and rage. Regrettably, the experiential domain has been much neglected in contemporary psychology, and perhaps the only branch of psychological enquiry which has of necessity always recognized the need to sample the three universes of discourse is psychopathology. Mental disorders are associated with disruption within the three universes, and it is accepted that attempts to induce a return to normality by tackling problems from one universe lead to observation of parallel changes of events in the others.

This three-universe approach of the psychophysiologist raises many difficulties in practical terms, for the psychophysiologist must maintain feet in several camps at once, without tripping himself up. He must have a comprehensive grasp of the state of play in a wide range of fields of enquiry, fields in which progress in theorizing, quantification and experimentation has reached varying degrees of sophistication. The psychophysiologist, more than workers in many other branches of psychology, is examining the 'whole man' and must be sensitive to the influence of a heterogeneous set of variables. He neglects at his peril advances in experimental psychology, individual psychology and techniques of phenomenological description. In a sense, he is somewhat parasitical upon other branches of psychology; his own special problems are often technical ones, but the questions he puts to nature are generally questions which have been devised by other workers.

But there is a payoff for all the effort involved in keeping up to date across the board, for the psychophysiologist may acquire the role of bridgebuilder and serve to synthesize and integrate information from several disciplines. In his parasitical search for problems to tackle, he is well placed to recognize the similarity between problems couched in different languages within apparently encapsulated disciplines. A nice example is presented by the study of attentional deficit in schizophrenia. Such a deficit is recognized by clinical, cognitive, physiological and phenomenological psychologists alike. At present, attempts to draw these differing views together have not achieved much more than a mere cataloguing of findings (e.g. McGhie 1969), and there has been little collaborative effort between those with different views of the problem. What is required is a synthesis of the available information in a language which serves as a common referent for all the differing approaches. The psychophysiologist, with the breadth of training which a three-universe approach necessitates, is well placed to perform such a task.

There are basically two alternative strategies for a psychophysiology of individual differences. Firstly, to manipulate existing variables and experimental procedures which are already well established in experimental and individual psychology, and to observe covariation of psychophysiological variables. Studies of extraversion and the EEG exemplify this approach, since the psychophysiologist may call upon a large body of established data concerning extraversion and performance. The second alternative is to break new ground and construct new psychophysiological tasks, i.e. tasks which owe their origin to psychophysiology rather than to any other discipline, and observe individual variation in performance or patterning of response during performance of the task. Consistency in such variation itself would serve as the descriptor of individual differences or provide a means of predicting differences on further tasks. For example, some recent research in schizophrenia has demonstrated the usefulness of employing performance on a psychophysiological task as a means of predicting performance on other tasks. Gruzelier and Venables (1971) show how the distinction between *responders* and *non-responders* in a simple GSR habituation experiment may be used to predict performance on a variety of further physiological and psychological tasks. Findings like these provide new means of drawing objectively defined distinctions between categories of patient, since they start not with traditional diagnosis categories but with a psychophysiological task. They therefore represent a possible conceptual disentanglement from earlier studies in psychopathology, which were obliged to employ the dubious clinical distinctions of paranoid/non-paranoid, chronic/acute, reactive/process, and so on, which may have led to much obfuscation of research.

Studies of the Relationship between Extraversion and the EEG

There have been more than a dozen studies of this relationship and they have yielded three classes of outcome. Extraverts have been shown to be less aroused than introverts, more aroused than introverts, or equally aroused. Arousal in this case is measured operationally in terms of the amplitude and frequency of the EEG. Can one make any sense out of such discrepant findings? Would the cynic be correct in asserting that the varied results of such investigations merely demonstrate that such investigations are worthless? One's answer to such a challenge must be along the following lines. First, we may ask whether the EEG is a characteristic of individuals or of groups which is as invariable and immutable as eye colour? Is it reasonable to expect the EEG of extraverts to be *always* differentiable from that of introverts and for the difference *always* to be in the same direction? Or to put another question, is performance on tasks universally superior for extraverts or introverts? The answer clearly is no. For example, Colquhoun and Corcoran (1964) have shown how time of day and group or individual testing on attentional tasks can reverse such relationships. Under certain conditions extraverts perform better than introverts, under certain conditions they perform worse. Studies of body temperature illustrate how even a simple measure can show both diurnal variation and crossover effects in relation to this personality dimension. Only a careful specification of the conditions of testing and an understanding of the effect of such conditions upon the subject groups allows for adequate prediction of the outcome. Since we may safely assume that the activity of the nervous system is differentially affected by experimental conditions and since the EEG is a reflection of central nervous activity, it is not surprising that the EEG should vary also. Thus on different occasions, as with performance, the extravert EEG may be greater or lesser in magnitude than the introvert EEG. The problem is whether the variation observed is explicable in a systematic manner. It is necessary to review the existing studies in detail in order to gain insight into the problems of such research and to identify the crucial variables. There are many serious defects in these studies. After reviewing them, I shall end with a list of recommendations for future work. I shall focus upon several procedural points. The rationale or different theoretical justifications for the studies will be considered later. The reader should look out for the following features: method of subject selection, personality assessment, EEG measures, EEG sampling and scoring, experimental procedures and conditions of testing, and statistical procedures and tests.

The EEG is a complex waveform, made up of a number of constituent frequencies. Understandably, therefore, techniques of analysis are extremely complex. I shall only mention those features which are of direct concern for the comprehension of this chapter. The EEG as recorded consists of moment-to-moment fluctuations in voltage. The simplest descriptors are amplitude and frequency. Visual techniques of analysis involve measuring amplitude variation by joining peaks and measuring envelope area, and simply counting the number of cycles per unit time to estimate frequency. Traditionally, four bandwidths have been studied: delta (1.5–4.5 Hz), theta (4.5–6.5 Hz), alpha (7.5–13.5 Hz) and beta (13.5–20.0 Hz). These different frequencies have been differentially associated with different levels of sleep. The frequency most studied in the waking state is the alpha frequency and most of the studies in this review are concerned with alpha. The psychological significance of the different bandwidths is not really understood. Alpha activity is influenced by visual stimulation specifically and also responds to generalized changes of state. Generally speaking, high amplitude and low frequency are said to be indicants of low arousal, whereas low amplitude and high frequency indicate high arousal.

The most popular form of electronic analysis is low-frequency automated integrated analysis. The primary waveform passes through selective filters, whose activity is then integrated, to produce a measure which, roughly speaking, indicates the area under the curve occupied within a particular frequency over a fixed period. This measure is often referred to as 'abundance' and may, of course, relate either to the whole measured range or just to a limited frequency band. Another descriptive term employed is 'index'; in the case of alpha index, this would simply mean the proportion of time occupied by alpha waves above a criterion voltage. This measure is often used in studies based upon hand-scoring techniques. In one or two studies in this review, measures different to those above have been used, and these will be explained when they occur. The key terms to remember are alpha, theta, beta, frequency, amplitude, abundance and index.

Gottlober (1938)

The first detailed report in the literature is by Gottlober (1938). Gottlober mentions an informal study by Lemere which reports no differences in prediction of alpha waves between extraverts and introverts. He observes that Lemere employs no adequate criterion for distinguishing personality groups and provides no precise account of how the EEG was quantified. Regrettably, such features remain as a constant source of frustration to those who would wish to replicate studies in this field. Gottlober employs two rating procedures, self-report (the Nebraska Personality Inventory) and ratings by clinical judges, including himself. It is unfortunate that the procedures employed by the raters are not specified at all, particularly since these have superior predictive power for EEG differences in his study. The subject reclined on a bed in a dark room with his eyes closed. He was instructed to keep his mind 'as free from thought as was possible'. A thirty-second sample was taken for each subject. Gottlober divided EEG alpha activity into the four categories of dominant, subdominant, mixed or rare, on the basis of per cent time during which alpha activity is found to be present within an individual record. Visual analysis was employed to score the EEG record. Gottlober concluded that most subjects (48) were in the dominant/subdominant classification (i.e. exhibited a large ratio of alpha activity) and few (19) were of the mixed/rare variety (total N was 67). A significantly larger proportion of the extravert group (as so classified by rating rather than by self-rating) had a high per cent of alpha, whereas the introverts were equally divided between the high and low categories. The questionnaire scores were unrelated to per cent time alpha. Interesting features of this study were: (i) the EEG was scored by eye, (ii) the subject lay with his eyes closed, (iii) the experimenter knew the subject's personality score prior to the experiment, (iv) the more objective method of personality assessment failed to yield a significant result, and (v) extraverts showed a significantly higher proportion of subjects in the high per cent alpha categories. Thus, in modern terms, Gottlober showed extraverts to be less aroused than introverts.

Henry and Knott (1941)

Henry and Knott (1941) attempted to replicate Gottlober's data. The only material differences in their study were the use of a five-minute testing period and a refusal to employ 'non-objective' methods of personality assessment. They obtained a negative but non-significant relationship between the NPI extraversion score and alpha index. They then reworked Gottlober's data and claim that the presence in his study of a *large proportion of extraverts* and an unduly high proportion of subjects with *high per cent* alpha led to an apparent but unacceptable result. The chi-square statistic employed by Gottlober was, they claim, inappropriately applied and his conclusions were therefore invalid. They also added their data in with his but still obtained no significant effect for the combined data. They are particularly critical of his use of raters, which they point out makes his study in principle non-replicable.

Although one must object to the use of raters without any indication of the criteria they employed, it does not follow that use of raters is necessarily 'non-objective' or valueless. If persons are able to distinguish groups of other persons in a manner which leads to a differentiation of their EEG, then this capacity of itself is a phenomenon of considerable interest. Our approach should not be to reject the use of raters but rather to attempt to find out systematically how they achieve this feat and whether it may be accomplished reliably. What cues are employed in the perception of others to yield such information? Complete rejection of Gottlober's findings demonstrates quite nicely the lost opportunities which arise when a person primarily engaged in physiological work is unaware of activities in other branches of psychology. In view of current research by social psychologists upon cues involved in the perception of other persons, we might reasonably expect that such a study might now be carried out. For example, I suspect that many an EEG technician, working in the hospital setting, will assert that he is capable of knowing in advance 'what sort of an EEG' a patient will have after only a short encounter prior to recording. A study of this alleged capacity would be relatively straightforward, but so far as I am aware it has never been attempted. Most of the studies in this review, and the later ones in particular, depend upon self-rating techniques. The authors assume that these are more 'objective' than ratings by others, in that they provide a measure of the individual's capacity to sample and report upon his own dispositions reliably. In the only study which in fact attempts to measure this reliability by using a parallel version of the same test, the outcome is quite unencouraging. (See study by Gale, p. 233 below.) Henry and Knott do not point out that since Gottlober was acquainted with his subject's personality ratings in advance (indeed he rated some of them himself), bias may have entered the procedure at the recording stage. Gottlober observed a low correlation between alpha index and the emotionality score of the NPI but fails to speculate about its relationship with extraversion. Although Henry and Knott employed the NPI, they do not report having tested for a relationship between emotionality and EEG. Thus, Henry and Knott replicate Gottlober's failure to demonstrate a relationship between the extraversion score of the NPI and the EEG, and claim that the relationship which he obtained between ratings and extraversion was in fact a spurious one. Thus they show no difference in arousal for extraverts and introverts. These two studies make a nice pair. It is unfortunate that in a recent collection of readings on extraversion–introversion only the Gottlober paper appears (Eysenck 1971), for as far as I am aware, no response was made by Gottlober to Henry and Knott's criticisms.

Mundy-Castle (1955)

The next study which is relevant is by Mundy-Castle (1955). This is not strictly speaking an experiment involving extraversion–introversion, but rather, primary–secondary function (Biesheuvel 1949), which Eysenck (1953) claims is virtually synonymous with extraversion–introversion. Subjects showing primary characteristics would be equivalent to extraverts, and those showing secondary characteristics introverts. 'The general effect of secondary function is to give continuity and integration to mental activity since it favours persistence of attention and rate of work, relative stability of moods and interests and action in the light of past experience' (Mundy-Castle 1955, p. 95). Again, 'secondary function . . . is associated with a central nervous excitability characteristic' (p. 95). The following features of Mundy-Castle's study are of interest. (i) He recorded for a minimum of 20 minutes, but does not say how much of this period he sampled. (ii) The subjects' personality scores were known in advance. (iii) Alpha frequency was measured by hand, to the nearest half-cycle per second; no figures are given for scorer reliability. (iv) A negative correlation was obtained between secondary function and alpha frequency ($r = 0.464$, $N = 40$), i.e. the higher the EEG frequency, the lower the secondary function score. Given Eysenck's equation of this dimension (or typology) with the dimension of extraversion–introversion, this means that introverts had a lower alpha frequency. (v) No indication is given of the nature of instructions to subjects. (vi) Mundy-Castle claims that he is measuring an inherited characteristic and that alpha frequency is invariant for the individual and is unaltered by relaxation or stress. This study shows that extraverts are more aroused than introverts.

McAdam and Orme (1954)

McAdam and Orme (1954) report an EEG study on a group of 40 alcoholics. Personality was assessed by means of a structured interview which ranged widely over many aspects of the patient's life. Details of the topics covered in the interview are presented in the paper. The interview material itself revealed considerable heterogeneity within the group, the only thing common to the group being their unfortunate drinking habits. However, when different patterning of EEG characteristics was employed as a criterion, the patients fell into two groups, which the authors claim could be classified as 'extraverted' or 'introverted' on the basis of the interview protocol. The 'extraverted' group had a high beta index, a low alpha index and a low theta index (in other words a fast and activated record), whereas for the introverted group the reverse held. This finding then is consonant with that of Mundy-Castle. It is unfortunate that the interview data were not subjected to a more rigorous form of analysis, which, contrary to the eyeball test employed by the authors, might have revealed factors or clusters within the protocol scores. Alternatively, they could have followed up their hunch that the EEG had enabled them to distinguish extraverts and introverts by using a questionnaire specifically designed to measure this factor. The following points are of interest. (i) The EEG was employed as an independent variable to predict personality traits. (ii) Little information was given regarding sampling, instructions or recording technique. However, three frequency bands were measured, the alpha frequency with the aid of electronic analysis. (iii) A series of chi-squares were employed on statements (positive or negative answers during interview) and the EEG dichotomous classification; full details are not given, but several tests are said to be significant beyond the 5 per cent level. This study shows that extraverts are more aroused than introverts.

Savage (1964)

Savage (1964) presents one of the best designed and clearly reported studies in the literature and his work heralds us over the threshold of the scientific era. (i) The subjects were 20 female students. (ii) The MPI was administered prior to recording, which was performed 'blind', i.e. the experimenter did not know the personality scores of the subjects until recording was completed. (iii) Subjects were divided into four groups (high and low extraversion, high and low neuroticism) on the basis of the MPI score. (iv) Alpha abundance was measured automatically by means of electronic low-frequency analysis for a fixed period of 240 seconds. (v) Information appears to have been available for the calculation of alpha frequency but such calculations are not reported. This omission does not allow comparison with earlier work. Savage claims that frequency was not measured since 'studies using latter scores (frequency) have been inconclusive'. As we have seen above, studies of frequency have not been inconclusive, since they showed extraverts to be more aronsed than introverts; as we shall see below, Savage's findings show extraverts to be less aroused. (vi) The subject lay with her eyes closed. (vii) An analysis of variance revealed that extraverts had a significantly higher alpha abundance than introverts ($P < 0.01$), there was no relationship for neuroticism and alpha abundance, but finally, extraverted neurotics had a lower alpha abundance than stable extraverts. (viii) There was a positive but non-significant correlation ($r = 0.24$) between neuroticism and extraversion in this sample. The feature which mars this study is Savage's claim that his results are consonant with those of Mundy-Castle. In fact, the reverse is the case. Mundy-Castle's 'extravert' group had high frequency alpha, whereas Savage's extravert group had high alpha amplitude. Since amplitude and frequency are generally considered to be inversely related, the results of the two studies are contradictory. Eysenck (1967) absorbs this contradiction when accepting Savage's finding to support his theory of the neurophysiological basis of individual differences. (On page 311 of the 1970 edition of *The Structure of Human Personality*, a diagram is shown representing Mundy-Castle's findings. On page 441, however, a table is shown giving Savage's (contradictory) findings.) This study shows that extraverts are less aroused than introverts.

Claridge and Herrington (1963)

Claridge and Herrington (1963), in a study completed after that of Savage but reported earlier, failed to demonstrate any relationship between resting alpha abundance and either extraversion or neuroticism. This was a complex study, conducted upon a sample of normal and mixed neurotic subjects and involving figural aftereffect to an Archimedes spiral and measurement of sedation threshold. Low and insignificant correlations were obtained for both extraversion and neuroticism and alpha amplitude, frequency and index ($N = 54$). Although the EEG was hand-scored and the relationship between the EEG and personality traits was only a subsidiary concern, the study appears to have been done with considerable care. However, the authors explain that conditions of testing may have led to a failure to replicate Savage's findings. They also point out that many factors are known to influence the EEG. One of such factors, individual differences in imaging ability, was not, they admit, controlled for in their study. Data bearing upon this particular problem are presented later in this review. This study shows no difference in arousal between extraverts and introverts.

Marton and Urban (1966)

Marton and Urban (1966) report findings relating both to resting EEG conditions and to response to auditory stimulation. Their findings were: (i) extraverts had a higher alpha index than introverts and a lower alpha frequency, (ii) EEG response to a repeated auditory stimulus ceased earlier in extraverts (between trials 12 and 15 as opposed to between trials 28 and 45), and (iii) following this habituation, the extravert records showed signs of sleep. This report is particularly cryptic concerning a number of important procedural details, and its quaint presentation is particularly irritating because the set of findings presented are the *only* ones which totally conform to Eysenck's predictions concerning resting and response measures. We do not know how the subjects were allocated to the criterion groups, how exactly the EEG was measured or sampled (either in terms of resting activity or response), or which statistical tests were employed (even though the findings are said to be statistically significant). For example, there were 20 subjects in each group, but nine of the introverted group are said to have been 'without alpha rhythm'. Were these subjects included or excluded from the calculations of alpha index and frequency? Their exclusion would be difficult to justify and their inclusion would have a dramatic effect on the calculations of the mean for the group. In my own experience, although subjects may exhibit low amplitude records, there are very few in whom alpha activity (as measured electronically) is totally absent. Since 'response' is normally defined in terms of degree of alpha-blocking, it is difficult to understand how introverted subjects, who showed no alpha, were able to continue responding for more than 28 trials! If the study may be accepted at face value, it conforms with the view that extraverts are, physiologically speaking, lower aroused and less responsive. The resting measures for both amplitude and frequency are consistent with Savage's findings, the frequency data conflicting with those of Mundy-Castle.

Fenton and Scotton (1967)

Fenton and Scotton (1967) also report a study of both resting levels and response to stimulation. This study is reported in great detail. However, in view of the aims of the investigation, some features of it are puzzling. Subjects sat with eyes shut, and after a resting period of two minutes were subjected to 60 photic stimuli. There were 54 subjects, 30 of whom were male. The MPI was administered after recording was completed. Fenton and Scotton obtained no correlation between either extraversion or neuroticism and their EEG measures (alpha index during a prestimulation rest period, mean alpha amplitude derived from the same data and mean duration of alpha-blocking to stimuli). The following features of this study indicate that the results are not as straightforward as they appear. (i) There was in fact no true 'resting period', since subjects were under continuous auditory stimulation, designed to mask distracting stimuli arising presumably from the apparatus. (ii) Stimuli were not presented automatically according to a prearranged schedule, but were contingent upon 'presence' of alpha activity as defined by visual inspection of the record by the experimenter as the experiment was in progress. Presumably, therefore, the subject could have been inadvertently conditioning the experimenter to present him with stimulation. Thus we have no guarantee that testing conditions were identical or that testing was of the same duration for all subjects. This procedure is peculiar in view of the redictions to be tested. Since it was predicted that extraverts would exhibit a more pronounced alpha wave and that they would habituate to the stimuli quicker, the procedure adopted would ensure that extraverts completed the experiment more rapidly and also have a shorter average inter-stimulus interval. At the same time, given visual analysis and a response criterion dependent upon the visual sensitivity of the scorer, 'alpha-blocking' will be detected more readily in those subjects with prominent alpha than in those without, since a response will be easier to detect. Thus the method of stimulus presentation biases the study in favour of prediction and the method of scoring biases the study against prediction. Since we have at our disposal no objective measure of the effect of these biases, it would be unwise to conclude that they cancel each other out. (iii) The method of assessing habituation is puzzling. Fenton and Scotton collapsed average duration of alpha blockade for the first 25 trials and ran a correlation with personality score upon this measure. They repeated the procedure for the final 35 trials. This is not a measure of habituation, since it gives no indication of degree of response attenuation as a function of stimulus number. Some type of regression analysis or an analysis of variance treating stimulus number as a main effect would have been more appropriate to the question in hand. Extraverts *may* have given an initially high response which attenuated rapidly, whereas introverts *may* have given an initially low response which was sustained over time. The technique employed would not distinguish such patterns of responding. Moreover, analyses of habituation are more typically applied to many fewer trials, particularly for EEG, which, according to Sokolov, habituates the arousal response within 15 trials. It is also possible that EEG response is subject to the Law of Initial Value, which states quite simply that response magnitude is said to be a function of prestimulus level. Thus an analysis of differences in response between groups who are said to be different for pre-stimulus level is liable to be complicated and calls for something like an analysis of covariance design which eliminates the effect of such dependence. (iv) The figure given for alpha index is extremely high. Fenton and Scotton claim that the mean index, i.e. proportion of a 30-second sample occupied by alpha activity of 15 microvolts or more, is 83, with a standard deviation of 10. This figure is remarkably high, particularly in view of the fact that mean amplitude is particularly low (29 microvolts, standard deviation 8). It is possible that the presence of continuous sound stimulation throughout this period induced drowsiness in the subjects even before the experiment was under way. How different a population from that of Marton and Urban, in which 23% had no alpha activity at all! A major difficulty with this study is its dependence upon a hand-scoring technique. However, Fenton and Scotton report high test–retest reliability for scoring. But it is not clear from their report whether the reliability was *within subjects*, and/or within judges, or across judges. This study demonstrates no difference in arousal for extraverts and introverts.

Broadhurst and Glass (1969)

A study by Broadhurst and Glass (1969) also depends in part upon hand-scoring and in part upon an opsometric technique, in which a map reader is run over an enlarged epidiascope projection of the EEG trace. Fifty-one subjects were used, 43 of whom were males, and an MPI was administered between two and six months after testing. The EEG was recorded during a series of mental arithmetic tasks. Broadhurst and Glass performed two types of analysis upon their data: (i) analysis of variance design replicating that of Savage and (ii) correlations. Their results differ from those of Savage in three ways: (i) introverts had significantly higher alpha index and amplitude than extraverts, (ii) stable subjects had a higher index than neurotics and (iii) there was no significant interaction between extraversion and neuroticism. They point out that, unlike Savage, they were not blessed with equal groups for the ANOVA. In fact, Savage must have been particularly lucky to obtain a clearcut division of 20 subjects upon two independent criteria at the same time (i.e. to end up with four cells of five). Broadhurst and Glass do not indicate what the cell discrepancies were nor how they compensated for this in the analysis. Gross deviations from equality can, under certain circumstances, constitute a breach of the assumptions underlying the test. Certainly, they appear to have retained their full ration of degrees of freedom for the purpose of the analysis. It would be most helpful if the technique employed were made clear for the benefit of other workers, since equality of cell membership is not easy to obtain in personality studies. The correlational analysis yielded low but significant correlations between rate of change of potential and extraversion, which Glass and Broadhurst (1966) claim indicates that extraverts are less inhibited cortically than introverts. One puzzling finding is that although neurotics had low amplitude alpha as revealed by the ANOVA, they also had low frequency as shown by the correlational analysis. Such an association between low frequency and low abundance is rare if not unique in the literature. In attempting to reconcile their findings for rate of change of potential with those of Savage for abundance, they point out that the rate of change of potential technique (which measures alpha prevalence) is more sensitive than that used by Savage. His low frequency analysis confounds prevalence with amplitude; a given sample of the EEG may contain only a few waves of particularly high amplitude, or a relatively homogeneous set of waves of low amplitude, but the abundance measure (which averages the voltages over a period of time) will show the samples as identical. Thus abundance masks the information concerning variability which is given by rate of change of potential.

This study appears to have been done with great care so far as the measurement of the EEG is concerned, and the use of alternative statistical treatments is commendable since it allows for comparison with previous studies. The major difficulty is that recordings were taken during a task or rather at periods of rest between presentation of mental arithmetic tasks. The authors do not appear to consider this problem at all in their discussion of the results. It may well be that such testing conditions have a differential effect upon personality groups. The duration of the EEG samples is particularly brief, presumably as a result of the laborious nature of the scoring procedure. It is not clear from the report exactly how long the samples were. They appear to range from five, one-second samples for amplitude and frequency measurement to 200 seconds for index and rate of change of potential. Moreover, it appears that subjects were not tested under identical conditions. Some were given a buzzer to indicate completion of permitted calculation time for the arithmetic tasks, some were given a warning signal 15 seconds prior to arithmetic calculation, and some were financially rewarded for correct response (Glass 1964). We may be tempted to speculate, for example, that extraverts, when offered a financial inducement to perform well, might become more aroused than introverts, or that a warning buzzer may considerably raise their anticipation of the ensuing task. Broadhurst and Glass point out that differences with Savage's findings are not attributable to the sex-composition of the samples (Savage used females only), for their female subjects tended, if anything, to show the reverse of Savage's findings more strongly than the males. Again, we might speculate that in our culture, with its stereotype of female innumeracy, female subjects would always be more aroused than men when faced with arithmetic tasks. These, then, are some of the difficulties associated with *post hoc* application of new hypotheses to data which have already been gathered for other purposes (Glass 1964). Conditions of testing may well be a crucial source of variance in these studies, and experiments must be set up to test specific hypotheses from the outset. This study shows that extraverts are more aroused than introverts.

Nebylitsyn (1963)

Gray (1967) puts a strong case for the identification of extraversion–introversion dimension with either the strong–weak dimensions of Pavlov–Teplov (Gray 1964) or the equilibrium in dynamism of Nebylitsyn. Nebylitsyn (1963) employed a number of indices, including the EEG, to distinguish subjects with predominance of either excitation or inhibition in dynamism. The inhibited group had a low frequency, high amplitude and high index alpha, high theta frequency and also high beta (frequency, index and amplitude). This particular combination is rather different from those which we have observed before in this discussion. Now strong and weak nervous systems are not distinguishable on the basis of the EEG. Thus, if the EEG is to be employed as a basis for drawing analogies between Russian and Western personality dimensions, then extraversion and predominance of inhibition in dynamism could be good candidates. However, any overlap in the EEG context is not necessarily reflected in behavioural measures. Gray appears very much in this paper to be grasping at straws. Correlation even on a number of measures does not necessarily imply synonymity of the dimensions.

An estimate of the degree of non-agreement of the dimensions may show that the suggestion of identity of the dimensions is at present premature. Nevertheless, if there is a case to be made, then extraverts have high alpha, theta and beta, and are less aroused than introverts.

Gale, Coles and Blaydon (1969)

Gale, Coles and Blaydon (1969) introduce a number of novel features. (i) Their subjects were given a simple task to perform: opening and shutting their eyes upon instruction. (ii) The EEG was measured for the eyes open condition as well as for the eyes closed condition. During the eyes open condition, subjects were surrounded by a matt black enclosure. (iii) Subjects were restricted to those with only average or low neuroticism scores. (iv) Automated low frequency analysis was used to yield an alpha abundance score for a range of measured frequencies. (v) A new measure of mean dominant frequency (mdf) was employed. Finally, (vi) it is moderately easy for the reader to understand what procedures were followed. Gale, Coles and Blaydon preface their report with a brief review of the literature. They point out that studies relating the EEG to personality must satisfy three requirements: (i) adequate quantification of the EEG, (ii) adequate measurement of personality and (iii) provide a theoretical rationale for predicting what relation holds between these two variables. The EEG was recorded over a total of 20 minutes and integrated by a low frequency analyser over theta, alpha and beta frequencies. A 500-second sample was selected automatically from the total period. Alpha activity was measured both over its whole range (gross filter) and also over its individual frequency bands taken separately in single-cycle steps (discrete filters). For an initial eyes closed sample of 110 seconds, all frequencies were sampled and the mdf was calculated from this sample. For subsequent eyes open and eyes closed alternated trials, only theta, beta and the gross alpha filter were sampled. There were 10, two-minute trials in all (five eyes open and five eyes closed). Subjects were preselected to accord with certain criteria in advance, from a parent population of students, on the basis of EPI score. Two extreme groups of 12 extraverts and 12 introverts were set up, all the subjects having low neuroticism scores. Such samples are not easy to come by, and it is thus an unfortunate feature of this study that it contained 19 females and 5 males. The feature of low neuroticism scores was introduced for the following reasons. Eysenck claims that the factors extraversion–introversion and neuroticism are *orthogonal*. Nevertheless, care must be taken when studying the effects of one factor to ensure that the experimental population is not confounded for the other factor. Take, for example, studies of anxiety. A group of patients may be labelled 'anxious' by the experimenter and the group may contain subjects who are both highly introverted and highly neurotic. Differential response when contrasted with a normal group may be attributable either to neuroticism or to introversion or to an interaction between the two. Savage's design allows for detection of such effects. Indeed, he finds that the addition of neuroticism to high extraversion scores depresses the alpha amplitude rating of the group. Since Gale, Coles and Blaydon were concerned only with the effects of extraversion, neuroticism was controlled for simply by eliminating high scores from the sample.

There were two reasons for employing an eyes open condition. First, the recording period was particularly long. When lying supine in a soundproofed room with eyes closed, the subject tends quite rapidly to become drowsy. Glass and Broadhurst (1966) point out that Savage's main finding for extraversion may have been attributable to the presence of large, high-voltage, but relatively infrequent waves. Such activity would be characteristic of drowsiness and the early signs of sleep. Since we were not concerned with onset of sleep but with the relaxed, waking EEG, the introduction of this simple task increased the possibility of sustaining a constant level of arousal throughout the testing session. It must be pointed out that any study which employs extended sampling periods is suspect on these grounds. Unless sampling techniques are applied strictly and systematically, one may derive samples which are not truly equivalent. Gale, Coles and Blaydon included a measure of the effect of time in the task within their analysis. Secondly, it is claimed by Eysenck that extraverts are 'stimulus hungry'. For example, Gale (1969) has shown that extraverts will work for stimulation (press buttons to hear sounds) to relieve the tedium of mild sensory deprivation. It was predicted that the ̄monotony induced by the matt black enclosure during the eyes closed condition would differentially de-arouse the extraverts and would amplify the personality differences. The key findings were as follows. (i) The extravert EEG for eyes closed was greater in abundance across all the frequencies measured, apart from the upper spectrum of the alpha frequency. (ii) The effect for gross alpha, theta and beta was sustained during the whole session for both eyes open and eyes closed. (iii) The effect for alpha was strongest when eyes were *open* and for beta and theta when eyes were closed. (iv) Mdf was higher for introverts when within alpha comparisons were made (extraverts 10.25 Hz, introverts 10.80 Hz). This study confirms Savage's key finding for abundance and at the same time contradicts the frequency findings for Mundy-Castle, Broadhurst and Glass, Claridge and Herrington and Fenton and Scotton. It is also consonant with the findings of Marton and Urban and the Russian studies of subjects with predominance of inhibition in dynamism. The defects in this study are (i) the experimenter knew the subject's personality ratings prior to recording and scoring, (ii) the design was unbalanced for sex, (iii) mdf was not calculated for eyes open (where the stronger effects for abundance lay), (iv) although the EEG analysis was automatic, the scoring of the analyser record was performed manually, from ruled millimetre paper; the possibility of bias in scoring was still open therefore.

Finally, (v) although the exclusion of neurotic subjects made the results more straightforward to interpret and allowed for a direct test of Eysenckian views concerning the relation between arousal and extraversion, it represents a lost opportunity when comparison with other studies is required.

Gale, Coles, Kline and Penfold (1971)

Gale, Coles, Kline and Penfold (1971) studied resting levels and responses to repeated auditory stimulation in relation to extraversion and neuroticism. (i) Sixty males were preselected from a parent population and allocated to six equal criterion groups (three levels of extraversion, two for neuroticism) on the basis of EPI score. (ii) Recording, scoring of the analyser output and statistical analysis were all performed 'blind'. (iii) Recordings were made at two fixed times of day only, in the early and middle afternoon. (iv) Recording was for 48 minutes; during this period the subject heard 20 auditory stimuli presented at a regular rate of one per 120 seconds. (v) Resting and response measures were taken. (vi) Statistical analysis was by means of a series of ANOVA. (vii) The EEG was one of a number of physiological measures taken.

The key results were as follows. (i) There was no effect for resting abundance for extraversion, nor any meaningful interaction between extraversion and neuroticism. (ii) Neurotics had a significantly higher resting abundance than stables throughout the session. (iii) EEG response to the stimuli took two forms: for the first few trials the EEG was attenuated during stimulation, but for the remainder of the session the EEG was augmented during stimulation. (iv) For both attenuation and augmenting responses the magnitude of response was dependent upon the prestimulus level. When this effect was controlled for by means of an analysis of covariance, no differences in magnitude of response for the personality groups were observed. (v) There was no differential patterning of response for the different personality groups. (vi) Patterning of response for the other psychophysiological measures taken (heart rate, electrodermal response, finger pulse volume and respiration) yielded results both different from the EEG findings and different from each other. The implications of this finding are discussed below (see page 244).

This study is the most extensive and rigorous to be reported so far and it is difficult to fault it upon methodological grounds. It fails to differentiate the EEG for extraversion and produces an unique finding for neuroticism, since it demonstrates that on this occasion neurotics appeared in EEG terms to be more relaxed than stables. It also throws some doubt upon the concept of habituation, since following an initial attenuation of one type of response a new response pattern emerges which appears to be sustained (at least for the 20 trials measured). The use of a regular inter-stimulus interval of an unusually long duration may well have contributed to this new finding. Use of a regular interval was essential to enable extraction of regular inter-stimulus tonic samples for all the measures employed. Post-test dummy trials indicated that the subjects had not been conditioned to a time interval.

However, rigour is no guarantee of, nor substitute for, a good experiment. The principal defect in the Gale, Coles, Kline and Penfold study is that it embodies, albeit in a systematic manner, many of the faults and misguided assumptions inherent in previous work. One source of these difficulties is that, until recently, there have been few demonstrations of systematic variation in the human EEG during the waking state. Therefore, there has been little alternative other than to employ the so-called 'resting' or habituation paradigms. Some alternative experimental paradigms are presented in the final section of this chapter.

Gale, Harpham and Lucas (1972)

A recent study by Gale, Harpham and Lucas (1972) showed that when the Gale, Coles and Blaydon (1969) paradigm of alternating eyes open and eyes closed trials was used on several sessions, employing the same subjects, then no simple effect for extraversion and EEG abundance was apparent. This was a study of the effects of time of day upon the EEG. Subjects attended for a random sequence of four time of day visits (ranging between 0700 and 2200 hr) within a period of three days. Subjects knew from the outset that they would undergo an identical procedure on four occasions. There were no time of day effects nor any indication of an interaction between time of day and extraversion. However, two findings are of note: (i) the test–retest reliabilities of the individual subject EEG, as measured by rank correlations, were extremely high (of the 24 correlations between sessions, all were statistically significant, with 21 beyond the 1 per cent level), and (ii) extraversion was significantly related to session-to-session variation (product-moment correlations between EEG abundance range for session and extraversion being 0.414 for eyes closed and 0.476 for eyes open). Diurnal variation has been demonstrated by many investigators for both physiological and performance measures and the failure to produce results for the EEG was disappointing, particularly since work of this nature is extended and tedious for both experimenter and subjects alike. In fact, university students were unwilling to accept the constraints imposed by the procedure and the subjects were therefore young male army personnel in training. The sample was slightly biased in the direction of extraversion when compared with the university samples which have been employed in most previous work.

Winter, Broadhurst and Glass (1972)

Winter, Broadhurst and Glass (1972) present one of the most complicated studies in the literature, because they employ four experimental conditions and are able to estimate their differential effect upon four different personality groups. Thus interpretation of the outcome is difficult to follow. (i) Subjects underwent four tasks, eyes open and eyes shut, with and without mental arithmetic problems. (ii) A predominantly male sample was divided into four groups, following Savage's model, although unlike Savage the groups were unequal in size. (iii) The EEG was analysed by means of a time series analysis performed by a computer, which samples amplitude at a high rate. The working data for the statistical tests (analysis of variance) were the standard deviations for amplitude. The sample appears to have been of only five seconds' duration for each condition. Their key findings were as follows. (i) The effects of eyes open and arithmetic problems appear to be consistent for all groups when high neurotics, low neurotics, extraverts and introverts are treated separately. Both the eyes open and arithmetic tasks lead to heightened arousal. (ii) Neither extraversion nor neuroticism emerged as significant main effects in the analysis of variance, and correlation coefficients were similarly non-significant. (iii) They claim that a significant interaction between extraversion and neuroticism ($P<0.05$) could be attributable to the possibility that neurotic extraverts were more aroused during the eyes open, arithmetic, condition than neurotic introverts and that stable introverts were more aroused than stable extraverts. There are, however, certain problems in interpreting the results of this study. (i) The authors present a very moderate significant interaction term together with a graphical illustration of the group means for the different conditions. They perform no multiple comparison tests upon the data. Thus their speculation concerning the origins of the significant interaction goes beyond the data as presented. Another problem which obfuscates interpretation is that analyses for different experimental conditions were performed separately, yet their discussion of the data presupposes a single analysis in which personality groups and experimental conditions were manipulated within one factorial design. (ii) It appears that there were in a sense more than four tasks, since subject and experimenter engaged in conversation in between the different experimental conditions. Although they take no measure of the effects of conversation upon the EEG, there are likely to be effects during the succeeding experimental periods. They do not report that these 'conversational' periods were standardized. Thus the authors employ very careful methods of EEG sampling but fail to consider the psychological implications of their procedures. This study demonstrates no differences between the criterion groups. The authors make the useful point that extraversion and neuroticism may have complex interacting effects under different experimental conditions. However, they present no theoretical rationale for predicting exactly what might happen. As we shall see below, such prediction is essential if Eysenck's theory concerning the neurophysiological bases of extraversion and neuroticism is to be empirically defined in terms of operational procedures and observations of data. It appears that these subjects were employed by one of the authors in an earlier study. It is unfortunate that they do not take the opportunity of presenting test–retest reliability coefficients for the EEG, since they have data unavailable in earlier work.

Finally, two unpublished studies are worthy of mention since they have considerable bearing upon our discussion. Morris and Gale obtained a correlation of 0.464 ($N = 32$) between extraversion and alpha abundance during a simple imaging task. But they also obtain a correlation of 0.445 between extraversion and vividness of imagery score as measured by the Betts Questionnaire upon Vividness of Imagery. Now imaging is known to suppress the EEG (Gale, Morris, Lucas and Richardson 1972). The study also showed that experienced imaging during this task was significantly and inversely related to alpha abundance. Thus, within the extravert, two opposing forces may be at work under certain circumstances, for extraversion as such elevates the EEG, whereas imaging suppresses the EEG. This is the sort of problem which Claridge and Herrington (1963) considered and which most authors have neglected.

Gale attempted to replicate the study by Gale, Coles and Blaydon, using a design which would allow for comparison of the differential effects of sex upon extraversion. Only the first half of the experiment, involving the female subjects, was completed. Two extreme groups of 11 were selected from a parent population on the basis of the EPI Form A score. They attended the laboratory for EEG recording, undergoing five eyes closed and five eyes open trials. The experiment was performed 'blind', i.e. the EPI Form A scores were unknown. The subjects then completed Form B of the EPI. To my horror, six of the subjects rated as introvert on Form A were now clearly extravert on Form B, and two extraverts had become introverted. The Form A (first administration) extravert group had a mean score of 17.8 (S.D. 1.2, range 16–23), the introvert group had a mean of 9.5 (S.D. 1.3, range 4–12). On Form B (second administration) the extravert figures were now 16.9, 4.61 and 10–22 and the introvert figures 13.73, 4.17 and 5–19. Nine introvert scores were raised (average increase 4.18, $P < 0.01$, t-test). Changes within the extravert group were not significant (a mean reduction of -0.82). The test–retest correlation (Form A : Form B) was $r = 0.51$. The EPI manual indicates that mean scores for Form B tend to be higher than for Form A. The sample now contained 15 extraverts and seven introverts. t-tests on the Form A scores and the EEG proved to be well below significance.

All was not lost, however. After log transformation of both EPI Form B scores and EEG scores to reduce skew, a product-moment correlation between EEG and extraversion emerged ($r = 0.454$, $P < 0.025$). The log transformation is not, strictly speaking, legitimate and the manner of subject selection constitutes a breach of the assumptions underlying the use of the correlation coefficient. Nevertheless, the example is instructive. Although the test–retest correlation for the two administrations was 0.510, there had been a significant shift in the introvert group score over a period of eight weeks (the interval between the administration of Forms A and B). These were first-year students, who completed the EPI at one month and three months after their arrival at University. It may be that during that time the subjects, in adjusting to new ways of life, became more extraverted. This hunch can apply only to the introverted group, however. The extravert group scores were extremely high for the extravert group on Form A and left little room for increase. There was, in fact, a discrete but non-significant decrease in score for this group. Extreme groups are used, of course, to ensure a reasonable interval on the scale between extraverted and introverted groups. Nevertheless, in this case such precautions were to no avail. This is the only study upon the EEG and extraversion in which an attempt has been made to test for the reliability of personality score in the group employed.

Sources of Experimental Error in Studies of Extraversion and the EEG

We have now come to the end of this serial comedy of errors. We have witnessed a strange phenomenon: a dozen or more studies which apparently were designed to ask the same question yet which yielded very different answers. The question, 'Is there a relationship between extraversion and the EEG?' appears to be quite simple and straightforward. However, a little 'unpacking' of the question reveals a horde of difficulties. The problem areas are: selection of subjects, choice and use of inventory, techniques of EEG measurement, implicit set within the subject, bias within the experimenter, experimental instruction, experimental paradigm, statistical tests, and finally, the rationale for the whole procedure.

The Possibility of Suppressed Hypotheses

It is impossible to know, when one reads the final and published report of a research study, whether there were at the outset subsidiary or even major hypotheses which were tested for but then discarded and not reported. Although such subsidiary hypotheses may not have borne fruit, they may well have influenced the procedures and outcome. Such subsidiary hypotheses may well constitute a hidden source of error variance. We can only guess at their existence. However, we have seen that on occasion questions concerned with personality and the EEG were themselves a subsidiary concern, or even a *post hoc* consideration.

Subjects

It is a common criticism of Freud that his 'experimental subjects' were middle-class, middle-aged, Victorian, Viennese, sexually frustrated/inhibited,

Jewish women. According to Schultz (1969), an exceptionally high proportion of contemporary experimental psychology is conducted upon middle-class, late adolescent, intelligent, sophomore, first-year psychology, American, male, Caucasian undergraduates. It is often the latter variety of psychologists who criticize exponents of the former variety for overgeneralizing well beyond the limits of their sample!

Studies of extraversion and the EEG are no exception. From the evidence available, it would appear that subjects in these studies consist preponderantly of 18–30-year-old subjects of very much more than average intelligence, who either work or study within a university environment. A high proportion are likely to be psychology students, strongly motivated by a desire for social approval (Rosenthal 1965). There are no studies of children, early adolescents or the aged. Thus there is no substantial evidence at present for a general relationship between extraversion and the EEG within the population at large. It requires only a superficial comparison with sampling techniques employed in the standardization of psychometric devices to realize how limited in scope the EEG findings are. This criticism applies to the EEG as a measure in its own right. There are no satisfactory developmental data derived from adequate non-clinical samples, nor any robust normative data concerning the patterning of EEG characteristics in the adult. One advantage from which psychometric studies have derived benefit is that their professed aim has often been their ultimate application within the educational or vocational sphere. Thus the justification for gaining access to samples of adequate size and stratification is easier to present to the appropriate authorities. It is not easy to persuade a local educational authority or a headteacher to make available the population of even one school for the purpose of EEG measurement.

It is not altogether clear how, or whether, the biases observed in the existing samples influence the outcome; however, we shall see that consideration of the procedures employed in studies of extraversion and the EEG allows for a *prima facie* case to be made for such an influence. Certainly, the samples *are* biased and do not allow for the formulation of general statements concerning extraversion and the EEG.

Personality Inventories

The following features are general in the studies we have reviewed. (i) Subjects are classified on the basis of a single score which takes about five minutes or less to obtain. Thus there are no attempts to combine or compare scores derived from different inventories nor to test for the retest reliability of the inventory used. Only one unpublished study used a parallel form to test reliability and the results were not encouraging. Where 'extreme group' designs are employed, a difference of only one or two points (on a 24-point scale in the case of the EPI) may determine whether the subject is classified as 'extravert' or 'introvert'. (ii) No study has attempted to look more closely at the composition of the extraversion score, researchers being satisified with a global rating at the lowest possible level. Jung recognized many categories of extraversion; although Eysenck is careful to say that his extraversion is not the same as Jung's extraversion, they are clearly not talking about two completely different kettles of fish. The unitary nature of extraversion has been subject to considerable criticism (e.g. Carrigan 1960). Of late, Eysenck himself has recognized the value of considering sociability and impulsivity separately in certain circumstances. Cattell's approach has always been to distinguish different varieties or factors.

This is clearly an important issue which has considerable bearing on the studies under discussion. This is not the place to enter into a detailed consideration of the merits and demerits of the concept of extraversion. Suffice it to say that the studies we have reviewed simply refuse to acknowledge that any such problems exist, and accept the notion of extraversion as a global unitary factor as given.

There is some evidence that less formal methods of evaluation (e.g. structured interviews) can yield results of value. The evidence seems at least good enough to warrant further enquiry, the results of which could be of considerable interest.

We cannot chastise earlier workers for failing to take account of Eysenck's later theorizing. However, Eysenck's evidence concerning the orthogonality of extraversion–introversion and neuroticism must be taken into account when interpreting the earlier work. One source of difficulty is that earlier studies believed they were measuring extraversion alone whereas they were probably confounding extraversion and neuroticism, that is, when setting up groups based on clinical criteria. This criticism does not apply to much of the more recent work.

The EEG

(i) We have seen that a number of different measures have been taken. In many cases all the measures could have been derived from the raw data available. The only limitation upon including all these measures appears to be the labour involved. It is likely, however, that one thoroughgoing and exhaustive study is worth several piecemeal snippets of information. Since so many studies each employ different measures, only a study which includes all the measures would provide an adequate means of comparing the different findings. One problem is that there are few if any studies which have explored systematically the relationship between the measures themselves. Thus folklore, rather than fact, tends to be the basis for interpretation. Again, studies in this field compare unfavourably with psychometric measures and psychometric enquiries.

(ii) Secondly, there is a tendency for these studies to use the term 'EEG' as if the record is constant and invariable wherever the electrodes are placed on the cranium. This is not the case, since different electrode placements yield characteristically different EEG patterns. Although there are as yet no sound theoretical grounds for distinguishing waveforms derived from different placements or relating them to different personality characteristics, it would still be worthwhile to establish the consistency of such differences so far as personality is concerned.

(iii) Even at one location, different EEG frequencies are observed. The larger proportion of the studies reviewed are concerned only with the alpha range. There is at present little theoretical rationale for distinguishing the different frequency bands, but again the time will probably come when such differences become meaningful and past failure to observe variation across the measured range will be regretted.

(iv) None of the studies reviewed employs a measure of the retest reliability of the EEG. This is surprising, in view of the claim that the EEG is an invariable and inherited characteristic. A developmental but longitudinal study would provide information of considerable interest. In fact, other studies reveal that test–retest reliability coefficients for the EEG are of greater magnitude than for other measures of individual differences (Gale, Harpham and Lucas 1972). The EEG score could be more stable than the EPI score.

(v) Finally, hand-scoring techniques provide a strong source of error. Sampling must be according to a prearranged time schedule, it must be performed 'blind' and measures of within and across scorer reliability must be provided.

Experimenter Effects

Ideally, neither the experimenter nor the subject should be aware of the purpose of the investigation. Schultz (1969) recommends the establishment of disinterested data-gathering institutions. Since their establishment is highly unlikely, we shall be obliged to continue administering our own experiments. 'Blind' procedures are unlikely to yield freedom from bias. After all, extraversion is very much a measure of ease of social interaction. Thus, interaction between experimenter and subject (which involves explaining why it is necessary to attach wires to the subject and connect him to complex electronic machinery) is likely to be differentially affected by the personality of both parties. It is reasonable to assume that it might be easier for the experimental procedure to be gone through when both the subject and the experimenter are stable extraverts. It has been recognized for some time that in studies of anxiety and the EEG it is difficult to establish whether the record of the anxious subject is a reflection of a permanent characteristic or merely a transient state induced by a stressful experimental procedure.

Designs which allow for administration of the inventories after EEG recording are preferable, and if interview techniques are employed, interviewer and experimenter should be different persons.

Experimental Instructions

Apart from studies of sensory deprivation, studies of extraversion and the EEG are unique in their instruction to the subject to 'do nothing'. A typical set of instructions would be, 'I am going to record your brain waves while you relax with your eyes shut. Try to keep your mind clear. Do not fall asleep but do not think about anything. Do not open your eyes. Do not worry. Nothing unpleasant will happen to you'. If the task is a habituation task, the subject will receive in addition the following instructions. 'Now and then you will hear a sound. Take no notice of it. The sound will be repeated but will not change in any way. Do not count the sounds. Do not try to assess the interval between sounds or guess when they will occur. Do you understand?' Because the instructions sound so straightforward, the subject invariably answers 'Yes' to this final question.

I myself have employed instructions of this sort. They are quite ludicrous and, possibly, meaningless. Even if the subject 'understands' them, he cannot possibly satisfy them. They probably constitute a major source of error variance, and, of course, we cannot predict the effect of instructions which are impossible to carry out upon our different personality groups. Their ambiguity means that the subject is unlikely to be clear of the 'demand characteristics' of the experimental situation (Orne 1962). In psychometric terminology, the situation lacks face validity.

Such instructions owe their origin to that psychological philosophy which conceives of the subject as a stimulus-response lump rather than a thinking being. It is somewhat paradoxical that although subjects are selected on the basis of statements concerned with how they think and feel on different occasions, none of the studies reported includes a post-test questionnaire which enables them to describe how they thought or felt during the experimental procedure. Schultz puts the problem rather nicely (Schultz 1969, p. 217): 'This image of the subject-as-object is reinforced by the mechanomorphic tendencies of behaviourism whose model of man is that of an organic machine—an inanimate, determined, reacting, empty organism. The tendency to view subjects as mechanical objects to be poked, prodded, manipulated, and measured, causes the experimenter–subject dyad to be of the order of Buber's I–It relationship. The relationship is not that of person-to-person, but rather that of person-to-thing, with its attendant tendencies of domination, manipulation and control'.

We can only speculate about the subject's response to this situation. The following set of statements are I think a good set of possible reflections during an habituation task. I think it likely that firstly, different statements might be associated with different patterns of physiological response, and secondly, that extroversion–introversion and neuroticism will be differentially likely to lead to the generation of particular statements. I trust that the reader will forgive this quasi-literary excursion. I have jumbled up the statements almost at random, since possibly they might occur in that manner. Many of the statements were inspired by Schultz' enlightened paper (1969).

On Being a Subject

Let us consider what happens to the subject when he enters the psychophysiological laboratory, and in addition what he may feel or think before, during and after the visit. Firstly, how exactly did he come to be there? He may be responding to an advertisement in the student newspaper, he may have received a letter telling him that he was selected at random from the university list, he may have been asked to come during a tutorial meeting, he may have been accosted on the campus by a complete stranger, he may have been asked to volunteer in a lecture. How then does the subject perceive the experimenter? Is this a research assistant doing a job, or a postgraduate student doing this for a higher degree, or a lecturer who is in the position to evaluate me? Such factors, I suggest, must affect the way in which the subject perceives and interprets the demand characteristics of the task and also the extent of his cooperation. Again, if he has heard that psychologists on the campus are conducting experiments which involve deception, he may be suspicious of the nature of the experiment and may even have decided from the outset to pretend to cooperate while inwardly scowling with amusement. He sees, as he comes in, a number of electronic gadgets equipped with moving parts and flashing lights. He is informed that he is to be attached to this machinery. He is informed that no harm will come to him. Strange or unusually smelling substances are rubbed into his skin. He may have been asked to remove some part of his clothing. Electrodes are placed on to him and wires clipped on to them. In all probability, he has been placed in a room which is devoid of all stimulation; possibly, the lights are turned out and he is shut in and alone. If the cubicle is not perfectly soundproofed, he may hear persons commenting on *his* brainwaves, or *his* heartbeat, they may talk of getting 'rid of the hum' or 'switching up the gain' and so on. May we now speculate about what this person is thinking? The situation bears fair resemblance to a projective test. He may, in fact, be asking of himself the sorts of things the subject is asked to ask of a TAT picture. 'Who are these people? What do they want? What is going to happen? Why are they here?' A number of possible thoughts, questions, statements and answers may be running through his head. 'This is horrible.

9

This isn't as bad as I thought. This is a waste of time. When is it going to end? What is going to happen? Are my brain waves normal? Can they see anything wrong with them? What will he think of me if I don't do things correctly? She's very attractive, I wonder if I could ask her for a date? It was rather nice when she rubbed the jelly in. I said I understood when he told me the instructions, but now I'm here, I'm not sure that I do understand. What exactly is this experiment trying to measure? I hate it in this dark room. How nice it is to lie back and relax. Now what was that problem I was working on before I came in? Did I put jam on the shopping list? Ouch, what a horrible noise. Oh, that one wasn't too bad. What a bore, I hope it will finish soon. I just can't keep my mind free, I hope it doesn't matter. I'm tempted to count the tones. I can't stand this any longer. This is all pointless. What a ridiculous way to spend a morning. Is that a fan I hear. It's getting close in here; I hope my deodorant works. Am I really supposed to do nothing? Oh dear, I nodded off; I wonder if they can tell. Shall I say anything afterwards?'

We may well ask upon reading this, are there really such things as 'resting', 'basal' or 'tonic' levels? Looked at from the phenomenological point of view, the subject is not only not at rest, but is free to experience a broad range of experiential events. He is certainly not under stimulus control. He is no less 'mentally active' than he would be during a nightmare.

The Habituation Paradigm

The habituation paradigm, which is the most popular procedure employed for studies of individual differences in physiological responsiveness, typically involves presentation of a one to five-second tone at a rate of two or three per minute for an experimental period of around 20 minutes. This means that given a three-second tone and 40 stimuli and a 20-minute testing period, the subject is under experimental control for only 10% of the total testing period. Thompson and Spencer (1966) present the classic rationale for the habituation paradigm. The main argument concerns the ubiquity of the habituation phenomenon, firstly across species, and secondly within the organism in terms of the different categories of description or levels of analysis employed. Habituation may be considered as an attenuation in the response of the whole organism as demonstrated in the behavioural component of the orienting response, or it may be considered in terms of general physiological responding as measured by the indices we have already mentioned in this chapter, or lastly in terms of the attenuation of responsiveness of the individual nerve cell. It is claimed by Thompson and Spencer that these different exemplars of habituation resemble each other closely and that the time course of the phenomenon is common to all. Thus habituation is a universal process. In a recent volume devoted to consideration of short-term changes in the nervous system (Horne and Hinde 1970), several of the contributors point out that the Thompson and Spencer original case is not as yet supportable in terms of the experimental evidence. Hinde (1970) demonstrates that a fine-grained examination of habituation and its component phenomena does not allow either for (i) a description adequate enough to allow for assumption of similarity between phenomena at the different levels of analysis, or (ii) for the explanation or description of the mechanisms involved. There is, in fact, little evidence to show that behavioural, physiological or neuronal habituation bear much resemblance, nor is there much support for the view that habituation is a simple form of negative learning which shares features in common with the classical extinction phenomenon (Kling and Stevenson 1970). It is clear that habituation requires a good deal of close and detailed examination before any general statements may be formulated. The trouble is that once a phenomenon acquires the reputation of being straightforward, considerable effort is required to convince people that it is, in fact, complex. I have generated a good deal of data employing the habituation paradigm, and on occasion it is tempting to believe that 'habituation' is perceived in data whether it is there or not. For example, in a recent study of GSR habituation, carried out by one of my students, all 10 of the subjects employed achieved a criterion of two consecutive non-responses. However, eight subjects continued to respond after this point and in six of them the mean magnitude of post-criterion response was greater than that of the pre-criterion responses. No subject showed a smooth attenuation of response magnitude as a function of stimulus number, although the group curve for the first few trials fitted this notion quite nicely. In the study by Gale, Coles, Kline and Penfold (1971), it was observed that following initial attenuation, EEG abundance actually increased in response to stimulation on subsequent trials. Since earlier workers have looked for attenuation, and presumably have stopped sampling the data once their criterion of response-cessation has been reached, the possibility of a different sort of response (augmentation) has passed their notice.

Apart from these considerations, we have seen that a good case can be made out for the view that, phenomenologically speaking, the habituation paradigm just does not make sense. I am not suggesting that the habituation paradigm is a useless experimental procedure; indeed, data of interest have been generated. However, *some*, if not a considerable proportion, of the error variance in such studies may be due to the defects I have mentioned.

Sampling the Record

Because the primary record is so complex, hand-scoring bears with it the problems familiar to those who would wish to score the Rorschach. Sampling only those parts of the record which are 'scorable' or actually excluding subjects whose records are not 'scorable' must lead to considerable bias. Large bursts of alpha activity are more likely when the subject has become so relaxed that his state borders upon drowsiness. Thus it is crucial, when comparing criterion groups for the incidence of alpha activity, that pre-experimental resting periods are of uniform length. Some sort of task, to which the subject must give attention, is essential if the experiment is not to measure speed of sleep onset rather than resting EEG.

Statistical Tests

I shall here limit myself to the comment that comparison of extreme groups, analysis of variance of continuous samples, product-moment correlations and chi-squares all ask rather different questions of the data and therefore allow for different conclusions to be drawn. For example, a t-test comparison of two extreme groups does not allow one to conclude that there is a general relationship between extraversion and the EEG. So far as possible, studies which wish to resolve some of the contradictions in the earlier work should be designed in a manner which allows for comparison of the outcome of different statistical procedures. It is also important that the reader be given some notion of the psychological significance rather than statistical significance of a particular finding. Whereas this can be estimated at a glance from a product-moment correlation, F ratios are rarely accompanied by an assessment of the variance attributable to the significant factors.

The Theoretical Rationale for Studying the Relationship between Extraversion and the EEG

I have already pointed out that the procedures employed in these studies reflect the paucity of experimental paradigms in psychophysiology. If only we had available to us standard testing conditions which reliably induce systematic variation in the EEG, then we could measure the influence of personality on the variation. Another problem is the paucity of adequate theorizing in relation to extraversion and arousal. Much of the theorizing is barely removed from the vernacular description of personality traits. And yet, one clearly requires a means of predicting the outcome of experiments and of accounting for discrepant findings. The most advanced theory concerning the neurophysiological basis of extraversion is undoubtedly that of Eysenck (1967). However, it is not altogether certain that the theory allows one to predict experimental outcomes since the basic assumptions are not made wholly specific, the rules for relating the assumptions are not mentioned and the capacity to generate empirical or operational definitions is therefore inhibited.

Although Eysenck has not hesitated in the past to employ neurophysiological terminology (e.g. 'excitation', 'inhibition'), it is only comparatively recently that he has engaged in full-blooded neurophysiologizing. In *The Biological Basis of Personality* (1967) he relates extraversion and neuroticism to two individual but related 'circuits' in the brain.

Eysenck draws a distinction between 'arousal' and 'activation' or, more particularly, between 'cortical arousal', 'reticular arousal' and 'limbic/autonomic activation'. Both reticular arousal and limbic/autonomic activation lead to cortical arousal. The former relates to and sustains the normal range of activity required for day-to-day functioning of the individual; it is mediated largely by the reticular activating system which has an ascending influence upon the neocortex. 'Activation' is essentially dependent upon systems in the brain related to emotional response and intimately involved in the functioning of the autonomic nervous system. Since the neocortex, the reticular system and the limbic system are richly interconnected, cortical arousal may result either from reticular arousal (day-to-day variation in alertness) or limbic/autonomic activation (emotional response). Reticular arousal leads to cortical arousal but not necessarily to limbic/autonomic activation. However, limbic/autonomic activation will lead necessarily to both reticular and cortical arousal, either through limbic–neocortical connections or via limbic–reticular–neocortical loops. Extraversion–introversion is identified with the first system, and since it is claimed that the reticular system of introverted persons is more aroused than that of extraverted persons, it follows that introverts are more aroused cortically. Neuroticism is identified with the second system. Thus it follows that given a low level of stress and absence of emotional stimulation, variation in behavioural or physiological measures of cortical arousal is attributable to extraversion–introversion and its substrate the reticulo-cortical loop. Under conditions of emotion and/or stress, observed variation is attributable to an interaction between extraversion–introversion and neuroticism, since both arousal and activation occur. Thus it would appear that the only conditions under which the orthogonality of extraversion–introversion and neuroticism can be demonstrated are those which result from a manipulation of extraversion–introversion alone, for as yet we are not able to distinguish by means of psychophysiological measures which changes relate to activation and which to arousal. If we assume a simple additive model for extraversion–introversion and neuroticism and a common scale and units for reticular arousal and limbic/autonomic activation, then given a measure of arousal A and a constant high stressor we would expect in a 2×2 factorial design (high/low extraversion, high/low neuroticism) that A would be greatest for neurotic introverts, least for stable extraverts, with stable introverts and neurotic extraverts tieing. Given the total absence of stress, then neuroticism should have no effect and both introverted groups would display more A than both extraverted groups.

The big problem, of course, is the definition of 'stress', since the capacity to distinguish arousal from activation hangs upon the capacity to specify stress. Presumably one requires a circular definition, since only a large body of empirical studies of the effects of different stressors upon activation and arousal will allow prediction of the empirical conditions under which activation and arousal may be discriminated.

My own view is that it is parsimonious to study initially groups which vary upon the dimension of extraversion only, and hold neuroticism constant by employing subjects with low N scores. Secondly, highly situation-specific hypotheses should be tested. I refer to such possibilities in the final section.

As it stands, Eysenck's theory is not capable of generating clearcut experimental hypotheses.

The Problem of Arousal

Throughout this chapter the term 'arousal' has been employed without qualification. This brief section is included to remind the reader of the grim fact that there is little evidence to support the view that 'arousal' is a unitary concept. Few studies have demonstrated concomitant variation of the different psychophysiological indices of arousal, and it has been demonstrated that different individuals are responsive only in relation to one particular index (Lacey 1967). Stark facts of this sort make direct prediction from Eysenck's theory very difficult. However, there are occasions when discrepancies between the different indices can make sense, although, regrettably, *post hoc* explanations are essential. We may take the studies by Gale, Coles, Kline and Penfold (1971) and Coles, Gale and Kline (1971) as an example. In these studies, neurotic subjects were shown to be more relaxed than stables for the EEG (a unique finding) and more aroused than stables for GSR (a typical finding). Other data, as yet unreported, indicate that there were no differences for heart rate and finger pulse volume, but that for respiration neurotics were more responsive than stables, but only for the first of 20 habituation trials. The *post hoc* explanation goes as follows. The subjects were university neurotics and thus their inherent neuroticism (as measured by the EPI) had not crippled them academically. Indeed, they may have learned by virtue of 'self-control' responses to keep within bounds those autonomic reactions of which they were *aware*. Thus heart rate does not discriminate between high and low neurotics, since these neurotics have learned to contain heart rate variability. However, only the initiated are aware of GSR responses, and self-control of such responses can only be achieved while observing a record of one's own response patterns. Thus GSR responses in this experiment discriminated high and low groups. Respiration presents a nice intermediate case; after an involuntary acceleration to the first stimulus, the subject, reassured that the stimulus is quite tolerable, is henceforth able to impose voluntary control. The de-aroused EEG is a concomitant of self-relaxation and reflects the inhibitory control of the neocortex over lower brain centres involved in arousal and activation. Such control is discriminative and is exercised only in relation to those aspects of autonomic response of which the person is aware. Relaxation is moderately easy in this experimental context, since the subject is supine on a comfortable bed and insulated from the world for an hour, during which he has nothing to do. The experiment bears some resemblance to clinical relaxation techniques. If the reader is willing to accept *post hoc* explanations of this sort, then the contradictory findings yielded by the different measures of 'arousal' may be reconciled. Only further experimental study will clarify the matter.

A Post Hoc Attempt to Reconcile Contradictions in Studies of Extraversion and the EEG

Since I have expressed disquiet concerning a number of procedural features of these studies, it might appear that I wish to consign all of them to the laboratory dustbin. However, certain consistencies may be observed and I shall therefore present a tentative, but rather loose, hypothesis to account for the results. The crucial point is the procedures employed and the associated instructions to the subject.

My general proposition is that when extraverts are either too bored with the procedure or too interested with the task, they will be more aroused than introverts. That is to say, a moderate level of arousal is required to optimize on the personality differences in this context. Where the extravert is too bored (habituation tasks, or simply lying with eyes closed) boredom leads to self-arousal, possibly involving imaging, which in its turn activates the EEG. Where tasks are interesting (performing arithmetic problems, watching the Archimedes spiral, talking to the experimenter) the extravert becomes aroused. With moderately arousing tasks (opening and shutting eyes upon instruction, or a simple eyes closed recording procedure in a laboratory which does not preclude sound of the experimenter's activities) the extraverted subject is more able to obey the instruction to relax and keep his mind clear. Even where measures are taken for different conditions within one session, mere knowledge that other conditions are to be used will influence the record as a whole, since the subject knows from the outset that interesting things are going to happen. Again, a moderately arousing task will become tedious if the subject knows he must repeat it in several experimental sessions. Table 1 shows how the studies which have been reviewed may be arranged in accordance with a threefold classification of the conditions of testing (highly arousing, moderately arousing and boring).

This general view *could* account for some of the discrepancies in the literature. However, only an empirical study could serve to show whether it is substantiable. In many of the previous reports we do not have all the evidence, since a precise specification of the conditions of testing is essential. One defect is that this view makes no prediction concerning introverts but merely attempts to account for differences between extraverts and introverts in terms of changes in the extraverted subjects. There is evidence that the behaviour of extraverts is more *variable* than that of introverts. Gale (1969) argues that

TABLE 1. Studies of Extraversion and the EEG

(a)		(b)	
Gottlober (1938)	+	High arousal	
Henry & Knott (1941)	−	Claridge & Herrington	−
McAdam & Orme (1954)	−	Broadhurst & Glass	−
Mundy-Castle (1955)	−	Winter, Broadhurst & Glass	−
Claridge & Herrington (1963)	−		
Nebylitsyn (1963)	+	Moderate arousal	
Savage (1964)	+	Gottlober	+
Marton & Urban (1966)	+	Nebylitsyn	+
Fenton & Scotton (1967)	−	Savage	+
Broadhurst & Glass (1969)	−	Marton & Urban	+
Gale, Coles & Blaydon (1969)	+	Gale, Coles & Blaydon	+
Gale, Coles, Kline & Penfold (1971)	−	Gale (unpublished)	+
Gale, Harpham & Lucas (1972)	−	Morris & Gale	+
Winter, Broadhurst & Glass (1972)	−		
Gale (unpublished) (1972)	+	Very low arousal	
Morris & Gale (1973)	+	Henry & Knott	−
		McAdam & Orme	−
		Mundy-Castle	−
		Fenton & Scotton	−
		Gale, Coles, Kline & Penfold	−
		Gale, Harpham & Lucas	−

(a) The studies are arranged in chronological order. Where the study is classed as positive (+), it supports the hypothesis that extraverts are less aroused than introverts; a negative classification (−) indicates that the study either failed to reject the null hypothesis or contradicted the alternative hypothesis. (b) The studies are rearranged in terms of the experimental conditions which *may* have prevailed. Full details of the instructions and/or the conditions of testing are not available in every case.

extraverts, by virtue of an inherently low level of arousal, are obliged to search for stimulation in order to sustain behavioural efficiency. This is the origin of the 'stimulus-hungry' behaviour of extraverts. Thus, if the extraverted subject is not to simply fall asleep during a boring experiment, then he is obliged to arouse himself with whatever sources of stimulation are available in the laboratory. Social contact with the experimenter will be arousing. When all such contact is precluded, the subject is obliged to engage in self-induced mental activity. In both cases the EEG will be activated. Thus studies of this sort must sustain a delicate balance between the underarousal and over-arousal of the extraverted subject.

I should like to offer this proposal as a working hypothesis, to assist in the construction of new experiments in this field. The hypothesis has the advantage of being testable. The fact that extraverts have been shown to be more aroused than introverts on some occasions and less aroused on others is not surprising. The problem is to explain such variation. The one thing which is absent in all these studies is a questionnaire which asks (systematically) how the subject felt during the task. Those who shudder at such a 'subjective' procedure are invited to recall that the very criterion measure for subject selection asks him to report his feelings and reactions upon a variety of experi-mentally uncontrolled occasions.

Recommendations for Future Work

It is unlikely that further studies set within the mould of previous work will clarify the problems which have been raised. The following recommendations must be considered as necessary prerequisites for any future study of the rela-tionship between extraversion and the EEG.

Subjects

Subjects must be selected in accordance with adequate sampling procedures. Since it is claimed that extraversion is inherited and that its relation to the EEG is fundamental, subjects should not only cover both age and ability spectra, but should also be selected for familial relationships; as yet, there have been no twin studies. Longitudinal studies of both extraversion and EEG would be particularly informative. Since sex is a likely source of variation in earlier work, samples should be balanced for this factor. Studies which sup-port the view that extraverts are low aroused tend to have preponderantly female samples. This may be attributable to an interaction between sex and extraversion or to a superior capacity in females for obeying ludicrous instructions. Samples based upon university students do not allow for general statements.

Personality should be assessed by means of a battery of tests and proced-ures, and evidence should be presented demonstrating the unitary nature of extraversion for the sample. Parallel forms of inventories should be used where available and their retest reliability confirmed. The discriminability for the EEG parameters of different questionnaire items should be examined. Where interviews are used, precise criteria for allocation to groups must be given. The person recording the EEG should not know the inventory or other personality scores of the subject. Since *other* personality factors have been shown to influence the EEG (e.g. scores of vividness of mental imagery, Gale,

Morris, Lucas and Richardson 1972), questionnaires measuring such factors should be included if only to allow for their partialling out.

The EEG

The EEG should be recorded on at least two separate occasions for each individual and details of retest reliability provided. On all occasions, recordings from different placements should be obtained and the full measured range should be analysed. Although electronic analysis is essential, measures should also include those visually derived indices which have been employed in earlier work, firstly to provide comparison and secondly to establish the relationships between the different measures of EEG activity. Thus estimates must be provided of alpha, theta and beta abundance, alpha index and mean dominant frequency, together with some measure of moment-to-moment variability.

Experimental Conditions

In order to clarify some of the problems raised by earlier work, the study should include some sample of the conditions under which earlier data were derived. Thus 'resting' conditions, response to simple repeated stimuli and performance upon some of the simple 'tasks' already used should all form part of a repeated measures design. Clear predictions, based upon a sound theoretical formulation, should be stated at the outset, in an attempt to eliminate the embarassingly *post hoc* quasi-explanations of paradoxical findings evident in the existing literature. In view of the working hypothesis presented above, experimental conditions should include boring, mildly arousing and very arousing treatments. The subject should complete a post-test questionnaire which assesses the incidence of different subjective experiences under the various experimental conditions.

However, use of such paradigms will only help to clear up past mistakes; they are unlikely to yield much additional information of value. New experimental situations which capture conditions under which behavioural differences between extraverts and introverts have already been demonstrated are required to extend our knowledge of psychophysiological differences. Thus tasks involving social interaction, sustained attention, stimulus hunger and perceptual complexity would be both empirically based and readily derivable from theory.

Further studies along the lines of existing work can only add to the confusion.

Experimental Situations Which Yield Systematic Variation in the EEG

This final section is a mixture of established fact and to-be-substantiated experimental hunches. The literature concerning extraversion and the EEG is confused because of an excess of theoretical naïveté and a paucity of experimental paradigms. These studies have been dominated by the simplistic view that since extraversion is inherited it will, like body build or eye colour, be observable in an invariable and constant state under all conditions. Thus it is assumed that whatever the experimental arrangements the extraverted EEG will be 'lower aroused' than the introverted EEG. The working hypothesis presented above provides a means of reconciling the apparently discrepant findings.

I now present, very briefly, some alternative paradigms. Figure 1 illustrates a variety of situations which lead to systematic variation in the EEG. The different experimental paradigms cover a range of situations and involve individual differences, perceptual phenomena, subjective experience, social interaction and performance. Most of the designs are for an intra-subject analysis, but all may be adapted for inter-subject comparisons as a treatment or main effect.

EEG Correlates of Vigilance

Gale, Haslum and Penfold (1971) have demonstrated that the EEG varies systematically during an inspection task as a function of the stimuli to which the subject is exposed. Where the subject is instructed to respond rapidly to a sequence of three odd and unequal numbers, the EEG becomes progressively more aroused as each odd number in the sequence is presented. If even numbers intrude into the sequence, or if the subject has just responded, then the EEG becomes de-aroused. This phenomenon has been demonstrated for both auditory and visual presentation of digits, and similar variation within the subject is observed for both skin conductance and heart rate. Moreover, the better the fit of physiological response to stimulus content, i.e. the better the physiological measures discriminate the differential cue value of stimuli throughout the task, the faster the reaction time of the individual. These studies are relevant in the present context for two reasons. First, there is a large body of established data concerning performance differences in vigilance for extraverts and introverts (e.g. see the review by Davies and Tune 1970), and second, previous attempts to relate physiological indices of arousal to variation in performance have been very disappointing. The question asked by Gale, Haslum and Penfold (1971) was, 'Does the subject's arousal wax and wane as a function of the cue value of the stimulus?'. They examined EEG response to every individual digit in a sequence of some 400 digits. The subject was asked to report how he felt when exposed to different stimulus sequences and his report matched stimulus content. Thus three measures of the person were taken: performance, subjective report and EEG. Other studies, adhering closely to classical findings in vigilance research, have asked questions like, 'Do vigilance tasks which yield a decrement also yield a physiological change?', 'Does rate of decrement relate to rate of physiological

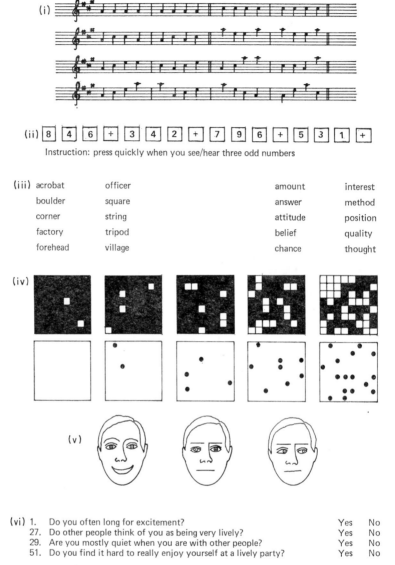

Instruction: press quickly when you see/hear three odd numbers

FIGURE 1. Six situations in which stimuli have systematic effects upon the EEG.

(i) *Simulated Music.* The less repetitive the pattern of sounds the more the subject is able to relax. (ii) *Vigilance Task.* Where the subject must respond to three consecutive odd numbers, the EEG waxes and wanes as a function of the cue value of the numbers. The '+' is a rest period. (iii) *Words and Imagery.* High imagery words suppress the EEG more than low imagery words. (iv) *Stimulus Complexity.* EEG abundance is inversely related to the number of objects in the pattern. This is not a brightness effect since the same relationship holds for white or black objects. (v) *Social Interaction.* The EEG of the subject is most aroused when the experimenter smiles and least aroused when he averts his gaze. (vi) *Extraversion–introversion.* Extraverted subjects have greater EEG abundance than introverted subjects.

change?', 'Can pre-signal levels differentiate between detections, omissions and false positives?' and 'Do individual differences in patterning of physiological response differentiate between good and poor vigilance performers?'. The answers to these questions have not as yet been forthcoming, largely, I suspect, because physiological measurement has been used as a mere accompaniment or handmaiden to existing tasks and an attempt is made to relate it to performance in a *post hoc* manner. In our task, however, stimulus control of the psychophysiological variables is determined in advance and is less affected by uncontrolled subject variability. Since systematic variation in our task has now been replicated on several occasions, questions concerning personality and physiological variation may now be asked. What was required beforehand was evidence of a replicable *general* effect. The paradigm may now be manipulated, varying those parameters of the vigilance task which performance studies have already shown to be of importance for individual differences in extraversion–introversion.

EEG Correlates of Social Interaction

There is now a growing body of evidence concerning modes of non-verbal interpersonal communication and the cues employed in our perception of the other person. Variation in physiological arousal as a function of certain social variables could make sense of much of the data (Zajonc 1965). Extraversion is, of course, a measure of sociability and it has been shown to influence aspects of social behaviour in experimental situations (e.g. see Cook 1971). It is not easy to devise experimental paradigms in social psychology which allow for psychophysiological measurement. However, Gale, Lucas, Nissim and Harpham (1972) have achieved some moderate success while measuring variation in the subject's EEG as a function of the degree of eye contact imposed upon him by the other person. Thus the EEG is least aroused when the other person's gaze is averted, moderately aroused when the other person stares at him and most aroused when the other person smiles. This effect has been replicated for both males and females, although the females appear to be less affected than men by the smiling condition. Since extraversion can account for some of the individual differences in patterning of eye gaze and tolerance for the gaze of other persons, there should also be systematic variation in the EEG within this experimental situation as a function of extraversion. We are able to measure the EEG of both subjects while they undergo a variety of experimental conditions. Thus personality, sex and degree of eye-to-eye contact may all be varied within one design.

Stimulus Complexity and the EEG

Berlyne (1960) considers in detail those properties of stimuli which may influence the arousal of the subject. Several studies demonstrate that variation in stimulus complexity influences the EEG; the more complex the pattern of stimulation, the more arousing its effects upon the EEG. Gale, Christie and Penfold (1971) demonstrated such an effect as a function of the number of elements in the display. The effect appears to be independent of the brightness of the stimulus, since it holds for both white blobs on a black background and black blobs on a white background (Gale, Bramley, Lucas and Christie 1972). Since it is claimed that extraverts are 'stimulus hungry' (Gale 1969), it would be interesting to monitor the EEG during tasks in which either the complexity of stimulation was manipulated by the experimenter or in which the subject himself were to work for exposure to different stimuli in order to stave off the monotonous effects of sensory deprivation. In another study employing simulated music, in which four tones were presented either singly, in pairs, triplets or quadruplets, complexity and a hedonic scale of 'irritating-ness' appeared to have opposing effects. Simpler combinations of sound stimuli, which the subjects rated as more 'irritating' than the more complex stimuli, had greater arousing effects upon the EEG, presumably by virtue of their negative hedonic value. Since extraverts are claimed to have higher sensory thresholds and to be more tolerant of painful stimuli in general, this task provides yet a further means of exploring physiological concomitants of behavioural effects. Both these tasks provide a suitable testing ground for the effects of either stimulus hunger or noise (excessive stimulation) upon the subject.

EEG and Imagery

There has been a recent resurgence of interest in imagery. Individual differences in imaging ability, differential instruction to image and the imaging-inducing properties of words have all been shown to influence performance in memory tasks. Golla, Hutton and Walter (1943) claimed that different EEG waveforms related to individual differences in cognitive strategy in problem-solving. One of the problems in EEG studies is the difficulty in setting up experiments which manipulate imaging *per se* rather than arousal, since specifically visual effects and general effects upon alpha activity may be confounded. Gale, Morris, Lucas and Richardson (1972) showed that for easy (low-arousing) tasks, imaging of high-imagery words reduces EEG abundance, whereas in difficult (high-arousal) tasks content which yields imagery only with effort reduces abundance more than content which is easy to image. This demonstrates how generalized arousal and imaging interact as a function of experimental instruction. The study also showed a relationship between individual differences in imaging capacity and the m.d.f. of alpha activity.

An incidental finding was that extraverts reported richer imagery experience than introverts. This was puzzling since both Jungian and Eysenckian accounts of extraversion–introversion would lead one to believe that the introvert rather than the extravert is dependent to a large degree upon an inner world of experience. However, the notion of 'stimulus hunger' in extraverts relates to the notion that seeking for stimulation provides a means of raising arousal to an optimum level in order to achieve what Eysenck has termed a 'maximisation of hedonic tone' (Eysenck 1967). Previous accounts of such stimulus-seeking have emphasized external sources; however, seeking for stimulation could also include internal sources, and Morris and Gale (1973) suggest that the extravert indulges in imaging to elevate arousal when stimulation from external sources is not available. Conversely, since it is claimed that introverts are 'stimulus aversive', imagery may be suppressed by introverts (as are external sources of stimulation) in order to lower arousal and maximize hedonic tone. Such an interpretation is more consistent in arousal terms, since according to Eysenck, introverts are inherently overaroused (and stimulus aversive) and self-induced imaging would therefore serve to elevate arousal above an already high and intolerable level. It may be the case in certain clinical groups (i.e. phobics, obsessionals and compulsives—all falling in Eysenck's dysthymic group) that high neuroticism acts as a disruptive drive and serves to remove the inhibition upon imaging, thus increasing the already high level of arousal of the individual. There appears to have been little objective study of extraversion and imaging capacity. However, since both imaging capacity and extraversion have been shown to influence the EEG, the paradigms already developed for imaging studies may be usefully taken over for consideration of our central problem. At the same time, it is clear that speculation concerning imaging suffers from the fact that precise operational definition of imaging experience has yet to be achieved. Gale, Morris, Lucas and Richardson (1972) differentiate a number of different imaging experiences. It is not clear how different types of imaging experience are related to one another or whether individual differences in imaging relate to a unitary factor. I am therefore not altogether happy about my speculations in this section.

Concluding Remarks

Of all the paradigms outlined above, the vigilance paradigm is possibly the best candidate for immediate research, since it may call upon a body of established data. However, the remaining paradigms may be worked upon to yield useful data. All these tasks represent a considerable shift in ecological validity when contrasted with the 'eyes closed' and habituation paradigms. The only justification for further work along the lines of the existing studies would be merely to clarify their equivocal findings. We may end this case study in experimental mismanagement with a glimmer of optimistic, if not fervent, hope.

References

Berlyne, D. E. (1960), *Conflict, Arousal and Curiosity*, New York, McGraw-Hill.
Biesheuvel, S. (1949), 'An observational technique of temperament and personality assessment', *Bulletin of the National Institute of Personnel Research*, **1**, 9–27.
Broadhurst, A., and Glass, A. (1969), 'Relationship of personality measures to the alpha rhythm of the electro-encephalogram', *British Journal of Psychiatry*, **115**, 199–204.
Carrigan, P. M. (1960), 'Extraversion–introversion as a dimension of personality: a re-appraisal', *Psychological Bulletin*, **57**, 329–60.
Claridge, G. S., and Herrington, R. V. (1963), 'An EEG correlate of the Archimedes spiral after-effect and its relationship with personality', *Behaviour Research and Therapy*, **1**, 217–29.
Coles, M. G. H., Gale, A., and Kline, P. (1971), 'Personality and habituation of the orienting reaction: tonic and response measures of electrodermal activity', *Psychophysiology*, **8**, 54–63.
Colquhoun, W. P., and Corcoran, D. W. J. (1964), 'The effects of time of day and social isolation on the relationship between temperament and performance', *British Journal of Social and Clinical Psychology*, **3**, 226–31.
Cook, M. (1971), *Interpersonal Perception*, Harmondsworth, Penguin.
Davies, D. R., and Tune, G. S. (1970), *Human Vigilance Performance*, London, Staples.
Eysenck, H. J. (1953), *The Structure of Human Personality*, London, Methuen.
Eysenck, H. J. (1967), *The Biological Basis of Personality*, Springfield, Thomas.
Eysenck, H. J. (1970), *The Structure of Human Personality*, 3rd edition, London, Methuen.
Eysenck, H. J. (1971), *Readings in Extraversion–Introversion: Volume 3. Bearings in Basic Psychological Processes*, London, Staples.
Fenton, G. W., and Scotton, L. (1967), 'Personality and the alpha rhythm', *British Journal of Psychiatry*, **113**, 1283–9.
Gale, A. (1969), 'Stimulus hunger: individual differences in operant strategy in a button-pressing task', *Behaviour Research and Therapy*, **7**, 265–74.
Gale, A., Bramley, P., Lucas, B., and Christie, B. (1969), 'Differential effect of visual and auditory complexity in the EEG: negative hedonic value as a crucial variable?', *Psychonomic Science*, **17**, 21–4.
Gale, A., Christie, B., and Penfold, V. (1971), 'Stimulus complexity and the occipital EEG', *British Journal of Psychology*, **62**, 527–31.
Gale, A., Coles, M., and Blaydon, J. (1969), 'Extraversion–introversion and the EEG', *British Journal of Psychology*, **60**, 209–23.
Gale, A., Coles, M., Kline, P., and Penfold, V. (1971), 'Extraversion–introversion, neuroticism, and the EEG. Basal and response measures during habituation of the orienting response', *British Journal of Psychology*, **62**, 533–43.
Gale, A., Harpham, B., and Lucas, B. (1972), 'Time of day and the EEG: some negative results', *Psychonomic Science*, **28**, 269–71.
Gale, A., Haslum, M., and Penfold, V. (1971), 'EEG correlates of cumulative expectancy and subjective estimates of alertness in a vigilance-type task', *Quarterly Journal of Experimental Psychology*, **23**, 245–54.
Gale, A., Lucas, B., Nissim, R., and Harpham, B. (1972), 'Some EEG correlates of face-to-face contact', *British Journal of Social and Clinical Psychology*, **11**, 326–32.
Gale, A., Morris, P., Lucas, B., and Richardson, A. (1973), 'Types of imagery and imagery types: an EEG study', *British Journal of Psychology*, In Press.

Glass, A. (1964), 'Mental arithmetic and blocking of the occipital alpha rhythm', *Electroencephalography and Clinical Neurophysiology*, **16**, 595–603.

Glass, A., and Broadhurst, A. (1966), 'Relationship between EEG as a measure of cortical activity and personality measures', *Electroencephalography and Clinical Neurophysiology*, **21**, 309.

Golla, F. L., Hutton, E. L., and Walter, W. G. (1943), 'The objective study of mental imagery. I: physiological concomitants', *Journal of Mental Science*, **89**, 216–23.

Gottlober, A. B. (1938), 'The relationship between brain potentials and personality', *Journal of Experimental Psychology*, **22**, 67–74.

Gray, J. A. (1964), 'Strength of the nervous system as a dimension of personality in man: a review of work from the laboratory of B. M. Teplov', in J. A. Gray (Ed.), *Pavlov's Typology*, Oxford, Pergamon, pp. 157–287.

Gray, J. A. (1967), 'Strength of the nervous system, introversion, extraversion, conditionability and arousal', *Behaviour Research and Therapy*, **5**, 151–69.

Gruzelier, J. H., and Venables, P. H. (1971), 'Two-flash thresholds, heart rate, skin temperature and blood pressure in schizophrenics with and without skin-conductance orienting responses', *Bulletin of the British Psychological Society*, **25**, 48–9.

Henry, L. E., and Knott, J. R. (1941), 'A note on the relationship between "personality" and the alpha rhythm of the electroencephalogram', *Journal of Experimental Psychology*, **28**, 362–6.

Hinde, R. A. (1970), 'Behavioural habituation', in G. Horne and R. A. Hinde (Eds.), *Short-term Changes in Neural Activity and Behaviour*, Cambridge, Cambridge University Press, pp. 3–40.

Horne, G., and Hinde, R. A. (1970), *Short-Term Changes in Neural Activity and Behaviour*, Cambridge, Cambridge University Press.

Kling, J. W., and Stevenson, J. E. (1970), 'Habituation and extinction', in G. Horne and R. A. Hinde (Eds.), *Short-term Changes in Neural Activity and Behaviour*, Cambridge, Cambridge University Press, pp. 41–61.

Lacey, J. I. (1967), 'Somatic response patterning and stress: some revisions of activation theory', in M. H. Appley and R. Trumbull (Eds.), *Psychological Stress: Issues in Research*, New York, Appleton-Century-Crofts.

McAdam, W., and Orme, J. E. (1954), 'Personality traits and the electro-encephalogram', *Journal of Mental Science*, **100**, 913–21.

McGhie, A. (1969), *Pathology of Attention*, Harmondsworth, Penguin.

Marton, M., and Urban, Ya. (1966), 'An electroencephalographic investigation of individual differences in the processes of conditioning', *Proceedings of the 18th International Congress of Experimental Psychology, Moscow*, 106–9.

Morris, P., and Gale, A. (1973), 'A correlational study of variables related to imagery', *Perceptual and Motor Skills*, In Press.

Mundy-Castle, A. C. (1955), 'The relationship between primary–secondary function and the alpha rhythm of the electroencephalogram', *Journal of the National Institute of Personnel Research*, **6**, 95–102.

Nebylitsyn, U. D. (1963), 'An electroencephalographic investigation of the properties of strength of the nervous system and equilibrium of the nervous processes in man using factor analysis', in B. M. Teplov (Ed.), *Typological Features of Higher Nervous Activity in Man*, Vol. 3, Moscow, Acad. Pedagog. Nauk R.S.F.S.R., pp. 47–80.

Orne, M. T. (1962), 'On the social psychology of the psychology experiment: with particular reference to demand characteristics and their implications', *American Psychologist*, **17**, 776–83.

Rosenthal, R. (1965), 'The volunteer subject', *Human Relations*, **18**, 389–406.

Savage, R. D. (1964), 'Electro-cerebral activity, extraversion and neuroticism', *British Journal of Psychiatry*, **110**, 98–100.

Schultz, D. P. (1969), 'The human subject in psychological research', *Psychological Bulletin*, **72**, 214–28.

Thompson, R. F., and Spencer, W. A. (1966), 'Habituation: a model phenomenon for the study of neuronal substrates of behaviour', *Psychological Review*, **73**, 16–43.

Winter, K., Broadhurst, A., and Glass, A. (1972), 'Neuroticism, extraversion and EEG amplitude', *Journal of Experimental Research in Personality*, **6**, 44–51.

Zajonc, R. B. (1965), 'Social facilitation', *Science*, **149**, 269–74.

CONCLUDING REMARKS

PSYCHOLOGICAL TESTING is one of the oldest branches of psychology, beginning as it does at the turn of the century with Binet in Paris. Now as we look at its most recent developments some seventy years later, what conclusions can we draw? Is it moribund like many other technical innovations of that time, for clearly, unlike steam, psychological testing is not actually dead? The picture seems promising: in almost all fields psychological assessment is thriving. Thus clinical ingenuity continues to produce new projective tests. The Rorschach seems at last to be demonstrably as powerful a technique as its adherents have intuitively believed, rescued, ironically enough, by sophisticated statistics. Objective tests too are useful and entirely new measures. Intelligence and ability-testing continues to develop in the hands especially of Cattell, so that even this most well-worked seam is not exhausted. With these techniques psychodynamic hypotheses are yielding to scientific quantification, while psychophysiological measurement, as yet in its infancy, has an obvious future. Perhaps more important than all these developments is the fact that psychologists are questioning the very assumptions of testing itself, both those who realize there are areas to which it cannot effectively reach and those who are attempting to reformulate the statistical models implicit in psychological measurement so that it be more suited to its purpose. Our book has accurately portrayed all these manifold endeavours, and we feel confident in concluding that psychological measurement has still an important part to play in the development of psychology.

AUTHOR INDEX

SUBJECT INDEX